Monopoly, Competition and the Law

Monopoly, Competition and the Law:

The Regulation of Business Activity in Britain, Europe and America

Tim Frazer

Professor of Commercial Law,
University of Newcastle upon Tyne

HARVESTER WHEATSHEAF

ST. MARTIN'S PRESS

First published 1988 by
Wheatsheaf Books Ltd
Reprinted by
Harvester Wheatsheaf
66 Wood Lane End, Hemel Hempstead,
Hertfordshire, HP2 4RG
A division of
Simon & Schuster International Group

and in the USA by
St. Martin's Press, Inc.
175 Fifth Avenue, New York, NY 10010

Printed and bound in Great Britain by
Billing & Sons Limited, Worcester

British Library Cataloguing in Publication Data
Frazer, Tim
   Monopoly, competition and the law: the
   regulation of business activity in
   Britain, Europe and America.
   1. Competition—Government policy
   I. Title
   338.6′048   HD3611

   ISBN 0-7450-0444-X

Library of Congress Cataloging in Publication Data
Frazer, Tim
   Monopoly, competition and the law.

   Bibliography: p.
   Includes index.
   1. Antitrust law—United States.   2. Antitrust law—European
Economic Community countries.   3. Restraint of trade—European
Economic Community countries.   I. Title.
K 3856.F73   1988   343.4′072   87–28837
ISBN 0–312–01671–9   344.0372

2 3 4 5   92 91 90 89

To Jan

The functioning of competition not only requires adequate organisation or certain institutions like money, markets, and channels of information...but it depends above all on the existence of an appropriate legal system, a legal system designed both to preserve competition and to make it operate as beneficially as possible.

Hayek, *The Road to Serfdom* (1974)

Contents

List of Tables

Preface

Competition policy inhabits something of a no-man's land between the territories of economics and law. Lawyers trained in traditional legal scholarship are perhaps disquieted by the need to take account of economic principles, and economists are deterred by legal methodology. But this state of affairs is changing rapidly; competition law and policy is taking its place among the mainstream subjects in degree courses in economics and in law.

A number of factors have contributed to this change. A growing scholastic alliance between economics and law has fostered an interest in a closer interdisciplinary scrutiny of many policy areas. There have also been some excellent recent publications to assist the new students of competition policy. But perhaps most of all, competition policy has adopted a much higher profile in society at large. The 'mega merger' wave in the UK has placed the issue of corporate acquisitions on everyone's breakfast table. The daily revelations concerning the merger activities of Guinness, and news of the behaviour of corporate managers in the UK and the US have fuelled this growing interest.

As a result of these developments, there is a general realisation of the importance of competition policy as an aspect of economic regulation. It is the purpose of this book to explain the principles underlying the competition policies of the UK, the EEC, and the US, and the way in which these principles are put into practice. The administration of antitrust—its processes and bureaucracy—are as important as its underlying theories in fashioning the practical policy. These three legal systems have been chosen because their contrasting styles and objectives highlight the often fierce debate concerning the proper goals and achievements of antitrust. The practical importance of these systems to firms and individuals throughout the trading world is beyond doubt.

I have attempted to write this book in a style which will appeal to both economists and lawyers, and I hope it will be of interest to students and practitioners of both disciplines. It is intended to be neither an encyclopaedia of competition law, nor a treatise on economic theory. It *is* intended to be a guide to the practice and application of a policy which is based on economics but which is effected through the law.

Competition policy does not stand still. In the UK, the government is undertaking a comprehensive review of its policy towards mergers and restrictive trade practices. In the US, there is speculation that the Wall Street scandals will precipitate a movement away from the permissive stance of Chicago economics, towards the closer regulation of business activity. These are exciting times!

Tim Frazer, February 1987

Table of Cases and Decisions

Black Bolt and Nut Assoc. Agmnt. (No. 3), LR 6 RP (1965).
Blanket Manufacturers Agmnt., LR 1 RP 271 (1959).
Boat Showrooms of London Ltd. v. Horne Brothers (Boat Builders) Ltd, 1980 (*unreported*)
BPCL/ICI *Decision*, OJ 1984 L 212/1.
BP Kemi: ATKA v. BP Kemi, [1979] 3 CMLR 684.
Brasserie De Haecht S.A. v. Wilkin (No. 1), [1967] ECR 407.
British Basic Slag Ltd v. Registrar of Restrictive Trading Agreements, LR 4 RP 116 (1963).
British Bottle Assoc. Agmnt., LR 2 RP 345 (1961).
British Heavy Steel Makers Agmnt., LR 5 RP 33 (1964).
British Iron and Steel Founders Agmnt., LR 4 RP 299 (1964).
British Jute Trade Agmnts., LR 4 RP 399 (1963).
British Leyland v. E.C. Commission, *The Times* 12 November 1986
British Paper and Board Makers Assoc. Agmnt., LR 4 RP 1 (1963).
Broadcast Music v. Columbia Broadcasting System, 441 US 1 (1979).
Brown Shoe v. US, 370 US 294 (1962).
Bull v. Pitney Bowes Ltd, [1967] 1 WLR 273.
Byars v. Bluff City News, 609 F. 2d 843 (6th Cir., 1979).

Camera Care Ltd. v. E.C. Commission, [1980] 1 CMLR 334.
Carbon Gas Technologies *Decision* [1984] 2 CMLR 275.
Carlsberg *Decision*, [1985] 1 CMLR 735.
Cast Iron and Steel Rolls, [1984] 1 CMLR 694.
Cellophane: US v. E.I. du Pont de Nemours and Co., 351 US 377 (1956).
Cement Makers Federation Agmnt., LR 2 RP 241 (1961)
Centrafarm v. Sterling, [1974] ECR 1147.
Chemist Federation Agmnt. (No. 2), LR 1 RP 75 (1958).
Chicago Board of Trade v. US, 246 US 231 (1918).
Clubtwo Ltd v. Ongakusha Ltd, 1983 (*unreported*).
Colgate: US v. Colgate & Co., 250 US 300 (1919).
Columbia Steel, US v. 334 US 495 (1948)
Commercial Solvents v. E.C. Commission, [1974] 1 CMLR 309.
Consten and Grundig v. E.C. Commission, [1966] CMLR 418.
Continental Can v. E.C. Commission, [1973] ECR 215.

1 The Policy of Antitrust

THE OBJECTIVES OF ANTITRUST POLICY

One of the fiercest and most persistent debates in American jurisprudence concerns the proper goals and objectives of antitrust policy. Such a debate is to a large extent absent from the antitrust policies of the EEC and the UK. In the EEC, the objectives of competition policy have been expressed clearly and have largely been determined by the needs of the Common Market. In the UK, it is accepted that the objectives of the antitrust laws are so wide and varied that there could be no useful debate as to their precise scope.

In the American debate, the opposing arguments are clearly defined: either antitrust laws are designed solely to maximise consumer welfare through maximising allocative efficiency in American industry; or they are designed to achieve and protect a bundle of social and political values, including in particular the avoidance of 'bigness' and the concentration of economic power in the hands of a few. The use of price theory to promote economic efficiency as the sole objective of antitrust is championed by economists of the Chicago school, and their supporters. There is no doubt that Chicago theories have the support of the Reagan administration; the antitrust enforcement agencies have been 'captured' by adherents of Chicago economics. Reagan appointees to these agencies have declared their allegience to economic efficiency as the sole aim of antitrust (Campbell, 1982; Baxter, 1983; Note, 1985). However, this does not mean that the debate has ceased. Not all courts are convinced by the arguments of the enforcing agencies, and the agencies are not the only initiators of policy. In the US, the vast majority of antitrust cases are brought by private plaintiffs, whose interests may well lie outside the narrow confines of economic theory. Further, many courts have shown a reluctance or inability to adopt economic analysis in antitrust cases, unless it is reduced to easily-applied 'rules of thumb' (Hay, 1985).

Where economic efficiency is regarded as the only goal of antitrust policy, no consideration is given to concepts of distributive equity, or 'fairness'. The basic assumption is that the competitive process will ensure the efficient allocation of resources, that it is essentially a self-correcting mechanism, and that intervention will be required only occasionally to correct temporary imperfections. Features which do not pertain to notions of efficiency based on price theory, sometimes characterised as 'vague and general invocations of the public interest' (Areeda, 1985), should not be considered as relevant or proper in antitrust analysis, even where they are capable of definition and measurement (see especially Bork and Bowman, 1965).

Critics of this view have characterised Chicago ideology as 'minimalist' and as an 'efficiency-based agenda of abstentionism' (Rowe, 1985). It is seen by many as tending towards the per se legality of practices hitherto regarded as potentially harmful (Blecher, 1985). The major criticisms of the Chicago view are that its assumptions are too simplistic for real-world economics and that, in any event, it fails to take account of a number of different values which ought to be included in the assessment of trading practices (see the range of papers in Tollison, 1980). Sometimes characterised as a 'populist' or 'Jeffersonian' ideology, the opposing view seeks to maintain a competitive economy composed of a large number of small units. The objections to 'bigness' are based on the fear that effective governmental power will pass into the hands of the private sector, at the expense of the democratic process. This view was well summarised by Justice Douglas in *US* v. *Columbia Steel* (1948): '[i]ndustrial power should be decentralised so that the fortunes of the people will not be dependent on the whim or caprice, the political prejudices, the emotional stability of a few self-appointed men'.

The debate continues fiercely. Some critics of the Chicago view ascribe notions of religious fanaticism to their opponents, referring to Chicago principles as 'revealed truth' (Schwartz, 1983), or 'theology' (Flynn, 1983), requiring a 'bending at the knee by bench and bar' (Flynn, 1977). A leading Chicago exponent has even been described as an 'Ayatolla' (see Bork, 1985). Efforts have been made to legitimate the opposing arguments by an historical analysis of the debates in Congress preceding the passage of the Sherman Act. Bork claims that there is 'not a scintilla of support' in the legislative history that Congress intended anything other than consumer welfare to be the antitrust objective (Bork, 1966), whereas Elzinga, analysing the same debates, comes to the opposite conclusion (Elzinga, 1977). In a sense, this search for historical justification is irrelevant. Antitrust has become fully politicised; the views taken by the enforcing agencies on its meaning and objectives will depend on current political influences and not historical analysis.

Populists regard antitrust law as an entrenched constitutional principle, a *grundnorm* of economic freedom. The Supreme Court in *US* v. *Topco* (1972) referred to the antitrust laws as the 'Magna Carta of free enterprise', and compared them to the Bill of Rights. Rowe describes antitrust as 'a vital component of our American culture'; and some members of the Attorney General's Committee described competition as 'desirable...for its own sake, like political liberty' (Attorney General, 1955). Learned hand, in the *Alcoa* case (1945) viewed the absence of competition as a 'narcotic' and rivalry as a 'stimulant' to industrial progress.

If the objectives of US antitrust are the subject of bitter controversy, those pertaining in EEC policy are fairly well settled and expressed. In its Ninth Report on Competition Policy (1979), the European Commission rejected a dogmatic approach in competition policy and stipulated three basic objectives. These objectives are fashioned by the particular tasks given to the EEC by the Treaty of Rome. The Treaty seeks the promotion of economic cooperation throughout the Community, through the unification of the separate national economies into one common market, within which goods are to move freely. Competition policy is one method of achieving the objective of economic harmony, but is not regarded as an end in itself. The three basic objectives of competition policy, in the Commission's view are these. Firstly, to keep the market open and unified. The unification of the national markets must not be reversed through the restrictive activities of firms re-dividing the market. Secondly, competition policy must maintain a competitive structure in Community markets. Free competition is regarded as an effective regulator of economic activity, a reference to the purely economic disadvantages of concentration and monopoly. If the Commission is correct in characterising this as one of the fundamental objectives of competition policy, it is all the more regrettable that there is still no effective policy in the EEC to control mergers. Thirdly, antitrust policy is there to maintain a degree of fairness on the market. Within the concept of 'fairness', the Commission includes a prohibition on State aids to firms, and a promotion of the position of small and medium-sized firms. This favourable attitude to small and medium-sized firms is a feature which runs throughout the Commission's enforcement of antitrust policy. It is a clear departure from the confines of economic efficiency, and in this regard bears similarities to the exceptional policy of the Robinson-Patman Act in the US. The concept of fairness also embraces the idea of consumer benefit. Competition is assumed to benefit consumers through lower prices and higher output; likewise, any restriction in competition will be permitted only if the particular advantages of the transaction are shared with consumers.

The variety of the tasks assigned to EEC antitrust policy separate it from the supposedly unilateral US policy, restricted for the time being to the objective of economic efficiency. EEC policy is essentially pragmatic and is designed to operate in harmony with other policies in order to achieve the basic economic, social and political aims of the Treaty of Rome.

The objectives of UK policy are very difficult to define, simply because their potential scope is so wide-ranging. The original common law on the restraint of trade has been developed in a jerky, piecemeal and haphazard manner so that the resultant jumble of statutes bears no common style and few common policies. It is clear, however, that antitrust policy in the UK is wholly entwined with other social and economic policies, and may not be regarded as a discrete element of government policy. Tebbit, as Secretary of State, confirmed this when he declared that the promotion of competition is 'part of the fabric of government policy; and every one of my ministerial colleagues must keep in mind the competition implications of policy decisions' (Tebbit, 1984 II). The various statutory definitions of public interest reveal the close relationship between antitrust policy and other government policies. Both the Restrictive Trade Practices Act 1976 and the Fair Trading Act 1973 require an assessment of trading practices which takes account of matters outside the area of economic efficiency, and outside the area of competitive injury. Public safety, local employment, regional disparities, and export effectiveness are among the items which may be used to assess trading conduct. This requirement to balance competition and non-competition matters separates UK policy from that in the US. In the EEC, anti-competitive effects may be offset by economic advantages relating to the production and distribution of goods, and to technical and economic progress. The latest UK antitrust statute, the Competition Act 1980 is similar in style to Article 85 of the Treaty of Rome, but even under the 1980 Act, competition is just one element in the assessment of the public interest.

The control of trading practices and market structures is very much within the political arena. Equally, the conduct of business has political consequences, and political objectives. Some members of the Attorney General's Committee stated this succinctly: 'power to exclude someone from trade, to regulate prices, to determine what shall be produced, is governing power, whether exercised by public officials or private groups' (Attorney General, 1955). The political consequences of size may be considerable, and are most clearly seen in the case of multinational companies, whose business strategies may be facilitated through international group trading, legal and fiscal manipulation, and effective lobby power. Trading behaviour is therefore not only determined by the economic motive of securing a return on capital. Political motives, at a local or national level, and psychological factors, may also have substantial influence. The latter may range from the desire for the quiet life to the desire for empire. The UK

Green Paper on Monopoly and Mergers Policy stated that how far corporate acquisitions are 'due to economic factors. . .and how far to factors such as ambition for status and power among business executives, or advantages in terms of taxation or legal status and so on remains an unresolved issue'.

THE MEANING OF COMPETITION

The notion of 'perfect competition' has no real use in practical antitrust policy. Perfect competition is said to exist where firms are too small to influence price through changes in output; where there is no product differentiation; where resources are perfectly mobile; and where there is a perfect flow of information between market participants. Such a model is useful in order to demonstrate price theory, but is unrelated to real markets where intractable imperfections are all but universal (see Demsetz, 1982). In the presence of such imperfections, the theory of second best suggests that the public interest will be better served by permitting other imperfections to exist as a counterweight, rather than to remove them. This theory is widely applied in antitrust policy in those cases where the pro- and anticompetitive aspects of a transaction are compared. Further, the term 'perfect competition' is misleading; it really denotes the absence of competition in the sense of a productive rivalry between firms (McNulty, 1968). This is not the nature of competition which antitrust policies seek to promote; the benefits to society of undistorted competition flow from the struggle between firms for market share, a struggle which promotes product development and price reductions.

Since perfect competition is neither attainable nor desirable, antitrust policy seeks to promote 'workable' or 'effective' competition, a compromise which takes account of irremovable imperfections, the nature of the market, and that degree of attainable competition which will satisfy public policy. Originally the concept of 'workeable competition' was fairly closely defined (Clark, 1940), but it now has no independent meaning outside the legal system or the market of which it forms part; '[w]orkable competition is a term economists give to that rather ill-defined market situation that is socially acceptable' (Stocking, 1961). In this regard, the European Commission refers to 'the right amount of competition' to fulfil the aims of the EEC. Similarly, the European Court of Justice has defined workable competition as 'the degree of competition necessary to ensure the...objectives of the Treaty', a degree which will vary according to the nature of the market (*Metro* case, 1978). In the UK, the Restrictive Practices Court has defined the socially desirable degree of competition as requiring 'a reasonable number of non-preponderant buyers and sellers who are subject to normal competitive pressures' (*Locked Coil Ropemakers*, 1964).

THE APPROACH OF ANTITRUST POLICY

Just as the objectives of antitrust policy may differ from system to system, so may the means by which these objectives are effected. Differences in method are common not only between systems but also within them. Such differences have led to a two-stage taxonomy for the classification of antitrust systems. Firstly, a system may adopt an abuse, prohibitive or per se approach (Swann, 1979); and secondly it may be form-based or effects-based. In an abuse system, no predetermined judgment is made with regard to the desirability of trading practices or market structures, but provision is made for their control where they are found to be operating against the public interest (however that may be defined). Monopoly and merger policy in the UK are typical abuse systems. In a prohibitive system, specific practices or structures will be prohibited, but there will usually be provision for the prohibition to be lifted where countervailing advantages can be shown. The control of restrictive trade practices in the EEC and (theoretically) in the UK is achieved by way of a prohibitive system, although differences exist in relation to the factors which will be taken into account when deciding to remove the prohibition. Finally, in per se systems, specified practices are conclusively presumed to be contrary to the public interest and are consequently prohibited. The control of restrictive trade practices in the US adopts such a system. However, the widespread use of the rule of reason in the analysis of restrictive practices requires the courts to balance the pro- and anticompetitive features of a transaction in order to determine whether the prohibition applies. Such a determination is therefore of a definitional nature, and is to be distinguished from the evaluative process involved in a prohibitive system.

Whichever of these approaches are adopted by antitrust systems (and each system may adopt more than one), the regulated practices or structures may be defined according to their formal characteristics, or by reference to their effect on the market. The Restrictive Trade Practices Act 1976 is a masterpiece of formality, whereas the whole of EEC antitrust policy is effects-based. Other important differences in approach relate to the method of enforcement and the access to enforcement procedures. Legal policy may be enforced through the civil or criminal courts, or through administrative agencies staffed by civil servants or independent experts. The initiative for enforcement may be retained by government in order to centralise and rationalise enforcement, or it may be made accessible to private parties injured by anticompetitive behaviour.

The methods and approaches adopted in the three legal systems, and the consequences of those choices, will be fully explored in the following chapters. However, it must not be forgotten that there are alternatives to antitrust for the regulation of market structures and trading behaviour. State ownership of resources and the regulation of markets will also achieve the orderly use and distribution of assets. The choice between regulation and competition may be dictated by the nature of the markets concerned, but it is a choice equally influenced by political and cultural values concerning the role of government in society.

2 Monopoly Policy

THE APPROACH OF MONOPOLY POLICY

The approach adopted by monopoly policy will be determined by the view taken by policy makers of the possible or certain social and economic consequences of monopoly. Monopoly may be viewed as an enduring and inherently detrimental phenomenon, which has no countervailing advantages and which necessarily leads to a misallocation of resources through lower output and higher prices. Where such a view is taken, then monopoly policy will be directed to the structure of the market; its objective will be to dismantle the position enjoyed by the monopolist or to prevent its occurrence. Because of its emphasis on the first part of the structure-conduct-performance paradigm, such a policy is known as a structural monopoly policy.

The alternative approach is based on a belief that a monopoly structure will not always operate to the detriment of consumers or the economy as a whole. Economies of scale may be obtainable only where the firm achieves a very large size in relation to the market. Further, monopoly may be achieved through efficiency, inventiveness and response to demand. In other words monopoly may be the final outcome of the competitive process, where the most successful participant has absorbed its less efficient rivals. This familiar paradox, whereby free competition leads to monopoly, is usually referred to as competition containing 'the seeds of its own destruction'. Where monopoly has been achieved in this way, it would be both inequitable and inefficient to require it to be

9

dismantled; even the threat of such action could stifle the incentive to compete.

However, monopoly power may be achieved not through free competition but through unfair competitive techniques which disable efficient firms from competing for market share. In any event, monopoly power, however achieved, may be *exercised* in an unfair or exploitative manner, so that society at large is no longer enjoying the most efficient alternative. In these instances, it will be the acquisition or the exercise of monopoly power that is regulated, rather than the actual structure of the market. A policy which pursues such objectives is known as a behavioural monopoly policy, and will concentrate on the conduct and performance of the dominant firm.

None of the three legal systems under review has adopted a policy directed against the very existence of monopoly power, but there have been occasional recommendations that monopoly policy be given a more 'structural' basis. In 1979, for example, an official US report recommended that the US government be given the power to dismantle persistent monopoly power in any industry.[1] Others have recommended that the persistence of a monopoly over a long period should at least give rise to a statutory presumption of unfair conduct (Noble, 1982). It is to be noted that both of these recommendations concern only those monopolies which persist over a period of time, and not those which are newly acquired. This is a reflection of current approach to the analysis of monopoly power.

The static analysis of monopoly has given way to a dynamic analysis which takes account of the temporal dimension of monopoly power. Economists have noted the tendency for monopoly power to be eroded and eventually eliminated over time by actual or potential competition on the market. Under this theory, a firm which attempts to enjoy the fruits of monopoly power, by increasing prices and lowering output, will lose its monopoly power through other, efficient, firms undercutting its prices, and through yet more firms entering the market, attracted by the high profits available there (Shaw and Simpson, 1985).

Where the dynamic competitive process operates in this

way, firms with monopoly power must behave *as if* the market was competitive. In these circumstances, monopoly power will not be an enduring problem for policy makers. Indeed, this view of the market as a self-correcting mechanism would allot a greatly reduced role for monopoly policy; intervention on the market would be an unwarranted intrusion on a self-contained 'eco-system'. The fact remains, however that there are many occasions when the market mechanism is not able to check the exercise of monopoly power either at all, or within a reasonable time. There remains a role for intervention whenever the market mechanism has been disabled in some way.

The ability of actual or potential competitors to inhibit monopoly power depends on their ability to increase their market share or to enter the market for the first time. If for some reason firms are not able to do this, in other words where the market is not 'contestable' (Kay, 1983), then government intervention to curb any excess on the part of the monopolist will be justified.

BARRIERS TO ENTRY

The contestability of markets is determined by the presence or absence of barriers to entry. The different forms and varieties of barrier may be grouped into two categories: those which relate to the activities of the dominant firm and the potential entrant; and those which are imposed by law or regulation.

The first group would include—on the part of the dominant firm—pricing policy, product differentiation and brand loyalty,[2] other strategic behaviour, geographical location, and efficient operation achieved through economies of scale[3] and experience of production techniques. For example, in its report on the white salt market in the UK, the Monopolies and Mergers Commission found that the market was not contestable, in spite of the availability of salt deposits and the willingness of an existing monopoly supplier to license technology to others. The large economies of scale enjoyed by the existing firms meant that any new entrant would have to capture a large market share in order to avoid a production cost disadvantage. In addition, new entrants faced time lags of three to five years for the development of raw material. Combined with the insuperable geographical advantage enjoyed by the existing firms, the fact that a large part of demand was foreclosed by long-term supply contracts, the existence of excess capacity, and a downturn in demand, these factors gave rise to a virtually impenetrable market (*White Salt*, 1986).[4] Brand loyalty is often found to be a barrier, discouraging entry either on its own (*Tampons*, 1986), or together with other features such as economies of scale (*United Brands* case, 1978).

With regard to the activities of the potential entrant firm, *exit* barriers applying in its existing market will comprise not only the costs associated with plant, but also any long-term contracts to which it is party and the value of long-standing business relationships which it enjoys (Harris and Jorde, 1983).

Barriers arising through law or regulation include the grant of patents and other intellectual property rights, the issue of licences of many descriptions, and the imposition of import tariffs. Demsetz ascribes the existence of monopoly power almost entirely to such government-provided restrictions on entry, rejecting the notion that non-government barriers have any long-term effect in excluding entry (Demsetz, 1974; see also Baden-Fuller, 1979).

Calvani identifies a 'hybrid' barrier, 'non-price predation' (Calvani, 1985). This consists of the use, by a dominant firm, of government agencies to block or delay entry by potential competitors. This may be done by the dominant firm habitually raising objections to the entry of new firms, where such entry must be sanctioned in some way by a government agency. Such a practice may involve the potential entrant in substantial costs, and the attempt to enter the market may be abandoned altogether.

The degree of contestability in particular markets may not be easy to assess. A preliminary difficulty may concern the proper characterisation of a market feature as a barrier or as an entry-facilitator. For example, advertising may be seen as an exclusionary practice designed to discourage new entry (Mann, 1974), or as the basis for new entry (Brozen, 1974).[5]

One way to measure contestability is to examine the behaviour of the dominant firm. If it exploits its monopoly power in an abusive way over a long period then this would indicate that other firms are being prevented from entering the market. The concern of such an enquiry will usually be the pricing practices, profit margins and operational efficiency of the dominant firm. With regard to pricing policies, the presence of monopoly power may be evidenced either by excessive or by predatory pricing, or by pricing policies which are not consistent with a competitive environment.[6] It is often difficult to determine whether pricing policies are indeed indicative of monopoly power. With regard to profit margins, high profits may be due to the dominant firm charging supracompetitive prices, but they may equally be due to efficiencies enjoyed by the firm which enable it to produce at a lower cost. The mere existence of high profits is therefore not necessarily indicative of monopoly power. On the other hand, the absence of excessive profits may be due either to the presence of inefficiencies in a dominant firm, or to the presence of competitive pressures.

It is a function of the competition authorities, within the context of a behavioural policy, to determine whether any advantages accruing to a dominant firm are due to anticompetitive features or to efficiency. Although there are great differences between the monopoly policies of the UK, the EEC and the USA respectively, they may all be classed as behavioural policies, seeking to distinguish benign and malign monopolies.

THE MEANING OF MONOPOLY

Market definition
However monopoly is defined (and the three legal systems adopt very different positions on this), a critical element of the definition will be the proper identification of the market in which the monopoly is thought to operate. A monopoly position and market power are not abstract concepts; they can only exist in relation to a market. The choice of the correct product and geographic market is therefore the essential first

step in the practical identification of monopoly power. It is crucial that this choice be correct, and that the market chosen be the *relevant* market. An overly broad definition of the market would serve to diminish the real market share of a dominant firm, whilst too narrow a definition would artificially boost a modest share. As the US Supreme Court has stated 'a high market share indicates market power *only if the market is properly defined* to include all reasonable substitutes for the product' (*Jefferson Parish Hospital* v. *Hyde*, 1984, emphasis added).

The necessity of correctly defining the relevant market as the first step in identifying market power, is not generally disputed. One American judge put it thus: 'the search for the "relevant market" must be undertaken and pursued with relentless clarity. It is, in essence, an economic task put to the uses of the law' (Fortas J. in the *Grinnell* case, 1966). In the leading American case *Berkey Photo* v. *Eastman Kodak* (1979), the US Appeal Court said it was a 'basic principle in the law of monopolization' that the first step in a court's analysis must be a definition of the relevant market. However, some commentators have suggested that a more direct route be taken in the identification of market power, without the need to define the relevant market. Turner suggests that market power may be identified through the persistence of supracompetitive profits over a period (Turner, 1980). Others have suggested measuring 'own-price elasticity', defined as the change in the demand for a product consequent on a change in its own price (Glassman, 1980; Werden, 1985). Because this does not enquire as to *where* such lost demand has gone, (or increased demand come from) market power is measured without a product market having first been defined. Both these approaches have been criticised on the basis of fundamental conceptual and empirical problems (Harris and Jorde, 1983).

Market definition must be achieved at two stages: identification of the product market and of the geographic market, respectively. The first stage is dogged with difficulty; the products chosen must form part of a group with characteristics which separate them in an economically sensible way from all other products. All products within such a group will not necessarily be homogeneous, but they will be, to a greater or lesser degree, interchangeable. There will, however, be no substantial interchangeability between these products and those outside the group. The degree of interchangeability may be assessed from both consumers' and producers' viewpoints. The first method of assessment—demand-side analysis—measures the willingness of consumers to substitute one product for another. If there is a high degree of substitution possible between the two products, then they will be considered to be part of the same market. Thus if it was found that consumers are willing, in certain price conditions, to substitute typewriters for word-processors then they will form part of the same market, because they will be competing for the same consumer pound or dollar. If however there is no such substitutability between typewriters and main-frame computers then they will fall into separate markets.

This degree of substitutability between products may be measured by using the concept of cross-elasticity of demand. This measures the extent to which a change in the price of one product will affect the demand for another product. If a relatively small change in price will cause a relatively large shift in demand, then there is said to be high cross-elasticity of demand, and the two products will be considered to be part of the same market. Where, for example, a small change in the price of coffee causes a substantial increase in the demand for tea, then the two will be competing goods in the same market.

There are great difficulties involved in this demand-side analysis, concerning the choice of products to be used as comparators, and where to draw the line between 'good' substitutes and 'poor' substitutes. With regard to the choice of products, the use of 'pair-wise comparison' whereby substitution is measured between widgets and gidgets, then widgets and didgets, then widgets and doobies, and so on, has been criticised on the grounds that a product (here, widgets) may have no close substitutes at all, and yet have a host of poor substitutes (Werden, 1985). However, the use of the alternative 'own-price elasticity' test, whilst it avoids this problem, gives no indication as to *where* demand, lost through an increase in price, has strayed and will be of no assistance in defining the relevant market.

Any enquiry into demand substitution will almost always result in a chain of substitution, at one end of which may be products which are perfectly substitutable, and at the other those which are hardly substitutable at all. At some point a line must be drawn enclosing some products within the market under consideration, and excluding the others. The decision on where to draw that line will be an arbitrary one, rarely capable of justification on any sound economic basis (Needham, 1969; Turner, 1980).

Sullivan points to a further basic difficulty in using cross-elasticity of demand to identify the relevant market. Such an exercise will only reveal the correct information if it is carried out by reference to prices closely related to costs. Current prices may already be set at a supracompetitive level, so that substitution which results from even higher prices may bring in products which would not be regarded as good substitutes had the exercise been conducted by reference to competitive prices (Sullivan, 1977 II).

Demand-side analysis will identify the products and the consumers, but in order to fully identify the relevant market, consideration must also be given to both actual or potential suppliers. Supply-side analysis seeks to identify those firms which are either supplying the products or which would be willing and able to supply the products if there were an increase in their price. Some firms may be able to switch production to the product in question by simple adaptation of their plant. Others may require more extensive and costly changes; and at the extreme, firms may need to make a quantum leap from one industry to another in order to start production. The likelihood of firms switching production to the relevant market depends on their perception of the gains to be made and the costs involved in the move. Both gains and losses will be influenced by the nature of barriers to entry and exit.

Because of this close relationship between barriers to entry and supply substitution, some analysts prefer to consider the possibilities of supply substitution only as a discounting factor when estimating the market power of a dominant firm in a market which has already been defined wholly on the basis of *demand* substitution. An alternative approach is to actually assign market shares to firms which are in a position to supply the product even though they do not presently do so. Werden refers to these two approaches as the 'share-interpretation approach' and the 'share-measurement approach' respectively (Werden, 1985). The market definition contained in the US Merger Guidelines uses a mixture of both such approaches.[7]

A factor which affects the operation of both demand-side and supply-side analysis as practical exercises is the choice of a time-scale over which to test substitutability. In most cases, the longer the time-scale the more likely is substitution to take place, but the choice made is likely to be as arbitrary as that relating to the break in the chain of substitution. Another fundamental difficulty is that gathering reliable and sufficient data may be all but impossible. Even where these difficulties can be overcome, it is important to note that the exercise is hardly likely to predict the *actual* movement in demand between products. Where a firm increases or lowers the price of its product, other firms are unlikely to hold their own prices constant, either because the price movements are caused by factors affecting the whole industry (and possibly others as well), or because other firms will take strategic decisions to maximise their own profit; such strategy will rarely be to do nothing. In addition, consumer choice will also be influenced by factors other than price, such as the transaction costs involved in switching from one product to another (Gyselen and Kyriazis, 1986) and sheer, non-rational, inertia. The failure of many market-definition tests to relate realistically to real life has often been criticised (see especially Korah, 1980; and Harris and Jorde, 1984).

When the product market has been determined, it is also necessary to assess the relevant geographical market. Even suppliers of identical products will not compete where they operate in discrete geographical areas. The choice of geographical market may involve a degree of arbitrariness, but is usually a more straightforward process than the choice of product market. In UK monopoly policy, the geographic market is usually defined as the whole of the UK. In EEC and US policies, the geographic market must be determined not only to identify the relevant market but also for jurisdictional reasons. Article 86 and section 2 of the Sherman Act apply only where the monopoly conduct or power has inter-State significance.

The geographic dimension of a market may be measured either from the consumer's or the supplier's viewpoint. The former analysis has regard to the area in which the consumer has effective choice between competing products, whereas the latter has regard to the location strategies open to suppliers. Thus, consumers of foodstuffs will regard their effective area of choice as being the locality round their homes or workplaces. It would not be worthwhile to travel outside these areas to purchase these products, since any saving would usually be outweighed by the costs of transport. However, foodstuffs suppliers may well compete nationally to supply retailers. In such circumstances the proper geographic boundaries are not entirely clear.

United Kingdom law In UK monopoly policy, under section 10(7) of the Fair Trading Act 1973 the choice of the relevant product market is one for the person making the reference to the Monopolies and Mergers Commission (MMC), which in practice is always the Director General of Fair Trading. The MMC will be bound by the definition of the product market, though it could prevail upon the Director General to vary the reference with regard to the definition if it was thought necessary. In practice a definition is suggested by the Director General to the firms likely to come under the scrutiny of the MMC enquiry. An opportunity is given for these firms to object to the proposed definition and to make alternative suggestions.

The product markets which have been the object of recent references to the MMC are set out in Table 1. The table also indicates the closest substitutes found by the MMC; in no case did the MMC consider that a substitute was so close that the initial product market definition was unworkable. It will be noted, however, that certain of the reports concern *groups* of markets with a common product. For example, liquefied petroleum gas (LPG) is a product which falls within many different markets, depending on the use to which it is put. Substitution between LPG and other products, and therefore the market power of the dominant supplier, will differ from market to market. Similarly, ready-mixed concrete will serve distinct markets, ranging from the do-it-yourself market to major engineering projects.

The geographic market is also specified in the reference to the MMC. In most cases the market will comprise the whole of the UK, but where appropriate the geographic market may be restricted in the reference to a part of the UK. Only one such 'local' monopoly enquiry has been undertaken in recent years, and that concerned holiday caravan sites in Northern Ireland. In its report on *Ready Mixed Concrete* (1981), the MMC did find some evidence of local monopolies but could not investigate them because the reference defined the geographical market as comprising the whole UK, where no monopoly was found to exist. Monopoly power which exists at a very local level may also be investigated under the Competition Act 1980.[8] Examples of the exercise of monopoly powers at a local level discovered on such enquiries include an attempt to keep new entrants from a local newspaper market,[9] and anticompetitive franchise arrangements at a railway station[10] and an airport.[11] With regard to product substitution, the MMC does consider the possibilities for new entry on to the market, but sometimes rather fleetingly (eg. *Postal Franking Machines*, 1986).

EEC law In the *United Brands* case (1978), the European Court of Justice (ECJ) had to determine the relevant market for bananas. The choice was between placing bananas in a specific market of their own, or including them within the wider market for fresh fruit. The court held that to regard the banana as forming a separate market 'it must be possible to be singled out by such special features distinguishing it from other fruits that it is only to a limited extent interchangeable with them and is only exposed to their competition in a way that is hardly perceptible'.[12] The court found that 'a very large number of consumers having a constant need for bananas are not noticeably or even appreciably enticed away from the consumption of this product by the arrival of fresh fruit on the market'. Without considering the position of bananas vis-à-vis consumers outside this category, the court found that the banana market was distinct from that for fresh fruit.

The test applied by the ECJ was clearly one of demand

Table 1:
Recent monopoly reports of the MMC

Product market	Competing products
Ready Mixed Concrete Cmnd 8354 (1981)	site-mixed concrete; other building materials
Concrete Roofing Tiles HC 12 (1981)	no effective competition
Liquefied Petroleum Gas HC 147 (1981)	other fuels, depending on use
Roadside Advertising Services HC 365 (1981)	advertising services in other locations
Contraceptive Sheaths Cmnd 8689 (1981)	contraceptive pill; sterilisation
Trading Check Franchise and Financial Services HC 62 (1981)	other forms of personal credit; mail order
Car Parts HC 318 (1982)	no effective competition
Films Cmnd 8858 (1983)	television; video; other entertainment
Holiday Caravan Sites Cmnd 8966 (1983)	untied caravan sites
Animal Waste Cmnd 9470 (1985)	substitutes depend on end-use
Tampons Cmnd 9705 (1986)	other forms of sanitary protection
Postal Franking Machines Cmnd 9747 (1986)	postage stamps
White Salt Cmnd 9778 (1986)	other forms of salt
Foreign Package Holidays Cmnd 9879 (1986)	none identified
Steel Wire Fencing Cm 79 (1987)	other fencing products

substitution, having regard to the 'characteristics' or 'special features' of the product.[13] The European Commission has adopted a similar approach to market definition. In Commission Regulation 1983/83, for example, the Commission defines a market as comprising goods 'which are considered by users as equivalent in view of their characteristics, price and intended use'.[14]

In the later *Michelin* case (1985), the ECJ defined a market, for monopoly purposes, as comprising 'the totality of the products which, with respect to their characteristics, are particularly suitable for satisfying constant needs and are only to a limited extent interchangeable with other products'.[15] In this case the ECJ supported the Commission's definition of the relevant market as being one which included tyres for heavy vehicles, but excluded those for cars and vans. The basis for this separation was the lack of interchangeability at user level, differences in demand structure, and the absence of supply substitution, between the two groups. However, within the relevant market, the ECJ also found there to be no interchangeability from the viewpoint of users, and no elasticity of supply, between the different dimensions of tyres for heavy vehicles. In spite of this, the ECJ refused to split the product group into smaller 'sub-markets' because, from the viewpoint of the intermediary retailer supplying the whole range, the difference in dimension and type were unimportant. This formulation by the ECJ necessarily qualifies its earlier statement that '[t]he concept of the relevant market implies that there can be effective competition between the products which form part of it and this presupposes that there is a sufficient degree of interchangeability between all the products ... in so far as a specific use of such products is concerned' (*Hoffman-La Roche* case, 1979).

In relation to monopoly control, the Commission uses the concept of substitutability to ensure that the market is drawn widely enough 'so as to include not only the products manufactured or marketed by the allegedly dominant producer but also those which are in effective competition with it' (*AKZO* decision, 1985).

Supply substitution will play a part in the ECJ's assessment of market power. Although it has not been very specific in relation to the importance it attaches to potential suppliers, it seems that the likelihood of substitution must be high before it is seen as depressing the market power of an apparently dominant firm. In the *Continental Can* case (1973), for example, the ECJ regarded potential suppliers as those in related fields who 'by a mere adaptation' could step into the market.[16] The Commission also has regard to the possibility of supply substitution. Like the ECJ it uses this concept in a less precise way than demand substitution (usually necessarily so because of the lack of reliable data). This factor is examined as one of many market features which determine the real market power of a firm with a significant market share. With regard to the geographic market, the ECJ defines this as 'an area where the objective conditions of competition applying to the product are the same for all traders' (*United Brands* case, 1978). In order to fall within the scope of Article 86, the dominant position must be one 'within the common market or in a substantial part of it'. The precise meaning of this phrase is not clear, but where the geographic market extends to at least one large Member State, this will be sufficient to bring an abuse within Article 86.

United States law   In US monopoly policy, two leading Supreme Court cases on market definition are the *Brown Shoe* (1962) and *Grinnell* (1966) cases. In *Brown Shoe*, the court held that in monopolization cases the 'outer boundaries' of a product market are to be determined by reasonable interchangeability of use or cross-elasticity of demand. However, the court went on to further divide this broad market into 'sub-markets', each of which may be treated as a discrete market for antitrust purposes. The Supreme Court laid down that courts may have regard to the following seven criteria to determine the existence of such sub-markets: (i) industry or public recognition of the sub-market as a separate economic entity; (ii) the peculiar characteristics and uses of the product; (iii) unique production facilities; (iv) distinct customers; (v) distinct prices; (vi) sensitivity to price changes; and (vii) specialised vendors.

Although these tests do have the advantage of clarity and ease of operation for courts and litigants, they may be criticised on conceptual grounds. If the 'broad' market is selected on the grounds of interchangeability, then it follows that all products within such a market are, to a certain extent, competing with one another; that is the whole purpose of delineating the relevant market. It therefore makes little sense to further divide such a market into smaller groups. If the 'broad' market was correctly chosen, then any subdivision will only exclude good substitutes from consideration (see Posner,

1976; and Walker, 1981). The situation in the *Grinnell* case (1966) was the reverse. Here the Supreme Court lumped together a cluster of different services to form a single relevant market. The market was defined as that for accredited central station protection services, and comprised burglary and fire protection services which were linked to a central monitoring facility and which were accredited for insurance purposes. There was clearly no interchangeability between burglary protection and fire protection but the court, noting that competitors were obliged to offer the whole range of services, held that the definition reflected commercial reality.[17] Two dissenting judges criticised this 'Procrustean' approach to market definition, tailor-made to fit the defendant's business. They regarded the court's market definition as a 'strange red-haired, bearded, one-eyed man-with-a-limp classification'.

The *Grinnell* case also shows the difficulty in selecting the correct geographic market. The services included in the market were offered on a very local basis, each central station having a service radius of a few miles only. Consumer choice was therefore limited to those services offered in the individual localities. In this regard the market bears similarities to markets for low bulk value or non-transportable products, such as ready-mixed concrete.[18] In spite of the localised nature of the service, the court found that the relevant geographic market was the whole nation, because planning, inspection and certification were carried out on a national basis. This approach was roundly criticised by two dissenting judges. They preferred to base the geographic market definition on the areas available to the consumer to search for competing services. Market definition in US cases emphasises demand-side analysis, but use of supply substitution data is made by some courts, such as *Telex* v. *IBM* (1975).[19]

The definition of monopoly

Having defined the relevant market in which the firm operates it is now necessary to consider the nature of monopoly. All three legal systems are concerned ultimately with the acquisition or use of monopoly *power*, but the approach of the respective legal systems differs in many respects. UK policy defines the scope of the legislation by reference to a specific market structure, whereas the EEC and the US legislation proceeds directly to an investigation of monopoly power (rather than market share alone).

United Kingdom law UK monopoly policy is an 'abuse' system; there is no presumption against monopoly, the policy seeks to regulate only those monopolies which, after individual examination, are found to be operating against the 'public interest'. In its definition of monopoly, the UK system adopts a largely form-based approach. In the taxonomy of competition policies, therefore, UK monopoly policy may be classified as behavioural, abuse, and form-based.

UK policy is contained in the Fair Trading Act 1973 ('the 1973 Act'), which provides the power to regulate 'monopoly situations'. The scope of the policy is naturally determined by the definition of a 'monopoly situation', the most striking feature of which is its concern with the position of the dominant firm within the market, rather than with the degree of monopoly power it actually enjoys. Since the possession of a monopoly market share does not necessarily connote the possession of monopoly power, it may be regarded as unnecessary to cast the policy net so wide as to include monopoly firms which have no significant market power. Although this may indicate the needless use of resources, it is important to note that not all monopoly situations will be investigated, and in selecting *which* monopoly situations to investigate the Director General will be influenced by features which indicate that the monopoly firm is indeed enjoying monopoly power. The Director General reviews the economic performance of possible monopoly firms, taking account of import penetration, price levels and movements, profits and market behaviour. He also takes account of complaints from competitors and consumers (Director General, 1986), and there is some indication that the 'postbag' provides a very real initiator of action.

The definition of 'monopoly situation' is contained in sections 6 to 9 of the 1973 Act, each section dealing with a different type of market. Section 6 relates to the supply of goods, section 7 to the supply of services, section 8 to exports, and section 9 to localised markets. Each of these sections is divided into a number of alternative definitions, so that in all there are some eighteen different definitions of a monopoly situation. However, sections 6, 7 and 9 are very similar in their terms, so the following examination will be confined to the terms of section 6. This defines a monopoly situation as being one where the following alternative criteria apply:

(a) at least 25 per cent of all the goods of a certain description which are supplied in the United Kingdom are supplied by, or to, one and the same person (section 6(1)(a)); or

(b) are supplied by, or to members of one and the same group of interconnected bodies corporate (section 6(1)(b)); or

(c) are supplied by, or to, members of one and the same 'section 6(2)group', (section 6(1)(c)); or

(d) one or more agreements are in operation, as a result of which goods of a certain description are not supplied in the United Kingdom at all.

The 25 per cent figure referred to in three of the definitions in section 6 is an arbitrary one; in the preceding monopoly legislation, the market share required to be shown was one third. It was said that the effect of making that change in 1973 was that 115 'industries', in which a single firm was believed to be responsible for between 25 per cent and 33 per cent, were brought within the control of the legislation.[20] However, on examination, it is clear that many of these industries (such as champagne perrys, chewing gum, and corned beef) would not be considered to be separate markets for the purposes of monopoly control. In recent years, the retention of a 33 per cent threshold would have made very little difference to the effect of the legislation; virtually all monopoly situations found to exist by the MMC have involved a market share of more than 33 per cent.

It is not always obvious just how to calculate the percentage market share which a firm enjoys. Section 10(6) of the 1973 Act provides an inexhaustive list of alternative criteria which may be used, and on some occasions the MMC uses more than one method of measurement where it is not obvious which one is correct. In *Contraceptive Sheaths* (1982) both quantity and weight were used, since imports were recorded by weight but home sales by volume. Both physical and financial criteria were used in *Concrete Roofing Tiles* (1981) and in *Roadside*

Advertising Services (1981); and both volume and value were used in *Tampons* (1986) and in *Postal Franking Machines* (1986).

The first two alternative definitions of a monopoly situation, contained in paragraphs (a) and (b) above, are purely structural definitions. They are directed to market share only and take no account of the behaviour of the monopolists or of the basis of the monopoly position. In this regard the definition of monopoly under these paragraphs is a mechanistic process requiring only sufficient market data for its completion.

The word 'person' used in section 6(1)(a) includes both natural persons (such as sole traders or partners) and legal persons (such as limited companies and other incorporated organisations). The 'group of interconnected bodies corporate' referred to in section 6(1)(b) is one which consists of at least two 'bodies corporate' (i.e. companies) all of whom are 'related' to each other as parent, subsidiary or sibling-subsidiary. The circumstances in which such relationship will exist are governed by company law;[21] briefly, a company will be regarded as the subsidiary of another if that other holds at least 50 per cent of its shares. In other contexts, therefore, interconnected bodies corporate are usually referred to as a 'group of companies'. Recent examples of monopoly situations enjoyed by such groups include *Animal Waste* (1985), *Postal Franking Machines* (1986) and *White Salt* (1986). In UK law, in common with most other legal systems, companies are regarded as being legally distinct from their shareholders; a wholly-owned subsidiary has a legal personality independent of its parent company. The provisions of section 6(1)(b) are therefore required so that companies are not able to evade the legislation simply by hiving off activities to a number of subsidiary companies. By regarding a group of related companies as one unit for these purposes, the 1973 Act is articulating the economic reality of commercial activity, rather than the technical legal position. This is the stance taken by other competition policies and may be seen most clearly in the meaning of 'undertaking' in EEC law.[22]

The second two definitions of monopoly, contained in paragraphs (c) and (d), go beyond a mere structural test for monopoly, and examine the nature of the monopoly through the conduct of the firms enjoying it. These monopoly situations are concerned with monopoly achieved through combination or collusion. Such enquiries are much more difficult and less mechanistic than the tests for 'scale' monopoly, and for this reason they are known as 'complex monopoly situations'.[23]

Section 6(1)(c) covers the situation where the critical 25 per cent share is captured by a group of persons whose identity as a group is based on some common anticompetitive activity. This provision (unlike section 6(1)(b)) concerns a group of independent actors, defined in section 6(2). This definition is drawn in very wide terms. For example, the anticompetitive conduct may be undertaken 'voluntarily or not'. It is not clear what would constitute involuntary behaviour in this context, but firms will be unable to plead that their behaviour was determined by such factors as the nature of the market, economic and financial considerations or the terms of an unfavourable contract. Under the terms of section 6(2), firms will also be unable to plead that there was no actual agreement between members of the alleged group. Collusive behaviour may take place in the absence of an agreement, either by way of a 'concerted practice' or through even looser forms of conscious parallelism or information exchange. In *Holiday Caravan Sites* (1983), for example, the MMC accepted that the conduct of the firms enjoying the complex monopoly comprised parallel but independent behaviour not predicated on any specific agreement.

In highly concentrated or oligopolistic markets, collusion or parallel conduct is more likely to take place and more likely to succeed. Such arrangements may well be capable of regulation under restrictive trade practices legislation. However, one important qualification to section 6(2) results from the very sharp distinction drawn between monopoly control and restrictive trade practices policy under UK law. Thus, in determining whether a monopoly situation exists under section 6(1)(c), no account may be taken of the provisions of any agreement which is registrable under restrictive trade practices legislation, even if such agreement is unlawfully unregistered.[24]

Recent examples of complex monopolies under section

6(1)(c) include: *Car Parts* (1982), where twenty-six firms shared 37 per cent of the market through exclusive purchase agreements with franchisees; and *Films* (1983), where the monopoly was maintained through agreed systems for offering films for first run and for determining their sequence of exhibition.

The second variety of 'complex monopoly situation', defined in section 6(1)(d), exists where the relevant goods are not supplied at all in the UK, as a result of one or more agreements. Such a monopoly has never been investigated by the MMC, and it is doubtful whether this definition will ever make a significant contribution to monopoly control.

Monopoly in service industries is defined by section 7 of the 1973 Act, in terms which correspond exactly with those of section 6. Recent 'scale' service monopolies found by the MMC include *Roadside Advertising* (1981), *Trading Checks* (1981), and *Postal Franking Machines* (1986). Complex monopoly situations found under section 7(1)(c) include: *Roadside Advertising Services* (1981), where the identifying conduct took the form of discussions between members of a distribution service, and joint marketing arrangements; *Trading Checks* (1981), where all suppliers within the group placed restrictions on the commercial terms offered by retailers to customers; *Holiday Caravan Sites* (1983), where spaces on caravan sites were reserved for persons purchasing caravans from firms connected with the site operators; and *Foreign Package Holidays* (1986), where tour operators accounting for over 70 per cent of the market refused to allow travel agents to discount prices.

In the reports published by the MMC since the beginning of 1978, very few have concerned service monopolies. However, in 1976 and 1978, the MMC undertook investigations into eight professional service industries, and out of its seventeen reports in those two years, eleven concerned service monopolies.

The third major category of monopoly situations is those in export markets. The export of services, such as financial and insurance services, has long been of considerable importance to the UK economy; it is surprising, therefore, that section 8 covers only the export of goods, not services. The MMC has not investigated any export monopolies, though in three references it has investigated both domestic supply and exports.[25] Section 8 is not identical in its terms to sections 6 and 7, but it does comprise definitions covering scale and complex monopolies.

In summary, the definition of monopoly in UK policy comprises a mixture of structural and behavioural criteria, far removed from the economic monopoly model represented by a single-firm industry. Indeed it is not uncommon to find more than one monopolist under the UK definitions of scale monopoly, e.g. *Concrete Roofing Tiles* (1981), *Films* (1983), and *Postal Franking Machines* (1986). In complex monopolies, there is no limit on the number of possible monopolists.

EEC law Under the Treaty of Rome, monopoly is expressed as a 'dominant position' but is not defined. Article 86 of the Treaty is the basic legislative source for monopoly policy and its prohibition is expressed as follows:

Any abuse by one or more undertakings of a dominant position within the common market or in a substantial part of it shall be prohibited as incompatible with the common market in so far as it may affect trade between Member States.

This style is characteristic of the Treaty of Rome; it is a '*loi cadre*', providing the framework of policy whilst leaving its detailed application to be effected by the Community institutions. In the field of competition law, in common with many other policy areas, the detailed application and analysis has been, and continues to be, undertaken by the EEC Commission and the ECJ. The policy, as interpreted and applied by the Commission and ECJ, is an abuse policy where it is the abuse of a dominant position, rather than the position itself, which is the subject of prohibition.

The concept of 'dominant position' has been defined by the ECJ as:

a position of economic strength which enables an undertaking to prevent, or at least hinder,[26] effective competition being maintained on the relevant market by giving it the power to behave to an appreciable extent independently of its competitors, customers and ultimately of its consumers.[27]

The most striking difference between this definition and those found in UK policy is that the meaning of dominant position is expressed in purely effects-based terms, without market shares being prescribed. Indeed there are no predetermined indicia of monopoly in EEC law; each dominant position is defined according to the individual circumstances pertaining in the relevant market. This open-ended approach permits the Commission and the ECJ to take account of a whole range of factors giving rise to economic dominance, of which market share will be but one. It should be noted that the definition is concerned with a position which 'enables' and which 'gives power'. At this, the definitional, stage it is only necessary to show that such opportunity or power exists, and not that it has been used. As in UK policy, there is a distinction between monopoly (permitted) and its exploitation (prohibited or regulated in certain circumstances). In practice, however, this distinction may well be blurred; action taken under Article 86 is likely to have been prompted by the allegedly anticompetitive behaviour of a dominant firm. In these circumstances the analysis may tend to consider the abuse before the dominance, rather than the opposite way round, as suggested by theory.

Dominance will not be defined in terms of market share alone, but this does remain an important consideration. In the *Hoffman-La Roche* case (1979) the ECJ explained that the existence of a dominant position 'may derive from several factors which, taken separately, are not necessarily determinative but among these factors a highly important one is the existence of very large market shares'. A firm which holds very large market shares over a long period will usually be taken to be dominant because consumers or trading partners will be unable to avoid doing business with it. This will allow the firm a large degree of freedom in determining its market strategy.[28]

This degree of freedom will, of course, depend on the ability of others on the market to compete. For this reason the ECJ will always examine the market shares of other firms on the market, and especially those of the largest competitors of the supposedly dominant firm. Evidence of a large market share relative to those of competitors will be a more reliable indicator of dominance than evidence of a large share in absolute terms alone; but the maintenance of a market share of any size may be due to effective competition as much as to monopoly. In *Michelin* (1985), the dominant firm was found to have a market share of 57 per cent to 65 per cent, compared with shares of 4 per cent to 8 per cent enjoyed by its main competitors. That market share constituted 'a valid indication of Michelin's preponderant strength in relation to its competitors'. In *Hoffman-La Roche* (1979), in at least one market the dominant firm had a market share as large as the aggregate share of its two largest competitors.

It will be noted that, as in UK monopoly policy, the existence of a dominant position does not call for the complete absence of competition from products on the market or from substitute products from contiguous markets. Even the presence of lively competition on the market will not preclude the possibility of a dominant position. What is essential to dominance is that the firm must be able to determine its market strategy without taking the activities of its competitors into account. In other words, the dominant firm must be immune to any detrimental effects as a result of its market behaviour. A clear example of competition precluding the possibility of dominance, therefore, is where price cuts by competitors force the firm in question to lower its own prices in order to preserve its market share (*Hoffman-La Roche*). The position is the same with regard to products which are excluded from the relevant market but which are partially interchangeable with the relevant products. In *Michelin*, the dominant firm argued that the relevant product, new replacement tyres, were subject to competition from retreads. The ECJ, noting the limited nature of that competition, held that Michelin was free to act on the market without having to take account of competition from retreads and without suffering any adverse effects as a result of its attitude. That freedom of action was indicative of dominance.

The question of competition from contiguous markets is really another way of expressing the fact that such other products are not 'good substitutes' for the relevant product. Had there been a greater degree of interchangeability, the definition of the relevant market would originally have been drawn to include all the products. This would have reduced the market share of the supposedly dominant firm and, by inference, its market power. Also relevant to the original definition of the market will be the question of potential competition through supply substitution to, or new firms starting up production of, the relevant product. In assessing the possible dominance of the market the Court will again have regard to the existence of barriers to entry in order to evaluate the impact of potential competition. In this regard the ECJ considers the need for a large capital investment to be a barrier to entry. This attitude has been criticised, especially by Korah, as being more concerned to promote the position of smaller undertakings than to assess the real possibilities of entry on to the market.[29] If firms can convince sources of capital, such as banks or shareholders, that the profits which may be made from entry are large relative to the associated risks, then a large capital requirement should not constitute a barrier.

Other factors which the ECJ will take into account in assessing dominance will include: technical lead through patent protection or know-how etc; the development of a sales network; and the degree of vertical integration.[30] The ECJ has, however, repeatedly stated that it will not regard profitability as determinative of dominance, since whereas an efficient firm may make good profits even in a competitive environment, temporary unprofitability may not be inconsistent with monopoly. Further, a firm may be no less dominant simply because it charges low prices.

United States law Section 2 of the Sherman Act is similar in style to Article 86 of the Treaty of Rome, in that it provides a very brief and general description of the law's policy but does no more. The development and application of the section's general terms have been left to the courts. The advantage of this approach is that monopoly policy can be constantly updated to accord with commercial reality; the disadvantage, especially in the context of the complex American judicial structure, is that many different interpretations and policies may emerge. Fortunately there is much agreement among the courts as to the definition of monopoly power.

The stark terms of section 2 are as follows:

Every person who shall monopolize, or attempt to monopolize, or combine or conspire with any other person or persons, to monopolize any part of the trade or commerce among the several States, or with foreign nations, shall be deemed guilty of a felony...

The target of American policy is 'monopolization'. The nature of this offence will be examined below; for present purposes it is essential to disclose the two elements that, together, comprise monopolization. In the *Grinnell* case (1966), the US Supreme Court stated that, for a violation of section 2, there must be a finding of (i) the possession of monopoly power; and (ii) the wilful acquisition or maintenance of that power. As with UK and EEC policies, therefore, the preliminary requirement in US monopoly control is the demonstration of monopoly power. As the judge in *Berkey Photo* v. *Eastman Kodak* (1979) put it, 'the key to analysis, it must be stressed, is the concept of market power'.

Monopoly power for the purposes of section 2 was defined in the *Cellophane* case (1956) as 'the power to control prices or exclude competition', a test which has been closely followed in subsequent cases. Although it appears that the test has two legs—prices and competition—*Cellophane* intended that they should be considered together, an approach which conforms to economic theory.[31] In measuring market power, courts will consider first the market share of the firm on the relevant market. In common with EEC policy, US law does not lay down any predetermined market share which, by itself, will be indicative of market power. Sullivan characterises the predetermined approach as a 'self-executing, two dimensional structural test for monopoly power' (Sullivan, 1977 II).

As discussed above, the sole advantage of such an approach to the definition of monopoly power is its ease of application by enforcement authorities. Perhaps bearing this feature in mind, the court in the *United Shoe* case (1953) said, in a somewhat wistful footnote:

this Court [does not] consider whether ... a bold, original court, mindful of what legal history teaches us about the usual, if not invariable, relationship between overwhelming percentage of the market and control of the market, and desirous of enabling trial judges to escape the morass of economic data in which they are now plunged, might ... announce that an enterprise having an overwhelming percentage of the market was presumed to have monopoly power...

In the *Alcoa* case (1945), Judge Learned Hand held that a share of 90 per cent would be sufficient to constitute monopoly, that it was doubtful that a 60 per cent share would, and that a 33 per cent share would certainly not be sufficient. This market share approach to the determination of market power was intended by the judge to apply only to the market under consideration in that case, and not as a prescriptive rule for all cases. It is clear that, as in EEC policy, the significance of market share will depend on all the circumstances of the market in question: analysis 'depends not only on the market structure, which remains under the cases a most important evidentiary fact, but on the way prices are actually formed and decisions made' (Attorney General, 1955).

In the *United Shoe* case (1953), the firm in question had a 75 per cent share of the relevant market, a factor to which the court gave 'some weight', but which was not dispositive of the issue. Other factors considered by the court included the firm's pricing practices, the relative financial resources of the firm and its competitors, the firm's 'learning' advantages, the variety of its products, and the fact that 90 per cent of a largely static demand was substantially tied to the firm through long-term leases. However, although market share remains only one of several factors in the determination of monopoly, very large market shares have been taken by some courts to be of singular importance. In *Berkey Photo* v. *Eastman Kodak* (1979), for example, the court found that Kodak's control of the relevant markets had 'clearly reached the level of a monopoly', with shares of 95 per cent and 60 per cent to 67 per cent in respective markets.

THE TREATMENT OF MONOPOLY

The manner in which monopoly power is regulated in the three legal systems differs radically, not only with regard to the policy objectives and goals, but also in the institutional apparatus by which policy is effected. In an area where significant differences exist, the most significant similarity between the systems is that none of them seek to prohibit monopoly *per se*. The institutional structure of UK policy is wholly administrative. The discretionary, pragmatic system is based on civil, rather than criminal, law. It involves few sanctions and depends to a large extent on a degree of cooperation between industry and the competition authorities. The objective of UK policy is to intervene on to markets where it has been determined that monopoly power has been exercised in a way contrary to the public interest. EEC policy is designed to regulate the exercise of market power once it has been acquired. The institutional structure has two phases—administrative and judicial—and is backed up by a power to impose swingeing fines. These fines are described, mainly for political purposes, as being of a civil nature, but they are certainly designed and applied as deterrents. United States policy is more concerned with monopoly power itself—the 'wrongful' acquisition of such power is prohibited, as well as its maintenance through improper means. The Sherman Act is a criminal law statute, and the institutional structure is judicial in nature.

United Kingdom law

Where a monopoly situation is identified by the Director General of Fair Trading, the matter may be referred by him, or by the Secretary of State for Trade, to the Monopolies and Mergers Commission. It is usually the function of the MMC to investigate the entire industry in question to determine whether a monopoly situation does indeed exist, and if so whether it is being exercised in a manner contrary to the 'public interest'.

The findings of the MMC must be reported to the Secretary of State and, where appropriate, will contain recommendations for action. The Secretary of State may thereafter direct the Director General to seek undertakings from the dominant firm with a view to promoting the public interest; failing this, an Order may be made directing the

dominant firm to take, or refrain from taking, certain action.
The operation of monopoly policy in the UK is characterised by its administrative nature. The three 'actors' are the Director General, the MMC and the Secretary of State. Unlike the operation of restrictive trade practices policy in the UK, there is no participation by judicial bodies in monopoly policy.[32] Another characteristic feature, which separates UK policy from that of the EEC and the USA, is that it is not possible for individuals or firms injured by the anticompetitive activities of a monopolist to bring a legal action in respect of those activities.

The Director General of Fair Trading The Director General is an office established by the Fair Trading Act 1973 to supervise and oversee the entire field of competition and consumer policy in the UK.[33] The Director General is so crucial that the practical strength of UK competition policy turns on the effectiveness of the incumbent of that office and of his staff in the Office of Fair Trading (OFT). In the parliamentary debates preceding the 1973 Act, one Member of Parliament described the Director General as being 'expected to be a venturesome knight sallying forth to protect the consumer ... an independent assessor of monopolies and mergers and a legal scrutineer of restrictive practices ... I am very sceptical as to whether a paragon with so many virtues exists as an individual'.[34] Another described the government's expectations thus: 'the Director General will be a great guy, a marvellous fellow, a genius'.[35] In fact the office has been very successful; no criticism has been made of the role or effectiveness of the Director General. The present incumbent is Sir Gordon Borrie, who is undertaking the task for his third consecutive five-year period.

The OFT is similar in many respects to the Federal Trade Commission (FTC) in the USA in that both bodies have open-ended remits to oversee competition and consumer interests. Unlike the FTC however, the OFT has no quasi-judicial function, being a purely administrative agency. The Director General and the OFT are independent of government, comprising a small but expert agency. This independent position was emphasised in the early years of the OFT's existence by a degree of outside staffing. However, Ramsay has found that, since 1976, staffing has been restricted almost entirely to civil servants, largely as a result of pressure from civil service unions (Ramsay, 1987). In its consumer role the OFT is perceived as a new 'player' in the consumer constituency (Ramsay, 1987). In its role as enforcer of competition legislation it is identified more closely with government, although it has been successful in persuading firms to consult informally across the whole spectrum of competition law, with a view to avoiding formal enforcement procedures. The overall budget of the OFT is approximately £9 million.[36] The Competition Policy Division of the OFT, which employs over seventy staff, has an allocation of £1.2 million.[37]

With respect to his functions in relation to monopoly policy, the primary duties of the Director General are to review, and collate data on, commercial activities in the UK in order to become aware of monopoly situations and uncompetitive practices.[38] Where, as a result of this review, the Director General believes that a monopoly situation may exist, and that it may be operating against the public interest, he has discretion to refer the matter to the MMC for it to investigate.[39]

The Monopolies and Mergers Commission The original version of the MMC was set up under legislation in 1948.[40] After having undergone a number of changes, both in name and functions, the present body is regulated by the Fair Trading Act 1973. Its functions are contained in the 1973 Act, and are supplemented by the Competition Act 1980. These functions comprise investigation, assessment and recommendation, in the context of monopoly policy, mergers, anticompetitive practices, (either generally or in relation to a specific firm) and the efficiency of public bodies. Although the MMC is an entirely passive body, relying on matters being referred to it, it does have a definitive role in the assessment of monopoly activity; the government is unable to act against a dominant firm unless the MMC considers that the public interest has been adversely affected.[41] In addition, there is no possibility for the private enforcement of UK monopoly policy. This control wielded by the MMC over the development of monopoly policy is tempered by the passive role played by the MMC in the initiation of investigations, and by the absolute discretion available to the Secretary of State on whether to follow the MMC's eventual recommendations.

The MMC comprises a maximum of thirty-two members[42] including a chairman and three deputies; it does not consider matters in a plenary fashion but divides into ad hoc groups, usually comprising five or six members. Members of the MMC are appointed by the Secretary of State, who also appoints the chairman and deputy chairmen. However the MMC is intended to be a body independent of government. This is confirmed by the 1973 Act, which states that members of the Commission 'shall not be regarded as servants or agents of the Crown.'[43] The independence of the MMC is an important feature of its role; the government remains free to ignore its expert assessment if it is expedient to do so on the basis of policy outside the scope of competition law. Likewise, the MMC is free to assess economic and commercial activity as it thinks best, without feeling the constraint that a government department may feel to follow the current policy 'line'. However, one Secretary of State stated his intention of bringing to bear his 'political opinion' on the MMC (Robinson, 1980 I).

Until the advent of the 'mega-merger' wave in 1984–5, the MMC did not enjoy a very high profile outside financial and legal circles; it is still a rather obscure body so far as the greater proportion of people are concerned. It can in no way be regarded as a stepping-stone to appointment to high office in government or industry. About half of the membership tends to comprise senior figures from commerce and industry; the other half is made up of senior academic or practising lawyers, economists and chartered accountants, together with trade union representatives. Many members of the MMC have also been, or are concurrently, members of other public bodies. The MMC has a sizeable support staff[44] and an annual budget of over £2 million.[45]

Monopoly references Monopoly references to the MMC take one of two forms, those limited to the facts[46] and those not so limited.[47] The limited form has not been used since the present MMC was constituted. The unlimited form utilises the expertise of the MMC not only to determine whether monopoly power actually exists but also to assess the effect, if any, which the dominant firm's conduct has had or may have on the 'public interest'. As will be discussed below, it is also left to the MMC to determine, on a case-by-case basis, exactly what are the requirements of the public interest.

In the most common type of reference, five specific questions are put to the MMC: (a) does a monopoly situation exist, and if so under which of the definitions supplied by the Act; (b) who is or are the monopolist(s); (c) how, if at all, is the monopolist exploiting or maintaining the monopoly situation; (d) how, if at all, is the existence of the monopoly situation attributable to the monopolist; and (e) whether anything found by the MMC operates, or may be expected to operate, against the public interest. This reference therefore generates a wide-ranging enquiry and evaluation taking in the whole industry and requiring the involvement and cooperation of the leading firms and probably any trade association as well.

There is also a more restricted form of reference, where the MMC is required only to determine the existence, and assess the effects, of an activity specified in the reference, such as pricing policy, refusals to supply, or discrimination.[48] Recent examples of these restricted enquiries include: *Contraceptive Sheaths* (1982) and *Tampons* (1986), both concerned with pricing policy; and *Car Parts* (1982), restricted to exclusive purchasing arrangements in the industry.

Once the wording of a monopoly reference has been formulated, often after consultations with the industry, it will be transmitted to the MMC. A summary will be published in the press, with an invitation for comments. The reference will contain a time limit, within which the MMC is to report, usually between eighteen months and three years. This may appear to be a relatively long period, but may be explained by the comprehensive nature of monopoly enquiries in UK practice and by the fact that the (part-time) members will be considering more than one matter simultaneously. Nevertheless, the lengthy process is often a source of great irritation and inconvenience to the industry under investigation, and the protracted uncertainty may affect the share value of the leading firms.

At an early stage in the investigation the MMC will issue a questionnaire addressed to the larger firms in the industry,[49] and, if appropriate, to any trade association. These questionnaires will often be long and detailed and may require expert assistance from lawyers, accountants, economists and other professional advisors. Their purpose will be to elicit information on all aspects of the market and the position of each firm within it. Information will be required on the existence of agreements and trading relationships, corporate ownership, major shareholdings, trading practices, profit figures, technical information on production and distribution processes, the structure of demand, and other aspects of the market.

This data-gathering forms the first part of the MMC's investigation. Once the facts are elicited, and where a monopoly situation has been found to exist, the MMC will progress to the next stage, in which the public interest aspects are considered. This stage will only concern the firm or firms who are found to be enjoying the monopoly situation. The recommendations of the MMC with regard to the effects of monopoly conduct on the public interest will be the critical element of its report. The firms involved at this stage will therefore be allowed to make representations to the MMC and to appear before it to make a 'case' with regard to the public interest. The role of expert advisors is particularly important at this stage.

The 'public interest' The approach of UK monopoly policy to the definition of the public interest is in complete contrast to that taken by UK restrictive trade practices policy.[50] Whereas the latter comprises a technical, formal definition, capable of application by a judicial body, the definition supplied by the 1973 Act for monopoly policy is open-ended and flexible. This reflects the administrative, expert procedure by which monopoly policy is put into effect.

Section 84 of the 1973 Act is not so much definitive as permissive; the MMC is required to take account of 'all matters which appear to them in the particular circumstances to be relevant'. There are certain matters to which the MMC must have regard, as a minimum. These criteria relate to the maintenance and promotion of: (a) effective competition between UK suppliers; (b) consumer interests with regard to price, quality, and choice; (c) cost reduction, technical development, and the reduction of entry barriers; (d) balanced distribution of industry and employment in the UK; and (e) export competitiveness. These criteria are not laid down as policy objectives; the MMC is merely directed to have regard to their desirability in each case. There is no presumption that these matters will always be desirable or desirable to the same extent. In its report on *Tampons* (1986), the MMC rejected the argument of the dominant firm that the first criterion—the promotion of competition—has a higher status than the others. In particular, the MMC regarded itself as being free to recommend price reductions even though this might have the effect of stifling new entry.

In its assessment of the public interest, therefore, the MMC takes an entirely pragmatic line, unrestricted by any objective policy preconceptions. This pragmatic approach is regarded by some as a weakness of monopoly policy (Pass and Sparkes, 1980; Sharpe, 1985), but it is deeply engrained in the UK system.

The Green Paper on Monopolies and Mergers Policy[51] reviewed the findings of the MMC between 1959 and 1978. Pass and Sparkes undertook a similar, more detailed review in respect of a shorter period and found that the single most common activity found to be against the public interest was price discrimination (Pass and Sparkes, 1980). This occurred in half of the sixteen reports in which the MMC found any activity contrary to the public interest, and varied between discrimination between brands and customers, 'delivered price' systems and discriminatory cancellation charges. Discriminatory pricing has not been a major feature in the reports published since this study where activity contrary to the public interest has been found. However, a practice with similar effects has been found in two reports. In *Credit Cards* (1980)[52] and in *Trading Checks* (1981), the MMC criticised the 'no discrimination' practice of the monopolists, whereby retailers supplied with the services in question were prohibited from discriminating between those customers who took advantage of the service and those who did not. The requirement to charge different groups of customers in the same way is a form of price discrimination forced on to the retailers, and was found to deprive customers of choice and to have the effect of raising prices generally.

The reports published since the Pass and Sparkes paper have found supracompetitive prices to be a more prevalent problem than price discrimination. High prices were the result either of the dominance of the monopolist, or of the absence of price competition in oligopolistic markets. The latter was the case in *Roadside Advertising* (1981), where pricing was discussed in trade association meetings; and in *White Salt* (1986), where the two monopoly firms maintained parallel prices through a complex system of information exchange.

Excessive profits were found in six of the reports surveyed by Pass and Sparkes, and in reports published subsequently. It may often be difficult to determine whether profits are 'excessive' in an objective way, since there is often no control group or comparator against which the margin may be measured. The profits achieved by other firms in the industry may not be a proper indication where the dominant firm benefits from economies of scale or other efficiencies. Figures for other industries are similarly unlikely to be helpful. In addition, profit figures declared for accounting purposes may not be appropriate where they do not take account of all items considered by economists to be 'costs' (McGee, 1974).

High profits may not be attributable to monopoly conduct but to low costs achieved through efficiency. This is recognised by the ECJ[53] and also by the MMC. In *Tampons* (1986), the MMC accepted that, in the absence of barriers to entry, high profits 'may be attributable to superior entrepreneurial ability, successful innovation, and more efficient techniques of production and organisation'. The MMC described these features as 'the very characteristics of competition which the Fair Trading Act seeks to promote, and it would be counter-productive to penalise their success'. Profit figures in isolation are not a reliable indication of the exercise of monopoly power; the efficiency, innovative activity and responsiveness of the firm to demand trends must also be examined.

Where the MMC does find prices or profits to be excessive, it is open to it to recommend price or profit regulation. The MMC recommended price regulation in two reports on *Contraceptive Sheaths* (1974[54] and 1982), where no price competition existed and where there was no likelihood of the dominant firm's market share being eroded. In that market, the dominant firm had a market share of 90 per cent to 95 per cent. As a result of the first report, the dominant firm's prices were regulated on the basis of a maximum permissible rate of return. This method of control was rejected by the second report as involving particular practical difficulties with regard to the calculation of capital costs and profit figures. Moreoever, the MMC accepted that regulation based on this method weakened incentives to improve efficiency: 'for a company in [the subject firm's] monopoly position, where the spur to increased efficiency is not provided by pressure from strong and effective competition, this point has some significance'. Price control was therefore based on an index of input costs. In *White Salt* (1986), where the market was shared equally by two producers who chose not to engage in price competition, one firm was a low-cost producer and could have put pressure on the high-cost producer through pricing. The MMC found that price regulation was the only practicable way to break the link between the high costs of one firm and the prices of the other. It again rejected the notion of regulating prices by reference to profitability as this would weaken incentives to improve efficiency. It therefore recommended that control should be by reference to the input costs of the efficient firm and would only limit the prices of that firm. This would mean that the industry price would be that of the more efficient producer; the less efficient firm would have to search for efficiencies or else lose market share.

Price regulation will be a solution where there is no possibility for reviving price competition among existing firms or facilitating new entry; but where the market has not been permanently disabled, the regulation of prices is likely to further remove the possibilities for a natural recovery of the self-correcting market mechanism. In *Tampons* (1986), the MMC recognised that price regulation 'may discourage investment, innovation and new entry that would otherwise be expected both to reduce future prices and to improve the range of goods and services available to the public'.

Other anticompetitive behaviour of monopolists has also been criticised by the MMC, including restrictions on outlets, tie-in sales and refusal to supply a competitor.

Public undertakings Public undertakings largely escaped regulation under antitrust legislation until the enactment of the Competition Act 1980. Section 11 of the 1980 Act strengthens the possibilities for the control of such bodies by providing a mechanism for investigating their conduct and performance. The Secretary of State is given the power to refer to the MMC any question concerning the efficiency and costs of such bodies, the service provided by, or possible abuse of a monopoly situation by, them. This power is therefore wider than the control of private monopolies under the Fair Trading Act, which is effectively restricted to aspects of the conduct of monopoly firms, rather than their performance. The section covers a wide range of firms which are managed by government appointees, together with bus operators, water authorities, and agricultural marketing boards. Great use has been made of this power; the MMC has made nineteen reports under section 11. Six have concerned electricity boards, four have concerned water authorities, and seven have concerned various transport undertakings or authorities. The remaining two concerned the National Coal Board and the Post Office. When Secretary of State for Trade and Industry, Tebbit described section 11 as 'an important instrument for dealing with nationalised industries which cannot for the time being be transferred to private sector' (Tebbit, 1984 II).

EEC law
Article 86 prohibits the abuse of a dominant position only where the abuse may affect trade between Member States. Where such conditions are thought to prevail, then action may be taken by the Commission of the European Communities ('the Commission'). Action of a very different nature may also be taken by any firm or individual who is affected by the prohibited behaviour. These private actions, although of some practical importance, are less significant in shaping

monopoly policy in the EEC.

Where the Commission considers that a firm is dominant *and* that it is abusing its dominance *and* that such abuse may affect trade between Member States, then it may commence an investigation. Procedural aspects of the Commission's enquiry are mainly covered by Regulation 17.

The Commission The Commission's functions within the EEC are of a hybrid nature, and it occupies a unique position among international bodies. Its primary task within the EEC is to initiate legislation by submitting proposals to the Council of Ministers. The Commission is composed of seventeen independent persons supported by an operational and research staff of over 12,000. Momentum is maintained in the EEC through a system of creative interdependency between the Community institutions. The Council of Ministers, the legislative body, represents the interests of the Member States; it is powerless to act except on a proposal from the Commission, which represents the 'Community' interest. In turn, the Commission is politically responsible to the European Parliament, a consultative body with some budgetary powers. In its initiating role the Commission acts as the 'motor of integration' (Pryce, 1973). In addition to this role, the Commission acts as the enforcing agency of the EEC and, in relation to tasks delegated to it, as the executive of the Council of Ministers. It is therefore both a political body and a bureaucracy.

The Commission's function in relation to competition law falls within its bureaucratic role;[55] it should nevertheless be noted that, although its style is administrative, its decisions directly affect the *legal* position of the addressees. Boyer, contrasting the approach of the Commission with that of the US Department of Justice, characterises the role of the Commission as being purely mechanical: 'it forbids or approves business dealings in the same way that lesser agencies process applications for passports' (Boyer, 1983). Coombes also describes the Commission's antitrust functions as 'basically mechanical activities' and draws a distinction between this 'reproductive decision-making according to settled policies and the taking of critical, innovative decisions needed to initiate new policies' (Coombes, 1970). These are both harsh judgments of a hybrid agency which is empowered to exercise a great deal of discretion both in its choice of defendant and in the interpretation of the relevant legislation.

With regard to its antitrust functions the Commission bears many similarities to the US Federal Trade Commission (FTC), which also combines investigative, prosecutorial and decision-making roles within the framework of an administrative agency.[56] The separation within the FTC of the administrative law judge and the investigative and prosecutorial staff does not feature in the organisation of the EEC Commission. Indeed, a recent reorganisation has eroded the separation between investigator and assessor.[57]

The section of the Commission dealing with competition policy is Directorate General IV, which has a self-contained hierarchy and an expert staff of about 260. Decisions of DGIV must be formally ratified by the full Commission before they have the force of law.

The Commission's investigation into the possible abuse of a dominant position may be initiated by its own monitoring of industry conduct and performance or through complaints received from consumers or competitors. In any event, the Commission's powers of investigation are extremely wide-ranging. Regulation 17 empowers the Commission to request information from any firm, by way of a letter or a formal 'decision', concerning all aspects of the market and its conduct and activities. This requirement is backed up by heavy penalties which may be issued by the Commission for false, delayed or incomplete returns. In addition, where the Commission considers that information may be concealed or destroyed, it may mount a surprise visit, or 'dawn raid', on the offices of the firm, in order to examine documents and to take copies. The Commission regards this power as essential for the successful application of competition law (Joshua, 1983). Joshua has found that the presence of any of the following factors may lead the Commission to proceed by way of 'surprise': (i) where the suspected infringement is likely to lead to a heavy fine; (ii) where the suspected behaviour is by its very nature likely to be practised in secret; or (iii) where the previous conduct of the firm indicates that surprise would be appropriate. This swingeing power is quite unlike anything available to the DGFT or MMC under UK law, and British firms took some time in accepting such process, following the UK's accession to the EEC.[58]

A firm may be unaware that an investigation is under way until a Statement of Objections is delivered to it. The firm has a right to be 'heard' on the objections, this 'hearing' taking a mainly written form, although there is provision for oral hearings. The process is designed for data-gathering; it is administrative in nature, rather than judicial or quasi-judicial.[59] The consequences of a Commission decision on competition law may be particularly adverse for the firm concerned, and for this reason there is some disquiet that the Commission procedure does not provide for the full legal protection that parties would enjoy in the context of judicial proceedings. The Commission responded to some such criticisms by the appointment of a Hearing Officer, whose function it is to ensure that due process is observed in the preparation of decisions on competition law. The emphasis of a Commission enquiry into possible monopoly abuse will be on the firm in question, rather than on the industry as a whole, and will usually be more speedy than a monopoly enquiry in the UK. When the draft decision has been prepared, it is submitted for comment to the Advisory Committee on Restrictive Practices and Monopolies. This is a body composed of expert representatives from each Member State, whose deliberations and opinions are kept secret.[60] Subsequently, the formal decision is taken by the full Commission, and may be challenged before the ECJ. EEC monopoly policy, unlike UK policy, is not enforced in an exclusively centrical way.

Private parties are also entitled to bring civil actions in the national courts in their own Member States to establish a breach of Article 86 and, if their national law permits, to seek damages for any injury. The *Garden Cottage Foods* case (1984) is an example of such an action in the English courts. It is a great departure from their tradition for the courts in the UK to consider the economic arguments that are inevitable in any application of Article 86. Indeed the legal style of the whole of EEC law has required the UK courts to develop new techniques of interpretation. There are certain advantages to private actions as an additional means of enforcing antitrust policy. They free firms from dependence on the antitrust authorities and enable abuses to be brought to light more quickly. Further, by shifting the costs of the action to the firms involved, private actions will only proceed to full adjudication where the abuse causes injury and where the parties take different views of their respective chances of success in court. In many cases the matter will be settled informally. Although the use of private actions does release pressure on the resources of the antitrust authorities, there are certain associated disadvantages. The multi-source development of the law by the various national courts may lead to differing, and even conflicting, interpretations. In addition the relative inexpertise of the national courts compared to the Commission and the ECJ may hinder the efficient development of the law. Fortunately, the effect of such disadvantages is mitigated by the ability (and sometimes the obligation) of the national courts to seek a ruling from the ECJ on the interpretation of EEC law, under a procedure laid down in Article 177 of the Treaty of Rome.

The 'abuse' Article 86 provides a list of activities which are likely to be abusive if carried on by a dominant firm. It was at first thought that this was exhaustive, but it is now clear that it comprises merely a non-exhaustive list of possible examples of abusive behaviour. No significance will therefore attach to the appearance or non-appearance of an activity; those which do appear will not be *per se* prohibited. The list is, however, a good guide to the policy of Article 86. It will be immediately apparent that EEC monopoly policy is directed at regulating the market power of a monopolist rather than at the market structure itself. There is no power to prevent a firm actually acquiring monopoly power, even by the most anticompetitive means. On the other hand, a firm will be subject to the limitations on its conduct imposed by Article 86 even where it bears no responsibility at all for the acquisition of its monopoly power. Thus, in the *Tele-Marketing* case (1986), the monopoly in question arose through a statutory prohibition on competition in the market. Notwithstanding this, the activities of the monopoly firm were held to be capable of regulation under Article 86.

The activities listed in Article 86, together with other activities found to be abusive, may be grouped into two broad categories: exploitative abuses and anticompetitive abuses (Vogelenzang, 1976; Bellamy and Child, 1978; Temple Lang, 1979). Exploitative abuses comprise activity which could not be carried on but for the dominance of the firm. The monopolist is, literally, *exploiting* its market position in a way which harms those at different levels in the market, be they suppliers, customers or consumers. Examples of exploitative abuses would include monopoly pricing (imposing excessively high prices on consumers or excessively low ones on suppliers), discrimination, tie-in sales, and the imposition of onerous conditions. It would be impossible to sustain any of these activities under competitive conditions (or, in the long term, in monopoly conditions where entry barriers are low), and they will all operate to the disadvantage of those who, because of the market structure, must deal with the dominant firm.

Anticompetitive abuses comprise activity which does not depend on the dominance of the perpetrator, but the effect of which on the market is accentuated by that dominance. Activity included within this category would include certain vertical or horizontal mergers by dominant firms, refusal to supply, fidelity rebates, and exclusive or selective distribution systems. All these activities may be carried on in a competitive environment, but would have little or no effect on the market. In the context of a dominant position such activities will serve to further weaken the competitive structure through the exclusion of those competitors which still remain, and may therefore be prohibited. A dominant firm is subject to a much stricter code of conduct; it has a responsibility to refrain from conduct which has an anticompetitive effect, even though identical activity would be condoned or even encouraged in a non-dominant firm. That is not to say that a dominant firm must refrain from competing vigorously. The Commission made this clear in its *AKZO* decision (1985):

a dominant firm is entitled to compete on the merits ... large producers should [not] be under any obligation to refrain from competing vigorously with smaller competitors or new entrants. The maintenance of a system of effective competition does however require that a small competitor be protected against behaviour by dominant undertakings designed to exclude it from the market not by virtue of greater efficiency but by an abuse of market power.

It is clear that the two categories of abuse are not mutually exclusive. An activity by which a firm exploits its dominant position may also weaken competition on the market, but the classification is useful if only to demonstrate the scope of EEC monopoly policy. The following paragraphs will analyse the ECJ's approach to the activities of dominant firms in relation to Article 86.

The pricing policy of dominant firms can be examined under a number of the paragraphs of Article 86. Excessive pricing is certainly abusive, being 'unfair' pricing within the meaning of paragraph (a). The objection is that the dominant firm is using its market position 'to reap trading benefits which it would not have reaped if there had been normal and sufficiently effective competition'.[61] The prohibition of excessive pricing by monopolists is therefore a consumer protection measure, rather than a device to protect competition (Siragusa, 1979). In the absence of high barriers to entry, high pricing may be regarded as pro-competitive in that it will attract new entry to the market (Gyselen and Kyriazis, 1986).

The calculation of 'excess' in relation to prices was first considered by the ECJ in the *General Motors* case (1976), where the Court confirmed that 'abuse might lie ... in the imposition of a price which is excessive in relation to the economic value of the service provided'. In that case the excessiveness of the price was deduced from the fact that, on receiving complaints, the dominant firm had reduced it to 25 per cent of its original value.[62]

In *United Brands* (1978), the ECJ, whilst confirming that excessiveness referred to the relationship between price and 'economic value', required a more sophisticated calculation. The Court required the Commission to have regard to production costs in order to determine the excessiveness of prices. If it can be shown that prices are excessive on this basis, then a price will be taken to be 'unfair' either on an objective basis—i.e. 'unfair in itself'—or when compared to the prices of competing products. The ECJ was aware of the difficulties involved in calculating and apportioning production cost figures, especially in the context of complex corporate structures with a wide product range or multinational production facilities. One commentator believes that the ECJ demonstrated a lack of understanding of economics in its judgment, and that it may have misunderstood the difference between economic costs and costs used for accounting purposes (Adams, 1985 I). Adams' main criticism was that the ECJ was willing to accept industry cost figures where the actual costs of the dominant firm could not be determined. The use of such figures could be misleading where the dominant firm enjoys low-cost production through efficiencies.

In spite of these criticisms it seems that production cost figures will be the most reliable and practicable indicator of excessive pricing by a monopoly firm, even though it requires the Court to make a judgment on what return would be 'excessive' in each case. Temple Lang suggests that the value received by a dominant firm must be 'grossly disproportionate' to the value given (Temple Lang, 1979). Adams' prediction that the onerous task of collating price information will dissuade the Commission from devoting resources to such cases, may well prove to be accurate.

Excessively *low* prices, maintained with the intention of driving out a competitor or preventing new entry, are also capable of being abusive, although the position is less clear. There is much debate in economics literature on the nature and proper measurement of predatory pricing,[63] and the ECJ has not had an opportunity to rule on this activity. The Commission has, however, levied the heaviest fine to date, in relation to predatory pricing.[64] In the *AKZO* decision, 1985, the Commission rejected the definition of predatory pricing as pricing below average variable cost (or marginal cost), as suggested by Areeda and Turner (Areeda and Turner, 1975). This test was thought to be too narrow and inflexible in relation to EEC competition policy, which is designed to protect a competitive structure rather than secure short-term efficiency gains.

On the one hand, the Commission argued that sales below

total costs will favour large firms to the prejudice of small efficient firms, because of the deeper pockets available to the larger firms through sheer size or through cross-subsidisation from other markets. On the other hand, the Commission emphasised that non-predatory (in cost terms) strategic behaviour by large firms can be effective in excluding competitors. The important element is 'the rival's assessment of the aggressor's determination to frustrate its expectations ... rather than whether or not the dominant firm covers its own costs. There can be an anti-competitive object in price cutting whether or not the aggressor sets its prices above or below its own costs'.

The position seems to be, therefore, that pricing policies engaged in by a dominant enterprise with the intent of harming residual competition on the market may constitute an abuse even where prices are above total costs. Pricing below costs may raise a presumption of an anticompetitive intent, but will not be *per se* abusive (*AKZO* decision, para. 80; cf. Ashley, 1983).

Other pricing policies which are capable of being abusive include fidelity rebates and discriminatory pricing. Fidelity rebates depend on a customer purchasing all or a certain proportion of its requirements for a product from the dominant supplier. These can be contrasted with quantity discounts which depend only on the amount purchased. Whereas quantity discounts are perfectly justifiable in economic terms, fidelity rebates have the effect of restricting the freedom of the customer and, perhaps more significantly, render access to the market by competitors more difficult. Moreover, fidelity rebates do not have all the efficiency advantages of exclusive purchase agreements.[65]

Because of these unjustifiable anticompetitive effects, dominant firms are at risk under Article 86 whenever a system of fidelity rebates is capable of affecting trade between Member States. The ECJ confirmed its policy on this practice in the *Michelin* case (1985). In that case, the 'tying' effect was intensified by the complex nature of the system, which put customers under heavy pressure to purchase exclusively from the dominant firm. The situation was similar in *Hoffman-La Roche* (1979), where the ECJ also pointed to the discriminatory nature of fidelity rebates, in that purchasers of equal quantities will be treated differently according to whether they obtained all their supplies from the dominant supplier.

The question of discriminatory pricing was addressed by the Court in *United Brands* (1978). In that case, a dominant supplier of bananas was charging its national distributors different prices according to the local conditions existing in each Member State. The ECJ regarded such a practice as abusive discrimination under Article 86(c). The Court was influenced by the fact that the supplier did not bear 'the risks' of the sales markets and was therefore not entitled to take them into account when setting its price. It is difficult to see the relevance of this reasoning. The most striking feature of the situation was that the distributors, and firms lower down the market, did not compete with one another since they operated in separate geographical markets without much possibility of sales between areas. Given this fact, the requirement of Article 86(c) that liability will arise only where the parties discriminated against are placed at a competitive disadvantage, seems hardly to be fulfilled.

The Court's reasoning has been severely criticised as having no sound economic basis (Bishop, 1981; Adams, 1985 I). Bishop regards the ECJ as an improper forum for determining economic policy, referring to the judges as 'a few talented amateurs'. However, the ECJ should not be regarded merely as a forum for the application of economic theory, just as EEC competition policy cannot be regarded as pursuing purely economic ends. Article 86 is just one aspect of the drive towards European integration, in a social, political, and ideological manner as well as in economic terms.

Pricing policies are not the only form of abusive behaviour relevant to Article 86. It was mentioned earlier that a firm in a dominant position is under an obligation to act in a more restrained commercial manner than firms operating in competitive conditions. A prime example of this concerns refusal to deal. When a dominant firm refuses to deal with another firm, then the excluded firm may be effectively prevented from obtaining any supply of the product or service. In addition, where the dominant and excluded firms are actual or potential competitors, then the refusal to deal may have the effect of enhancing the dominance already existing on the market. The legal prohibition on refusals to deal by dominant firms therefore has two bases, as a measure of consumer protection (in the sense that it protects customers of the dominant firm) and as a means to protect the competitive structure of the market.

The Commission takes the view that all such refusals by dominant firms are capable of being abusive, but the ECJ has not ruled in such comprehensive terms. In its judgment in the *Commercial Solvents* case (1974), the Court ruled on the refusal by a dominant supplier of raw materials to supply a firm which used the materials to produce derivatives. The refusal was inspired by the dominant firm's intention to enter the derivatives market itself. The ECJ ruled that for a dominant firm to refuse to supply in these circumstances, with the possibility of eliminating all competition from the other firm in the adjacent market, would be an abuse of its dominant position. It has recently had an opportunity to confirm this policy in the *Tele-Marketing* case (1986).[66] In *United Brands* (1978) the dominant supplier refused to supply a long-standing customer in order to discourage it, and other customers, from dealing in competing products. The ECJ found this to be discriminatory behaviour which may have eliminated the excluded firm from the market; it was therefore an attempt to strengthen dominance through abusive means. As well as the anticompetitive effect of the refusal, the Court was also anxious to protect the position of small and medium-sized firms. This is another example of the competition policy of the EEC concerning itself with matters other than economic efficiency.

Much was made in these two cases, and in the comments on them, of the fact that the excluded firms were regular customers of the dominant firm, rather than first-time customers. However, in *GVL* (1983) a firm having a *de facto* monopoly refused to provide services to certain others on the basis of nationality. Even though these were potential customers only, rather than existing long-term customers, the ECJ ruled that the refusal was abusive. The Court may have been influenced by the fact that the excluded firms were wholly unable to obtain the services elsewhere, or by the fact that the dominant firm had discriminated on grounds of nationality (Whish, 1985). The abolition of such discrimination is a policy fundamental to the EEC.

The breadth of the prohibition in Article 86 is perhaps best seen in the judgment of the ECJ in *Continental Can* (1973). This concerned the purchase by a dominant firm of 80 per cent of the capital of its major competitor, thereby virtually eliminating competition in a substantial area of the Common Market. The Commission decided that this activity was abusive under Article 86. In its appeal to the ECJ, the dominant firm asserted that Article 86 was not intended to, and was not capable of, regulating mergers. Further, it claimed that, in order to be actionable under Article 86, there must be a causal connection between the dominance and the abusive behaviour.

The Court addressed itself to the purpose and extent of Article 86; to that end it examined the wording of Article 3(f) of the EEC Treaty. It is the style of the Treaty to proceed from very general statements of policy to progressively more detailed measures of application. In interpreting these more detailed provisions, regard is always had to the general policy statements upon which they are based. Article 3(f) states simply that one of the activities of the EEC shall be 'the institution of a system ensuring that competition in the common market is not distorted'. The ECJ regarded this as the common theme of Articles 85 and 86; both being designed to protect or encourage effective competition in the EEC. Seen in this light, structural changes in the market effected by a dominant firm which further impairs or eliminates competition, are capable of being abusive even where the means of achieving the change do not depend on the economic strength of dominance.

The ECJ entirely rejected the argument that the interpretation of Article 86 depended to any extent on the examples of abuse which it provides. Any activity of a dominant firm which strengthens its dominance through an interference with the competitive structure is capable of being abusive. It should be noted however that Article 86 can only come into play, to control mergers or other structural abuse, where the firm is already in a dominant position. It is still not possible to prevent dominance *arising* through structural changes; no general merger control exists under EEC law, though the Commission has been calling for it for some time.[67]

An important feature of Article 86 is that it only applies to abusive behaviour insofar as it may affect trade between Member States. This is a jurisdictional feature which separates the respective spheres of Community and national law. The requirement that inter-State trade may be affected is explained in the chapter dealing with restrictive agreements in the EEC.[68] In relation to Article 86, the clearest statement on this matter appears in the ECJ's judgment in the *Hugin* case (1979).[69] The Court explained that:

> Community law covers any ... practice which is capable of constituting a threat to freedom of trade between member-States in a manner which might harm the attainment of the objectives of a single market between member States, in particular by partitioning the national markets or by affecting the structure of competition within the Common Market. On the other hand conduct the effects of which are confined to the territory of a single member-State is governed by the national legal order.

The ECJ has usually been very ready to find that monopolistic practices are capable of affecting inter-State trade. In *Commercial Solvents* (1974), the dominant firm claimed that its refusal to deal with a competitor was not caught by Article 86 because, *inter alia*, 90 per cent of the competitor's products were exported outside the EEC. The Court refused to accept that argument; the elimination of the competitor from the market was likely to have repercussions on trade between Member States, even though the practice complained of may have related to exports from the EEC.

The crucial test is the likely consequences for the effective competitive structure in the Common Market, a test confirmed in the *GVL* case (1983), where the dominant firm's refusal to deal with persons of non-German nationality was held to hinder the cross-frontier movement of services.

United States law

Section 2 of the Sherman Act provides for the criminal offence of monopolization. Where it is thought that a firm may be guilty of such offence, the Antitrust Division of the Department of Justice will initiate an investigation and, where appropriate, will prosecute an action in the ordinary courts. These criminal cases are designed to establish that an offence has taken place and to punish those guilty by way of fines and/or imprisonment. The Antitrust Division is also empowered to bring civil actions, the object of which is to seek appropriate court orders to dismantle the monopoly power or to prevent its future exercise.

A distinguishing feature of US antitrust legislation is its accessibility to private parties. It will be recalled that monopoly policy in the UK is entirely regulated by an administrative body (the MMC) and the government. EEC monopoly policy is mainly guided by the European Commission and the European Court of Justice, but it is open to individuals to bring actions in their own national courts to establish that a firm has abused its dominant position. In US law, section 4 of the Clayton Act enables a private party who has been injured by an act forbidden by the antitrust laws to bring a civil action for 'treble damages'. This punitive sanction, which may give rise to huge awards, is clearly designed to deter anticompetitive activity, while giving an incentive to private parties to invest the resources required to bring actions. Pollock has found that there has been a sharp drop in the number of cases brought by the Antitrust Division and the Federal Trade Commission, but that there remains a large number of private treble-damage actions.[70]

The Antitrust Division The Antitrust Division (AD) is a constituent part of the Justice Department, and hence part of the structure of government. It is headed by an Assistant Attorney General, a political appointee, who is assisted by a large staff consisting predominantly of lawyers. It has been described as 'essentially a large and specialised law firm representing the government in antitrust and related areas' (Oppenheim *et al.*, 1981, p. 108). Its task is to prepare and prosecute criminal cases in the ordinary courts under sections 1 and 2 of the Sherman Act. It also has jurisdiction to bring civil cases in respect of the same activities, either instead of or as well as the criminal prosecution. In addition, the AD enforces the merger provisions of the Clayton Act. It is simply a prosecutorial agency; it has no adjudicative role. It is therefore quite unlike either the Commission of the EEC or any of the British antitrust agencies.

The AD has a fairly free hand to choose cases for prosecution. As an arm of government, it would be reasonable to suspect that such choice would be influenced by Executive pressure. However, Weaver has found that Congress has not sought to influence the AD's policies or activities, either through budgetary restraints or more direct means (Weaver, 1977). Subsequent to this finding, Congress *has* sought to influence the AD, especially in relation to its stance on resale price maintenance. Although Assistant Attorneys General have sometimes sought to influence the AD's activities by planning the use of its resources, these influences have been short-lived and have excited resistance from staff attorneys. Weaver describes the AD as being staffed by prosecution-hungry lawyers constantly seeking enough evidence to bring a case, their chief constraint being the scarcity of evidence. In spite of the presence of fifty-nine economists on the AD's staff, she found that the agency was dominated by a 'lawyers'' approach to antitrust enforcement where success was measured by reference to the throughput of successful prosecutions rather than by the economic effect of the agency's activities (Weaver, 1977). The approach adopted is therefore mainly a reactive one, although the publication of the Antitrust Division's *Merger Guidelines* does indicate that this approach is being tempered by some programmatic input. Some commentators have called for the AD to extend its programmatic approach to all, or substantially all, its activities (Posner, 1971).

An action by the AD will originate from the Division's intelligence-gathering processes. The majority of such intelligence is acquired through complaints sent to the AD from those directly or indirectly affected by the anticompetitive behaviour of a firm. This list will include consumers, competitors or their advisors or representatives. Other intelligence will come from informal contacts between firms and the AD or through scanning the financial press.

If there appears to be a *prima facie* case, the AD must then decide whether to commence a criminal or a civil case against the firms. Criminal prosecutions, whose object is to secure a fine and/or prison sentence, will generally be reserved for particularly egregious activities and where the meaning of the law is clear (Oppenheim *et al.*, 1981; Zimmerman, 1982). Civil actions are aimed at securing injunctions to prevent similar future activity, and court orders affecting the structure of a firm. A criminal prosecution will usually be accompanied by a civil action.

In order to mount a case in the courts, the AD will require evidence in the form of documents or oral testimony. The investigative capabilities of the agency are very powerful, especially in relation to the criminal process. The procedure for gathering evidence is the same as that used in relation to any other criminal activity. Thus, subject to the usual procedural requirements, a search warrant may be issued, enabling a firm's premises to be searched and documentary evidence to be seized. Such an exercise will be similar to the 'dawn raids' carried out by the Commission of the EEC to secure evidence of a breach of Article 85 or 86. In addition, before an indictment may be made, the AD must secure the approval of a federal grand jury. This body, independent of any government agency, is designed to 'ferret out crimes deserving of prosecution' (*US* v. *Sells Engineering*, 1983) and is empowered to subpoena persons to appear before it and to oblige them to produce documents which contain evidence of a breach of the law. The AD uses this process as its main intelligence-gathering opportunity, search warrants being used only in exceptional cases where it is believed that documents are being withheld from the grand jury.[71]

Where no criminal prosecution is contemplated, the AD may not use the grand jury method for intelligence gathering, but may issue a 'civil investigative demand' which enables it to call for persons and documents. To all intents and purposes, this is as useful as a grand jury investigation; however, no search and seizure exercise may be carried out in connection with a proposed civil case. A civil investigative demand may be issued whenever the Assistant Attorney General *has reason to believe* that a person is in possession of documents or evidence relevant to a civil antitrust investigation. The objective standard implied by the italicised words, together with the requirement that the AD specify the documents requested with reasonable particularity, prevents the AD embarking on 'fishing expeditions'.

Monopolization The offence in section 2 of the Sherman Act is not the mere possession of monopoly power, but of 'monopolizing'. The difference between monopoly and monopolization is the key to understanding the objectives of section 2. In the *Alcoa* case (1945) Justice Learned Hand formulated a very strict test, which suggested that firms with monopoly power would be guilty of monopolization unless they could show that they were the unwitting possessors of such power. Such would be the case where a dominant firm had not 'intended to put an end to existing competition, or to prevent competition from arising where none had existed'. Firms may become monopolists 'by force of accident'. Learned Hand cited as examples instances of natural monopoly, or circumstances in which the dominant firm had driven out competitors by virtue of superior skill, insight and industry. In order to escape a charge of monopolization under the *Alcoa* test, in other words, the dominant firm had to show that monopoly had been thrust upon it.

In *United Shoe* (1953) this restrictive test was liberalised, so that monopoly power would be taken to be legitimate if it was acquired by superior skill, superior products, natural advantages, economic or technical efficency etc. The principle was stated even more simply in the *Grinnell* case (1966), which defined the offence of monopolization as having two elements: the possession of monopoly power, and the wilful acquisition or maintenance of that power as distinguished from growth or development as a consequence of a superior product, business acumen, or historic accident.

The policy of section 2 and the definition of monopolization were fully considered in *Berkey Photo* v. *Eastman Kodak* (1979), a monopolization case brought by a private party rather than the State. The Court distinguished section 2 from section 1 of the Sherman Act (which deals with restrictive agreements) by showing that section 2 is aimed primarily not at improper conduct but at a pernicious market structure 'in which the concentration of power saps the salubrious influence of competition'. Section 2 comes close to being a structural section: its objective is to deter the acquisition or maintenance of monopoly power, even though such power is not being exercised. However, the section is unable to pursue such a 'pure' policy, because it would be essentially self-defeating. If monopoly power were to be condemned *per se*, it would stifle incentive in industry; firms would be 'rewarded' for successful competition and efficiency by being condemned for the resultant acquisition of market power. As Learned Hand stated in *Alcoa*, the Sherman Act cannot be taken to 'condemn the resultant of those very forces which it is its prime object to foster.... The successful competitor, having been urged to compete, must not be turned upon when he wins'.

As mentioned in the introduction to this chapter, competition contains the seeds of its own destruction; in the long run there is a constant tendency towards concentration, as the more efficient producers increase market share at the expense of their less efficient competitors. Once in possession of such power, the possibility of abuse will alway exist. Of course, such abuse will itself stimulate competition from new entry to the market with the possibility that the monopoly power will be eroded by more efficient competitors. Competition, in these simplified conditions, will effect constant change, so that the most efficient producer will succeed but will be unable to abuse its monopoly power over any substantial period. Seen in these terms, the force of competition is described as the 'process of creative destruction' (Schumpeter, 1942). However, this scenario does not take account of barriers to entry and other market imperfections which will protect a monopolist from such forces and permit the abuse of monopoly power.

Section 2 has the task of promoting competition whilst discouraging monopoly power. Unlike UK and EEC policy, monopoly power of itself is regarded by US policy as 'inherently evil' because of the possibility that it will be abused, and because of the belief that it 'deadens initiative, discourages thrift and depresses energy'. The compromise achieved by section 2, as confirmed in *Berkey Photo* v. *Eastman Kodak*, is as follows. First, where monopoly power has been acquired or maintained through 'improper' means, it will be offensive under section 2 even though such power has not been used to extract monopoly profits. Secondly, where monopoly power has been legitimately acquired, the monopolist must not *use* such power to prevent or impede competition: '[o]nly considerations of fairness and the need to preserve proper economic incentives prevent the condemnation of section 2 from extending to one who has gained his power by purely competitive means ... such a monopolist is tolerated but not cherished'.

It is the use of market power which is the distinguishing feature; the monopolist is permitted to use its *size* to compete by way of efficiencies, but is prevented from using its *power* to diminish competition through such means as predatory pricing, price discrimination or exclusive buying arrangements. The exercise of power by a monopoly firm to pursue a course of conduct which would not be open to a non-monopoly firm will violate section 2. In addition to such exploitative conduct, monopoly firms may be liable if they engage in anticompetitive conduct, such as exclusive dealing, which would be tolerated or even regarded as 'honestly industrial' among non-monopoly firms.

This two-part approach to the conduct of a 'legitimate' monopolist is similar to the approach of Article 86 of the EEC Treaty, with its exploitive and anticompetitive abuses of a dominant position. So long as monopolists do not utilise their market power they are perfectly at liberty to compete aggressively and to exploit the efficiencies available to them through size, technical lead, or any other factor; indeed the *Berkey* case encourages such aggression (Noble, 1982). It is often difficult to distinguish permitted from undesirable conduct, and Halverson has noted that the uncertainty generated by this has led to an increased use of antitrust laws by firms as a business stratagem (Halverson, 1980). It may be that inefficient competitors bring antitrust actions in order to protect themselves from aggressive but efficient monopolists (Jentes, 1980). If section 2 is to have a socially desirable effect then such actions should not be permitted to succeed, a fact of which the courts are aware.

Although there is an abhorrence of monopoly power in the

United States (an antipathy based on constitutional principles and a politico-cultural dislike of 'bigness'), section 2 assesses monopolization in terms of conduct and not in purely structural terms.[72] In this respect, section 2 is similar to UK and EEC monopoly policy. However it is also clear that the scope and objectives of section 2 differ from those other policies. In EEC law, Article 86 does not apply at all to the acquisition of a dominant position, and in the UK the emphasis is on the way in which monopoly power has been used rather than how it was acquired. The application of section 2 of the Sherman Act to the manner in which monopoly power was acquired, as well as to how it is exercised, is therefore an important distinguishing feature. Another major distinction is that section 2 is a criminal provision; monopolization is a criminal offence in the same way as fraud or tax evasion. In consequence, the State as prosecutor must show a criminal intent as well as criminal conduct. However this last point does not seem necessarily to involve a close examination of the intentions of those directing a firm's activities; intent may be inferred in many cases from the nature of the conduct engaged in (Jentes, 1980; Noble, 1982).

As an example of this, the Court of Appeals in *MCI* v. *AT & T* (1983) rejected a subjective intent-based test as a proper approach in predatory pricing cases. Such a test was thought to be incapable of distinguishing competitive price reductions from predatory ones. Such a test was also held to be unworkable, in that it is difficult to identify those people within a firm whose intentions are relevant, and difficult to assess any such evidence even where it can be uncovered. The Court held that to 'encourage judges and juries to rely only on nonprobative data allegedly bearing on a firm's "state of mind" invites the twin mischiefs of (1) burdening litigation with thousands of documents about the firm's motives and calculations; and (2) encouraging inconsistent and quixotic results'.

The emphasis in US monopoly power in preserving the competitive structure of markets contrasts with the UK and EEC approaches, which are concerned with regulating the exercise of monopoly power. The difference in approach may be seen clearly in relation to excessive pricing by monopolists. It will be recalled that the MMC has sought to control excessive pricing as a practice which operates contrary to the public interest. The ECJ has likewise ruled that excessive pricing by dominant firms may be taken to be abusive behaviour because it is an exploitation of monopoly power. However, in the *Berkey Photo* v. *Eastman Kodak* case (1979) the United States Court of Appeals held that excessive pricing, although the use of monopoly power, is not *of itself* anticompetitive. The Court regarded excessive pricing as pro-competitive, in that 'there is probably no better way for [a monopolist] to guarantee that its dominance will be challenged than by greedily extracting the highest price it can'.[73] Unlike the policy adopted by the MMC and the ECJ, the prevention of monopoly pricing is not seen as an end in itself by American courts. Legitimate monopolists are free to set prices at profit-maximising levels. It is only when monopoly power has been acquired or maintained through anticompetitive means that excessive pricing will be taken to be offensive.

Otherwise, it is seen as a reward for successful competition and, at the same time, a mechanism for the restoration of a competitive structure. This reluctance of the courts to treat the avoidance of monopoly pricing as a policy objective of itself appears to be at odds with the deep-rooted loathing of monopoly enshrined in US law. However, the reluctance stems from an unwillingness to allow courts to act as business directors, substituting their own judicial decisions for those freely and expertly taken by firms themselves. The willingness of the MMC and the European Commission and the ECJ to do just this, may be regarded as an important distinction between the UK and EEC approach on the one hand and the US approach on the other (Adams, 1985 I).

The control of predatory pricing is, however, an exception to the general self-restraint of the US courts; they will interfere to limit price competition where a monopoly firm appears willing to suffer short-term losses in order to drive out competition or prevent its growth. The risk incurred by the monopoly firm by such strategy has led some commentators and courts to believe that predatory pricing is unlikely to happen often. Such was the view of the Supreme Court in the

Matsushita case (1986). However, where the courts are confronted with an action for predatory pricing they must determine how such practice may be defined. The *MCI* v. *AT & T* case (1983) shows the willingness of the courts to enter into economic theoretical arguments as to the proper cost standards to be applied. In that case the Court of Appeals determined that the definition of predatory pricing must be a matter of law, for the court to decide, rather than something to be put to the jury. The uncertainty that would be generated by the absence of an objective and authoritative definition would give rise to such uncertainty that it could cause firms not to make competitive price cuts for fear of facing treble-damage actions by unsuccessful competitors. Such tactical behaviour by higher price competitors would serve to chill price competition whilst preserving inefficient production (Areeda, 1980).

Many US courts follow the Areeda-Turner approach that pricing below short-run marginal cost (or average variable cost, used as a proxy since it is easier to determine) should be regarded as predatory, but pricing above such costs should be regarded as legitimate (Areeda and Turner, 1975). This rule has been criticised as giving too much emphasis to short-term assessment. In the *MCI* v. *AT & T* case, the court did not reject the Areeda-Turner rule as a relevant indication of predation, but moved away from it to consider definitions which took more account of long-term considerations.

The court emphatically confirmed that a monopoly firm does not have to maximise its short-term profits in order to escape a charge of predation. Such a requirement would deprive consumers of legitimate price cuts brought about to meet new competition, and would be unfair because the dominant firm may not have sufficient information to determine whether or not it was maximising its profits. Further, adoption of such a rule would involve the courts too closely in price regulation, a role which they abhor. The court in *MCI* v. *AT & T* described such a role as 'unseemly' and 'incompatible with the functioning of private markets'.

On the other hand, the court was at pains not to set the price 'floor' too high lest that allowed inefficient rivals to be sheltered from the stresses and strains of full price competition. The court chose long-run incremental cost as the proper cost measure in predation cases, virtually rejecting non-price evidence as being determinative of the issue.

Price discrimination by a monopoly firm is clearly capable of being unlawful under section 2, where it involves predatory pricing or where it consists of the use of market power to prevent or destroy competition. However, even non-predatory price discrimination by a monopolist may attract liability under section 2 of the Clayton Act (a section usually referred to under the name of an Act which amended it—the Robinson-Patman Act). This legislation prohibits price discrimination by any firm where the discrimination has an anticompetitive effect. Consideration of this legislation is undertaken in Chapter 6.

On non-price issues, the US approach to refusals to deal by monopolists also demonstrates the reluctance of the American courts to interfere in the market process except where absolutely necessary. The basic premise on this issue is to be found in the clear statement of the Supreme Court in the *Colgate* case (1919): 'In the absence of any purpose to create or maintain a monopoly, the [Sherman] Act does not restrict the long recognised right of a trader or manufacturer engaged in an entirely private business, freely to exercise his own independent discretion as to the parties with whom he will deal'. Refusal to deal will not, on its own, attract liability under section 2. However, a monopoly firm does not have total immunity in this respect. Refusal to deal will be unlawful where it is used to enhance or maintain the firm's monopoly power. In the *Lorain Journal* case (1951) a newspaper with a monopoly position refused to accept advertisements from persons who had also advertised with a local radio station. This refusal was unlawful because it was designed to maintain the newspaper's monopoly against the threatened competition. Similarly, in 'bottleneck' cases where a firm has exclusive control of a unique product or facility, it will be under a duty not to unreasonably refuse to deal (*Terminal Railroad* case, 1912). In the case of a vertically integrated monopolist, a refusal to deal with customers who compete in the downstream market may constitute an attempt to enhance or maintain market power and thereby attract liability[74] (*Otter Tail* case,

1973, and see Sullivan, 1977 II, p. 127). Apart from these exceptions, the courts have preserved the monopolist's right to refuse to deal. In the *Official Airline Guides* case (1980), the Court of Appeals rejected the notion that a monopolist will be liable *simply* because the refusal is arbitrary. In that case the refusal did affect competition, but in a market in which the monopolist did not participate. In the *Aspen Skiing* case (1985) the Supreme Court referred to a firm's 'cherished right' to select its own customers, and confirmed that a monopolist is free to refuse to deal with a competitor if valid business reasons exist for that decision, such as efficiency justifications.

The approach of the courts to this issue has been the object of criticism mainly on the basis that it does not promote efficiency (Chapman, 1981; Adams, 1985 II). Chapman finds no general economic justification for allowing monopolists to refuse to deal, and recommends a shift in the policy to a rule of reason analysis. Under such an approach, the motives of a monopolist would be irrelevant; the only justification for a refusal would be that any competitive advantages flowing from the refusal outweighed its adverse competitive impact. This seemed to be the approach of the Court of Appeals in *Byars* v. *Bluff City News* (1979). The Court held that the legality of refusals to deal by monopolists should be determined on efficiency grounds, although business justifications should be permitted to excuse anticompetitive refusals. It was also pointed out in that case that, even where an illegal refusal has been found to exist, the courts may find difficulty in making an effective order which would not put the court in the role of a price regulator.

NOTES

1. The Report to the President and the Attorney General of the National Commission for the Review of Antitrust Law and Procedures, 1979. For a discussion see Kirkwood, 'Pro-Monopolization Reform Proposals', 49 *Antitrust Law Journal* 1233 (1980).
2. In *Contraceptive Sheaths* (1982), the MMC found that the brand name of the dominant firm had become synonymous with the product. In *Liquefied Petroleum Gas* (1981), it was found that 'Calor' was widely

thought to be a commodity rather than a brand name.

3. Generally, economies of scale will create barriers to entry where the minimum efficient plant size pertaining to the industry is large compared with industry output. See Baden Fuller, 1979.

4. For references to recent reports of the MMC cited in this chapter, see Table 1, p. 20.

5. See *Berkey Photo* v. *Eastman Kodak* (1979), at p. 287 for a discussion on the circumstances in which advertising may give rise to an entry barrier. In its report on *Household Detergents*, HC 105 (1966) and *Breakfast Cereals*, HC 2, (1973), the MMC found that advertising had created a formidable entry barrier. For a discussion, see Pass and Sparkes (1980).

6. See Adams (1985 I).

7. Department of Justice, Antitrust Division, *Merger Guidelines*, paras. IIB1 and IIIB (1982).

8. Sections 3 and 5 of the Competition Act 1980 provide for investigations by the Director General and MMC respectively, into anticompetitive practices carried on by a firm with significant market power or of significant size. See Chapter 6.

9. Director General of Fair Trading, *Sheffield Newspapers*, (OFT, 1981).

10. Director General of Fair Trading, *British Railways Board—Brighton Station* (OFT, 1982).

11. Director General of Fair Trading, *British Airports Authority—Gatwick Airport* (OFT, 1984).

12. *United Brands* v. *Commission* (1978), para. 22.

13. For another clear example, see *Hasselblad* v. *Commission* (1984).

14. Commission Regulation 1983/83, Article 3.

15. *Michelin* case (1985), para. 37.

16. *Continental Can* case (1973), para. 33.

17. Compare this with the position taken by the ECJ in the *Michelin* case (1985).

18. See the MMC report on *Ready Mixed Concrete* (1981).

19. See Oppenheim, Weston and McCarthy (1981) at p. 340, and the references they cite.

20. *Hansard, Written Answers* [852] 5 March 1973.

21. Companies Act 1985, s. 736.

22. I.e. any economic entity engaged in trade or commerce, from a sole trader to a State trading organisation.

23. Fair Trading Act 1973, s.11.

24. See below, p. 129 *et seq.*

25. *Ceramic Sanitaryware*, Cmnd 7327 (1978); *Electricity Supply Meters*, Cmnd 7639 (1979); *Insulated Electric Cables and Wires* HC 243 (1979).

26. Original formulations by the ECJ used the word 'prevent', whilst more recent judgments require only a hindering of effective competition. See, for example *Michelin* (1985), confirmed in *Tele-Marketing* (1986).

27. *Michelin* case (1985).

28. At the other extreme the ECJ has confirmed that a market share of one per cent cannot be regarded as a dominant position. *Demo-Studio Schmidt* case (1984).

29. Korah (1986 II).
30. On this last point, see the critical comments by Baden Fuller (1979).
31. It is also the position taken by the MMC in UK monopoly policy: 'no distinction can usefully be drawn between discretion over prices and market power. Discretion to set prices at one level rather than another is a manifestation of market power' (*Tampons*, 1986).
32. Except that an Order of the Secretary of State may be enforced by the civil courts.
33. But not restraint of trade, which is entirely separate from central control.
34. J. Roper, MP, *Parliamentary Debates (Commons)* col. 522 (1972–3).
35. M. Hamilton, MP, *Parliamentary Debates (Commons), Standing Committee B* col. 106 (1973).
36. Supply Estimates 1986–87, Class XX Vote 16 (HMSO, 1986).
37. *Ibid.*
38. Fair Trading Act (1973), s.2(2).
39. Fair Trading Act 1973, s.50.
40. Monopolies and Restrictive Practices (Inquiry and Control) Act 1948.
41. Fair Trading Act 1973, s.56.
42. Monopolies and Mergers Commission (Increase in Membership) Order 1982.
43. Fair Trading Act 1973, schedule 3, para. 1.
44. As at 31 December 1985 it had 114 full-time and three part-time staff.
45. Director General (1986).
46. Fair Trading Act 1973, s.48.
47. *Ibid.*, s.49.
48. *Ibid.*
49. The MMC has the power to compel firms to supply information—Fair Trading Act 1973, s.85.
50. For a discussion on the meaning of public interest in relation to restrictive trade practices policy, see below, p. 138 *et seq.*
51. *A Review of Monopolies and Mergers Policy*, Cmnd. 7198 (HMSO, 1978).
52. MMC, '*Credit Card Franchise Services*', Cmnd. 8034 (HMSO, 1980).
53. See above, p. 32
54. MMC, '*Contraceptive Sheaths*', HC 135 (HMSO, 1974–5).
55. Henig classifies the Commission's antitrust function as part of its 'guardian' function, rather than its 'administrator' functions. See Henig, *Power and Decision in Europe* (Europotentials Press, 1980).
56. The FTC may be much freer from judicial constraint, especially in relation to its interpretation of the general terms of the Federal Trade Commission Act, s.5. See Muris, 'Judicial Constraints', in *The Federal Trade Commission Since 1970*, ed. Clarkson and Muris (Cambridge University Press, 1981).
57. See Editorial, 9 *European Law Review*, 293 (1984).
58. See the *National Panasonic* case (1980) for an account of a surprise visit.
59. See the ECJ's explanation and justification of this in the *Musique Diffusion* case (1983); See also the *IBM* case (1981).
60. *Musique Diffusion* (1983).

61. ECJ in *United Brands* (1978).
62. See also *British Leyland* v. *Commission, The Times* 12 November 1986.
63. For a summary of the arguments see Hurwitz and Kovacic (1982). For a general explanation, see Scherer (1980) Ch. 12. Gyselen and Kyriazis make the point that it may be difficult to distinguish predatory pricing from competitive pricing, since predatory pricing is engaged in as a *response* to perceived competition on the market (Gyselen and Kyriazis, 1986).
64. In the *AKZO* decision (1985). The fine of ECU 10 million was the largest ever levied on a single firm.
65. But see Adams (1985 I).
66. See Adams' criticisms of the Court's analysis (Adams, 1985 II).
67. See Commission of the European Communities, *Fourteenth Report on Competition Policy* (EEC, 1985) para. 43.
68. See p. 162 below.
69. See Bennett, 'Article 86: "effect on trade between Member States" re-examined', 4 *European Law Review*. 294 (1979).
70. According to Pollock, 1,084 new private treble-damage actions were filed in 1984 (Pollock, 1985).
71. Letter from Department of Justice to author.
72. For an interesting submission for a performance-based assessment of monopoly, see Brock, 231 *American Business Law Journal*, 291 (1983).
73. See also Gyselen and Kyriazis (1986).
74. The objection to this approach is that vertical integration may well enhance efficiency, unless it allows for price discrimination, the increase of entry barriers on the first-level market, or the evasion of monopoly price regulation. See *Byars* v. *Bluff City News* (1979).

3 Merger Policy

Policy on mergers is best regarded as an extension of monopoly policy. Both policies are directed against the wrongful acquisition and use of monopoly power, and towards the maintenance of effectively competitive markets. In the USA, merger policy is expressly directed against incipient monopoly; in the UK, the operation of merger policy is effected through the same methods and processes as monopoly policy. In the EEC however there is no effective general policy on mergers, and therefore no real control at European level over the competitive structure of markets.

Monopoly power is not considered to be necessarily against the public interest. The same is true of mergers; even mergers which increase concentration levels, and which therefore facilitate collusive behaviour, may have countervailing advantages. Economies of scale, innovation and learning effects are all efficiency-producing factors which have been put forward as possible advantages of mergers. As with monopolies, the approach of mergers policy may be structural or behavioural. A structural policy will lay down permissible concentration levels above which no merger will be permitted to take place. The ease of application of such a policy must be set beside the fact that many efficiency-producing mergers will be prohibited; consumer welfare may actually be harmed by this policy rather than promoted. Such a structural approach has also been attacked as an undue interference with the market process. It is claimed that the market is better able to deal with the anticompetitive effects of concentration than are policies administered by outside agents (McGee, 1974).

However, arguments of this nature seem to take insufficient account of the time lags inherent in the self-correcting mechanism of the market, and indeed the failures of such a mechanism in the presence of intractable imperfections. In the USA, a fiercely structural policy was recommended in the Neal Report but was not adopted (see Neal, 1968). Indeed US policy on mergers is becoming progressively less structural in its approach (George, 1985). A behavioural policy will examine mergers on a case-by-case basis to determine whether the dangers of concentration are offset by the particular advantages inherent in the transaction.

Merger policy must address three distinct types of merger, each with different policy implications. Horizontal mergers, between firms at the same stage in the market, create a larger player in the market and increase concentration, with its attendant disadvantages. The potential negative effects of horizontal mergers are clear and relatively easy to detect. The merger policies of the UK and USA, with their emphasis on the avoidance of monopoly power, are largely concerned in practice with horizontal mergers. Vertical mergers, involving firms at different stages in the same market, do not affect concentration levels but enable transactions to take place between the two previously independent firms outside the constraints of the market. Vertical integration can have great efficiency advantages, and will not usually take place unless such advantages are available. However, monopoly power at either of the market stages may be enhanced where the vertical integration raises entry barriers to non-integrated firms. The integration may also foreclose outlets or sources of supply to competitors at both levels, a feature which greatly concerned the UK Monopolies and Mergers Commission in its report on the *British Telecom/Mitel* merger proposal (1986). Finally, conglomerate mergers, between firms in different markets, although not affecting concentration levels, involve the risk of cross-subsidisation within the conglomerate firm, which facilitate predatory pricing campaigns against smaller competitors. Entry into a market by way of acquisition of an existing firm will also remove the bidder as a potential competitor, ready to enter the market independently should conditions make entry attractive. This potential effect has been recognised by the Department of Trade (Robinson, 1980 I). Other public policy issues, of a non-competition nature, may also be raised by conglomerate mergers (see Siegfried and Sweeny, 1982). The current emphasis of UK and US merger policy on the *competitive* impact of mergers, rather than their wider socio-political implications, means that conglomerate mergers will largely be permitted. This accords with the Chicago analysis of mergers, but other commentators have shown that conglomerate mergers do not yield efficiencies, and are mainly motivated by a desire for power and empire on the part of the executives (Rhoades, 1983), or are in the nature of an 'entrepreneurial ego trip' (Pertschuk, 1977). Rhoades predicts that if left unchecked, merger activity will move the US economy from a state of competitive capitalism to one of monolithic capitalism, dominated by large corporations.

UK MERGER POLICY

The close relationship between monopoly and merger policy in the UK is revealed by the fact that both are regulated by the Fair Trading Act 1973, and both are put into effect through the same procedure. Thus merger policy is enforced through a referral by the Secretary of State[1] to the Monopolies and Mergers Commission (MMC), which undertakes a cost-benefit analysis of the merger in the context of the public interest. This evaluation is communicated to the Secretary of State, who ultimately has the discretion to permit or disallow the transaction or to impose conditions.

The Fair Trading Act is not capable of regulating all mergers, but only those which qualify for investigation under section 64.[2] A referable merger is one which leads to the market share of any firm being increased to or beyond 25 per cent. Alternatively, any merger in which assets worth more than £30 million are taken over[3] will be referable. The measurement of market share is subject to the same problems as exist in relation to monopoly control under the 1973 Act[4] and the same wide discretions are given to the competition authorities to apply suitable criteria. The asset value criterion was increased in 1984 from £15 million to its present value.

This was a far larger change than required by inflation and was intended to reduce the number of mergers qualifying for investigation from 200 to 150 per year (Tebbit, 1984 I). In practice the asset value criterion is the easier to apply, and for that reason virtually every reference made to the MMC in recent years has directed the MMC to have regard only to that criterion.

In its definitional sections, the Fair Trading Act refers neither to 'firms' nor to 'mergers', but to 'enterprises ceasing to be distinct'. An enterprise is defined by section 63(2) as being the activities or part of the activities of a business. The legal persona of the firm and its economic identity are considered to be quite separate; merger policy is concerned only with the latter. A firm may have several distinct activities, and therefore several different enterprises, and these may be considered to be separate phenomena for the purposes of merger control. The 1973 Act is therefore capable of regulating a number of different types of transaction and is not confined to the situation in which a firm purchases all or a majority of the shares of another. The purchase of mere plant will not fall within the Act, but the acquisition of any sort of activity, such as goodwill, may well do so.

Enterprises will be considered to have ceased to be distinct where they are brought under common ownership or common control. Further, if one of the previously distinct enterprises ceases to operate at all, that too will count as a loss of distinctiveness. It is important to emphasise that the loss of distinctiveness which triggers the Act relates to the enterprises concerned and not to the firms which formerly controlled them. Common ownership is not a complex concept but the idea of common control is a difficult one to define because of the myriad ways in which firms can influence the activities of others. The Act does not attempt a definition but gives certain examples of when common control will be taken to exist. The following situations involving corporate firms would constitute enterprises being brought under common ownership or control.

(i) Firm A purchases the shares of Firm B, or brings it under its control. The enterprises of both firms cease to be distinct. Note that the enterprises continue under separate *ownership* in both cases.

(ii) Firm C purchases the shares of Firms D and E, or brings them under its control. Firms D and E become subsidiary companies of Firm C and the enterprises of all of them cease to be distinct.

(iii) Firms F and G place part of their respective activities under joint control, either formally by way of a joint venture company, or through some informal arrangement. The pooled enterprises (and only those) will cease to be distinct.

(iv) The shareholders of Firm H acquire ownership or control of Firm I. The enterprises of both firms will lose their distinctiveness.

The idea of control extends beyond the possession of a controlling interest, in the sense of owning enough voting shares to dictate policy through shareholders' meetings. Control can exist independently of ownership, where a person or firm can 'directly or indirectly...control or materially...influence the policy' of a company or of a person carrying on an enterprise. For example, in the *P&O/European Ferries* merger report (1986) material influence was exercised through a shareholding of only 20 per cent, where other shareholders had relatively small shares, and where the influential firm had close connections with other institutional shareholders. This demonstrates that the law is sufficiently wide to include transactions where firms remain separate and independent. The definition of control is very wide, and the Act recognises that changes in the intensity of control, within the confines of the definition, are significant for the purposes of merger policy. Thus if a firm moves from having control in the very loose sense of the definition, to having a controlling interest, or the ability to control the policy of a person, then that movement may trigger the operation of the Act, as in the *BETC/Initial* merger, 1985.

Initiation of investigation
In practice, merger investigations will concern proposed rather than completed mergers.[5] One reason for this is that firms and financial backers will be unwilling to commit resources to a merger transaction where there is a risk that it will be referred to the MMC and ultimately disallowed by the Secretary of

State. Indeed in at least one case (*Lonrho/House of Fraser*, 1985) the bidder reduced its current holding in the target firm pending the MMC report in order to reduce its financial exposure should the MMC's conclusion be adverse. Another reason is that share purchase offers which fall within the City Code on Take-overs and Mergers must contain a clause by which the offer lapses should the proposed transaction be referred to the MMC.[6] At the stage of its investigation, therefore, the MMC is confronted with a proposal which on the face of it is no longer extant. However, where there is an expectation that the transaction will be revived if clearance is given, then the MMC will assess the merger as if it had taken place immediately before the reference was made.[7]

The initiation of merger enforcement is in the hands of the Director General of Fair Trading, who is under a duty to acquire information on merger activity and to recommend to the Secretary of State that a reference should be made to the MMC where appropriate. Unlike US law, there is no obligation on firms to seek clearance on proposed mergers or even to bring them to the attention of the Director General. However, the Director General is able to secure comprehensive information from the financial press and other sources, including the parties themselves. In addition many firms will voluntarily seek the opinion of the OFT on a proposed transaction in order to keep the risks of a reference to a minimum. However, in the case of 'unfriendly' mergers, the attitude of the firms to the prospect of a reference may not be the same. The target firm may actively campaign for a reference to be made in order to frustrate or at least delay the proposal. Many proposals have been frustrated in this way, even where the MMC has ruled in their favour. The delay allows for a 'white knight' to be found to purchase the target shares in the place of the bidding company, or for the bidder to lose interest for some other reason. One of the most controversial bids in recent years, *Elders IXL and Allied-Lyons* (1986), was abandoned whilst the MMC was considering it, when the bidder found a more attractive (and compliant) target. Of the referrals made between 1970 and 1984, nearly 25 per cent were not completed because of the abandonment of the bids (OFT, 1985).

The major concern of the Director General's preliminary assessment (which takes about one month) is the likely competitive impact of a merger, although factors such as the likely impact on employment, international competitiveness and the target firm's survival will also be taken into account (OFT, 1985). Efficiency advantages of the merger will be considered at this early stage, but must be quantifiable if they are to have substantial influence. The parties to the transaction, and affected third parties, are given opportunities to make representations to the OFT on the factual background and the impact of the merger on the public interest. Expert assistance is often utilised by the firms at this stage. However the OFT has made it clear that it does not regard the preliminary procedure as an opportunity for firms to bargain about the making of a reference (OFT, 1985).

The decision to recommend referral is for the Director General, based on the advice of his officers and in certain cases by a committee known as the Mergers Panel, made up of civil servants from various interested government departments. This committee is shrouded in mystery, neither its working methods nor its recommendations being made public. The decision to refer is exclusively that of the Secretary of State, who is free to disagree with the Director General's recommendation. The 1978 Green Paper on Monopolies and Mergers Policy found that about 3 per cent of referable mergers were actually referred to the MMC, even though 25 per cent of referable mergers involved the creation or enhancement of a 25 per cent market share.

In 1984 the Secretary of State announced that henceforth mergers would normally only be referred on 'competition grounds'. This statement, which echoed a similar one made by a previous Secretary of State in 1980, was a response to criticism that the referral procedure had been too widely used and was impeding desirable mergers. It is to be expected that in future referrals will mainly concern horizontal mergers, where the competition issues are clearest and most urgent. However, the conglomerate *Elders IXL/Allied-Lyons* merger (1986) was referred expressly on grounds which had nothing to do with competition matters, relating to the way in which the proposed bid was to be financed. Other conglomerate merger reports have speculated on the continuing effectiveness of the target firm following the imposition of new management (*Charter Consolidated/Anderson Strathclyde*, 1982; *Taubman/Sotherby*, 1983) and on the loss of potential competition (*Hong Kong & Shanghai/Standard Chartered/Royal Bank*, 1982).

Investigation by the MMC

Because of the disruption to the business of the firms involved, and to the Stock Market, the MMC is obliged to complete its investigations speedily. It is normally permitted only six months to deliver its report to the Secretary of State. This report will confirm whether a referable merger has occurred or is proposed, and whether it is likely to operate against the public interest. The criteria against which the public interest is to be assessed, contained in section 84 of the Fair Trading Act 1973, are the same as those used by the MMC to evaluate monopoly situations. The same wide-ranging, discretionary and ad hoc approach is employed, unconfined to competition and efficiency and not inhibited by a purely economic approach.

Although usually relieved of the need to assess the market shares of the merging firms for the purpose of defining the merger situation, the MMC will need to evaluate the market power of the firms in order to assess the competitive impact of the merger. The MMC will not merely accept the market definition proposed by the firms nor adopt an *apparently* reasonable market definition where this cannot be shown to be the most appropriate for merger control. However, the sophistication and complexity of the market definition mechanism in the US Merger Guidelines are not to be found in UK practice. The MMC adopts a more instinctive and less mathematical approach to the measurement of substitutability between products. In recent reports, the MMC has found insufficient substitution between different types of brick,[8] between various textile services,[9] and between mail order and general retail sale.[10] Such redefinition rendered the mergers non-horizontal and therefore less likely to produce substantial anticompetitive effects. The MMC will also critically examine the geographic market definition in order to detect whether the merging firms really are present or potential competitors. The questions of product substitution and barriers to entry are usually addressed in the section of the report dealing with the likely effects of the merger on the public interest, rather than as part of the market definition process. The task of the MMC is to predict the likely effect of the merger on the public interest. It has to steer a path between an unduly permissive policy which might allow anticompetitive mergers and an unduly restrictive one which would sacrifice efficiency-producing mergers. A mere possibility that adverse effects will result will not give rise to an objection. As the dissenting members of the MMC stated in the *Charter Consolidated* report (1982) if only a possibility were required hardly any merger would be allowed to proceed, since such possibility is hard to exlude: '[t]he question is whether the evidence creates an expectation that the merger will operate against the public interest...the required conclusion is not, "This may happen", but "We expect that this will happen"'.

In the case of horizontal mergers the primary (but not sole) concern of the MMC will be the anticompetitive effect of the increase in concentration. Concentrating mergers will be permitted where the increase in concentration is insubstantial or where the strength of other firms already on the market means that effective competition is unlikely to be compromised. In such circumstances, neither the merged enterprise nor other firms are likely to engage in successful monopoly pricing (*Norton Opax/McCorquodale* report, 1986). At the other extreme, where a market is already highly concentrated, a horizontal merger involving the leading firm will almost certainly be taken to be against the public interest. In this instance the approach of UK merger policy is the same as US monopoly under the Sherman Act: an increase in market power to a position of considerable strength will not be permitted where it is achieved by acquisition, but may be perfectly legitimate where achieved through efficiency (*GUS/Empire Stores* report, 1983).

The significance of higher concentration levels will be affected by the presence or absence of barriers to entry, such as scale economies or excess capacity. Where there are only low entry barriers, the MMC will often be prepared to discount apparently high shares and permit the merger. Examples of this would include the *BET/SGB Group* merger (1986) and the *P&O/European Ferries* merger (1986), where high market shares and a history of collusion in an unattractive market were discounted because of the absence of barriers to entry. The MMC will also take account of the 'stronger player' argument whereby the merged enterprise will form a more effective competitor to an existing firm. Horizontal mergers in the retail sales market[11] and in the biscuits market[12] were permitted because they created more effective competition with dominant firms. In one case the MMC thought that this effect would actually slow down the rate of concentration in the market. Finally, the MMC will discount high concentration levels where there are countervailing forces in the market such as powerful customers or suppliers or, in one case, where the precarious financial condition of customers made a profitable price increase unlikely (*Dee Corporation/Booker McConnell*, 1985).

The MMC will also consider other public policy implications of horizontal mergers. The effect on employment is frequently considered, but will not cause a merger to be disallowed where loss of employment would occur in any event, or where redundancies would improve the prospects of the merged enterprise. Efficiencies are examined by the MMC. Access to improved management or new technology, increases in operational and marketing efficiencies, rationalisation and economies of scale have all been considered in merger reports. However, the very breadth of the public interest test makes it impossible to detect the weight given to these aspects or to determine exactly which efficiencies will be considered relevant by the MMC in any case.

With regard to vertical mergers, the MMC has tended to emphasise the possible distortion of competition which may result from the new relationship between the merged firms. In the *British Telecom/Mitel* report (1986), the MMC found that the proposed vertical merger would place a dominant customer (BT) in control of a multinational supplier. It was in the interest of both firms to maximise sales to BT customers, and there was therefore a danger that BT would given preference to its own subsidiary over other suppliers. The dominance enjoyed by BT would delay the correcting effect of competitive forces on this distortion. In other vertical merger enquiries, the MMC has received assurances that intra-group trading would be conducted at arm's length and without the imposition of exclusive purchasing or selling constraints.

Conglomerate mergers throw up a number of public policy issues, unrelated to competition in the strict sense. The effect of a merger on distribution of industry within the UK has given rise to adverse reports by the MMC. In the *Charter Consolidated/Anderson Strathclyde* merger (1982) and the *Hong Kong & Shanghai/Standard Chartered/Royal Bank* merger (1982), the MMC considered that the mergers would deprive depressed areas of Scotland of industry and employment. This factor led to adverse reports, in both cases in the face of strong minority dissents. In the *Hong Kong* case, the dissenting member pleaded that trade within the UK should be liberalised so that resources could be shifted from one locality to another. This criticism, echoed by George (1985), is really an argument that the role of the MMC should be confined to questions of competition and not touch on aspects such as regional policy, which are better regulated by specialist policies. Such criticism of the MMC is inevitable, given the open-ended nature of the public interest test. It goes to the very heart of competition policy in the UK, rather than merely the way in which the MMC carries out its task. In addition to questions concerning the distribution of industry, the MMC has also considered the desirability of foreign ownership of UK concerns and the perennial difficulty with regard to cross-subsidy between the various businesses of conglomerate firms. Exchange control regulations have been abandoned in the UK and there is no formal obstacle to the acquisition of UK firms by overseas concerns. The MMC has confirmed that foreign ownership is not of itself relevant to the public interest (*Taubman/Sotherby*, 1983), but in one case it recommended that a UK clearing bank should not be permitted to be controlled by a foreign bank because of the special financial and fiscal problems which might be caused (*Hong Kong & Shanghai/Standard Chartered/Royal Bank*, 1982). Cross-subsidy is a more difficult problem in that the opacity of group accounts may render it impossible to detect.

Where intra-group arrangements do lead to predatory pricing then it may be more appropriate to tackle it under the provisions of the Competition Act 1980 which regulate anticompetitive practices.[13]

The Secretary of State is not obliged to follow the recommendations of the MMC, but almost always does,[14] and is only empowered to take action to regulate or prohibit a merger where the MMC has made an adverse report. There is a wide variety of possible orders, including the total prohibition of a merger and divestiture of existing ownership. In addition, interim orders may be made to ensure that the investigation is not impeded. It is more usual to seek undertakings from firms rather than enforce policy through Executive orders, a practice typical of the consensual approach adopted in monopoly and merger policy in the UK.

Effectiveness of UK policy
The first major critical study of merger policy under the 1973 Act was the First Green paper in 1978. This found that the policy had failed to slow the rate of concentration in UK industry and that a more critical approach to mergers was required. The operation of the 1973 Act tends to favour mergers; the burden of proof is on the MMC to show specific adverse effects rather than on the firms to show positive benefits. However the Green Paper did not recommend a reversal of the burden, mainly on organisational grounds. Instead, it recommended the adoption of a largely structural, neutral procedure concerned mainly with the competitive impact of mergers and supported by a policy statement for the guidance of industry. In addition, the secretive Mergers Panel was to be issued with published, non-statutory guidelines.

No action was taken on these recommendations; the Tebbit statement in 1984 (Tebbit 1984 I) confirmed that the legislation would remain, with a shift of emphasis towards competition in the selection of mergers for referral. However, merger policy is currently part of a wide-ranging review of competition policy being undertaken by the Department of Trade and Industry. Having regard to the pressure on parliamentary time, it is likely that any reform which comes out of this review will be one requiring little or no legislative changes.

Table 2:
Recent merger reports of the MMC

1982
BTR/Serck. HC 392   mainly conglomerate
Hong-Kong & Shanghai/Standard Chartered/
Royal Bank. Cmnd. 8472   conglomerate
ICI/Arthur Holden. Cmnd 8660   conglomerate/vertical
Nabisco/Huntley & Palmer. Cmnd 8680   horizontal
Charter Consolidated/Anderson Strathclyde.
Cmnd 8771   conglomerate

1983
GUS/Empire Stores. Cmnd 8777   horizontal
Sunlight/Initial/Johnson. Cmnd 8868   horizontal
Linfood Holdings/Fitch Lovell. Cmnd 8874   horizontal/vertical
Lewis/Illingworth/Morris. Cmnd 9012   conglomerate
London Brick/Ibstock Johnsen. Cmnd. 9015   conglomerate
Taubman/Sotherby. Cmnd 9046   conglomerate
Pleasurama/Trident/Grand Met. Cmnd 9018   conglomerate/horizontal

1984
Hepworth Ceramic/Steetley. Cmnd 9164   conglomerate/horizontal
Trafalgar House/P & O. Cmnd 9190   horizontal
GKN/AE. Cmnd 9199   conglomerate/horizontal

1985
Dee Corp/Booker McConnell. Cmnd 9429   horizontal/vertical
BETC/Initial. Cmnd 9444   horizontal
Lonrho/House of Fraser. Cmnd 9458   conglomerate
Scottish & Newcastle/Matthew Brown
Cmnd 9645   horizontal

1986
British Telecom/Mitel. Cmnd 9715   vertical/horizontal
BET/SGB Group. Cmnd 9795   horizontal
GEC/Plessey. Cmnd 9867   horizontal
Elders IXL/Allied Lyons. Cmnd 9892   conglomerate
Norton Opax/McCorquodale. Cmnd 9904   horizontal
P&O/European Ferries. Cm 31   horizontal

1987
Tate & Lyle and others. Cm 89   horizontal
Trusthouse Forte/Hanson Trust. Cm 96   horizontal

Merger activity continues apace in the UK, and the value of target assets is rapidly increasing. The value of target assets in referable mergers was £5.8 billion in 1975, but had grown to £57.5 billion in 1985, with a peak figure of £80 billion in 1985. Indeed, at one point in December 1985 current merger activity amounted to £7 billion (Markus and Levi, 1985). This continued upward trend in merger activity does not *of itself* denote a failure of UK merger policy; the mergers permitted by, or not referred to, the MMC may have been efficiency-producing or lacking in anticompetitive effects. With regard to efficiencies, Meeks (1977) has shown that in most cases hoped-for efficiencies are not realised, and that mergers often introduce inefficiencies together with reduced profitability. Meeks' call for a less permissive merger policy has been echoed by others (e.g. Sharpe, 1983; George, 1985), amongst whom there is a widespread support for the reversal of the present presumption in favour of mergers. The adoption of such an approach, together with the publication of workable guide-lines, may go a long way to increase the effectiveness of UK policy.

The Tebbit statement did little to reduce the uncertainty concerning the circumstances in which a merger will be referred to the MMC. This uncertainty is made more acute by the remote and secretive nature of the Mergers Panel. There is a good case for the publication of detailed merger guidelines so that firms may be able to discern at the planning stage (even before any informal approaches to the OFT) whether it is likely that a proposed merger will be referred. Referral should not be restricted to narrow competition grounds. Whilst it is true that in most cases any adverse impact on the public interest *will* relate to the anticompetitive effects of a merger, other matters, such as a potential adverse effect on employment, may also merit a reference. It may well be that the MMC will regard perceived efficiencies as outweighing these other matters, but that is a matter which should be considered at the evaluation stage and not at the referral stage.

If merger policy is to be made more certain then, in addition to clarifying the grounds for referral, there should be a mechanism whereby the OFT is apprised of proposed mergers in a routine way. The present methods by which the OFT secures intelligence on proposed mergers could be usefully supported by a requirement that bidding firms give advance notice of intended mergers.

A more radical proposal would be to transfer the present merger functions of the MMC to the OFT. This would have the benefit of streamlining merger policy. One body would have the task of screening and evaluating mergers, rather than splitting the process in two. It would also promote the integration of the various aspects of antitrust policy, which in turn would lead to a more homogeneous and orderly regulation of industry. It is a proposal already adopted by one political party in the UK.

EEC LAW

Unlike the other two legal systems, the EEC has no effective mergers policy. Neither Article 85 nor 86 is applicable to mergers generally, and the European Commission has been calling for many years for the adoption of new legislation for merger control. In the present political climate, the chances of this occurring are remote. EEC law therefore remains incapable of regulating mergers of inter-State significance and is directed instead to regulating the activities of existing monopoly firms. There are, however, two instances in which mergers may be regulated under existing law, namely anticompetitive mergers involving dominant firms, and para-mergers in the form of joint ventures.

It will be recalled that Article 86 prohibits the abuse of a dominant position where this may have an effect on trade between Member States. In the controversial *Continental Can* case (1973) the ECJ determined that a merger may constitute abusive behaviour. In that case a firm with a very substantial market share acquired the only other significant competitor, thereby virtually eliminating competition on the market. In spite of the protests of the firm, the ECJ confirmed that Article 86 would apply to such mergers even where the dominance was not used to initiate the merger. Continental Can remains the only means of merger control under Article 86, and is subject to severe limitations. The judgment is only applicable to firms already in a dominant position, rather than to mergers through which dominance is achieved. Secondly it gives rise to *ex post facto* control only, although the Commission has found new powers to take interim measures to preserve the status quo in competition matters.[15] Retrospective control can only be enforced by divestiture orders, which can have disastrous financial implications for industry. Further, the lack of any exempting provision in Article 86 (unlike Article 85) makes it a rather brutal instrument for effective merger control (Reynolds, 1983). As a result of these deficiencies, the Commission has never used Article 86 to oppose a merger formally, though it has been able to persuade firms informally against undertaking abusive mergers.

The Commission was aware of the limitations of the *Continental Can* rule and within a few weeks of it being delivered it published a proposal for a merger Regulation to extend Article 86. This proposal, last amended in 1984,[16] provides that certain mergers are incompatible with the objectives of the Common Market and are therefore capable of being regulated by the Commission. Such mergers (or 'concentrations') are those between firms, at least one of which is established in the EEC, whereby the power to hinder effective competition in the EEC (or a substantial part of it) is acquired or enhanced and where trade between Member States may thereby be affected.

The proposal is aimed at mergers which have significance for the EEC as a whole. The potential anticompetitive effect is to be measured at a Community level, having regard to a number of criteria laid down in the proposed Regulation. In common with the US Merger Guidelines, the proposed Regulation is concerned mainly with horizontal mergers. It provides for a rebuttable presumption of compatibility where the market share of the merged enterprise is less than 20 per cent in the EEC or a substantial part of it. Further, the general presumption of incompatibility does not apply where the turnover of all firms involved is less than £750 million ECU (approx. £550 million). On the other hand the Regulation would apply to mergers involving a lower turnover where the market share involved is greater than 50 per cent in a substantial part of the EEC. This last provision is intended to prevent the acquisition of a monopoly position in a Member State and will therefore be largely coextensive with the various national merger policies. However, even anticompetitive mergers would permitted under the Regulation if they are indispensable to the attainment of 'a priority of the Community'. This wide discretionary power would enable the Commission to permit mergers on grounds unrelated to efficiency or competition. Factors such as the balance of industry and employment could be considered (Potter, 1985), which would bring EEC merger policy closer to the UK model. Two important provisions in the proposed Regulation concern the prior notification of larger mergers and the provision of merger guidelines 'to ensure that the application of the merger control instrument takes into account the evolution of economic realities and to provide optimum legal scrutiny for undertakings' (Fourteenth Report on Competition Policy, 1984).

In addition to Article 86, there is some role for Article 85 in merger control. Article 85 is the instrument for the control of restrictive trade agreements in the EEC and is examined in Chapter 5. In this regard the Commission analysed the position of mergers within EEC law in its memorandum on concentrations (Commission, 1966). In this discussion paper the Commission drew a distinction between cartels, which fall within Article 85, and concentrations, which do not. The difference between these two forms of transaction is that the latter effects a permanent loss of economic independence and a modification of the internal structure of the merging firms. A cartel, however, merely creates contractual obligations relating to the practices of the firms. Certain types of merger-like transactions may therefore be caught. Clearly a full merger between firms which results in the elimination of the separate identities of the merging firms will not constitute an agreement because, on its consummation, there will no longer be any parties to it. At the other extreme a short-term cooperation agreement between firms may be caught by the Article but could not be regarded as a merger. Somewhere in between these forms of transaction lies scope for Article 85 control. The transactions concerned are usually referred to as joint venture agreements.

This type of agreement can take many forms and may be used for different purposes, such as joint research and development or joint sales. The vehicle for the joint enterprise may be corporate, such as a newly-formed subsidiary, or wholly informal with no separate physical or legal identity. The joint venture is a popular vehicle, enabling the parent companies to undertake activities which they are unable or unwilling to do alone. Rationalisation is the most common motive for industrial joint ventures, followed by research and development, and joint production (Fifteenth Report on Competition Policy, 1985). Article 85 will not apply to a joint venture where it amounts to a partial merger, that is where it effects a permanent change in the ownership and control of the parts of the firms concerned. Where the parents lose their separate identities in the field covered by the joint venture, Article 85 will have no application. Thus in the *SHV/Chevron* decision (1975) the parent companies transferred distribution networks and related assets to joint distribution subsidiaries for fifty years. The two parents agreed not to compete with the subsidiaries in the distribution of the product. The Commission regarded this arrangement as effecting a lasting change in the structures of the parents, having regard especially to the length of time of the transfer. The undertaking not to compete did not cause Article 85 to apply since it was unlikely in any event that the parents would compete with their own subsidiary.

However, it is only where firms effectively abandon the area of the joint venture's operation that the arrangement will be regarded as a partial merger, and therefore outside the control of Article 85. Where they remain actual or potential competitors in this market, then the arrangement will be treated as a restrictive agreement under Article 85. In the *Henkel/Colgate* joint venture (1972), the parents transferred research activities to the joint venture but remained as competitors in the sale of the product; the agreement was subject to Article 85. The Commission is eager to classify joint ventures as agreements rather than partial mergers in order to retain control over them. It therefore has regard to the effect of the joint venture on the relationship of the parents outside the joint venture's field. Where a 'spill over' effect can be detected then this will cause Article 85 to apply.

The Commission recognises the potential utility of joint ventures and almost always grants exemption under the terms of Article 85(3).[17] The prohibition (either formal or practical) on competition between the firms and the joint venture may be acceptable where it is essential to its operation and especially where the parent firms were unlikely in any event to compete in the joint venture's field. Entry into high-risk or high-technology markets by way of a joint venture will not reduce effective competition in that market where the firms were unlikely to have entered alone. Korah has found that the Commission will examine the likelihood of potential competition between the firms in a more realistic manner than it has in the past (Korah, 1986 I).

Even when there is some diminution in potential competition between the venturing firms, existing effective competition on the market or low entry barriers will ensure that any efficiency gains will be passed on to consumers. In *Carbon Gas Technologie* (1984) at least some of the parent firms would have been able to undertake the joint activities alone, but the Commission allowed the joint venture to proceed because it permitted greater use of complementary specialisations and thereby enhanced technical and economic progress in the field of alternative energy supplies. Strong competition on the market ensured the maintenance of low prices. In addition, non-competition agreements are often regarded by the Commission as essential to the proper functioning of the joint project and the facilitation of market entry (*VW/Man* decision, 1984).

Merger transactions which are not actionable under Article 86, and which amount to more permanent arrangements than a joint venture, will not be capable of regulation under EEC law. The decision on the *Mecaniver/PPG Industries* merger (1985) is an example of such a situation. This must be viewed against the background of continuing sharp increases in merger activity in the EEC, with most mergers being large in terms of turnover (Fifteenth Report on Competition Policy, 1985). Rationalisation was the most common motive for mergers involving the 1,000 largest firms in the EEC in 1984–5, accounting for over 29 per cent of such mergers. This trend does not necessarily reveal a compression of competition in EEC markets, but it does give cause for concern at the lack of any effective regulation at Community level.

US LAW

Merger policy in the US is complicated to a certain extent by legislative and administrative overlaps. Both section 1 of the Sherman Act and section 7 of the Clayton Act may be used for the control of mergers, and the latter section may be enforced by either the Antitrust Division or the Federal Trade Commission.

Section 1 of the Sherman Act is principally concerned with restrictive trading agreements between firms but, unlike Article 85 of the Treaty of Rome, is also generally applicable to mergers. The wording of the section, with its prohibition of 'every...combination in the form of trust or otherwise' is appropriate to merger control. However, when the courts developed the 'rule of reason' in relation to antitrust disputes, Congress strengthened the law through the Clayton Act 1914. Section 7 of that Act is specifically directed at merger control and has become the central weapon in the merger enforcement armoury. It was thought for some time that the Sherman Act would have no further part to play in merger control, but the *Lexington Bank* case (1964) reaffirmed that section 1 renders illegal any horizontal agreement between significant competitors. Section 1 therefore continues to provide residual possibilities for merger enforcement, for use by government or private plaintiffs (Oppenheim, Weston and McCarthy, 1981) and indeed is often used by the Antitrust Division in tandem with an action under section 7 of the Clayton Act (Sullivan, 1977 II).

However, section 7 remains the most significant feature in merger control, especially since its amendments in 1950,[18] 1976[19] and 1980.[20] In contract to the Sherman Act, the Clayton Act provides for civil, not criminal, enforcement. Section 7 prohibits the acquisition by any person of the stock or assets of another where the effect of such acquisition may be substantially to lessen competition, or tend to create a monopoly, in any product or geographic market. The reference in the section to the acquisition of assets was added in order to plug a loophole being exploited by bidding firms. However, by such inclusion, US law is made to embrace a very wide variety of transactions. UK law would not classify the purchase of assets as a merger unless they were purchased as part of an 'enterprise', that is an operative organic activity. The breadth of the prohibition is sufficient to include horizontal, vertical and conglomerate mergers, although the emphasis of policy enforcement is largely on horizontal mergers. The concern of the section is with the competitive impact of a merger: whether it will substantially lessen competition. The meaning of this phrase is of critical importance to the understanding of the section, and it is a meaning which has not remained constant since its enactment.

The meaning of 'competition'

There is an analytical conflict between atomistic and effective competition: should competitive impact be measured purely in terms of concentration figures or should other matters be taken into account to assess the significance of such data? The first case to reach the Supreme Court following the 1950 amendment to section 7 of the Clayton Act was the *Brown Shoe* case (1962). The court took the opportunity to trace the legislative history of the amendment in order to evince the policy of the Act. It found the dominant theme to be Congressional fear of the 'rising tide of economic concentration in the American economy', a phrase which has been reiterated in many subsequent cases. There were other objectives, principally the desirability of preserving small, locally-owned businesses. This populist approach to competition policy was a revival of the objectives of the Sherman Act, which Congress regarded as having been frustrated by the courts' adoption of the rule of reason. It therefore sought to reimpose a stringent policy to maintain an atomistic economy even though this might be at the sacrifice of efficiency. It may make little sense in economic terms to preserve small units, but it was a policy rooted in the American psyche, with its fear of bigness and of the political power available to economically strong units. The desire was to preserve an economic environment that was being broken down by the dynamic force of concentration, with the consequent breakdown of ties between employers and employees, and between firms and localities (Cann, 1985). Although the court in the *Brown Shoe* case found that section 7 protected competition and not competitors, it kept returning to the notion that the Act's purpose was to preserve large numbers of viable, small, locally-owned business: 'Congress appreciated that occasional higher costs and prices might result from the maintenance of fragmented industries and markets. It resolved these competing considerations in favour of decentralisation. We must give effect to that decision'.

Given this atomistic policy towards mergers, the court considered that market shares in horizontal mergers was one of the most important factors in determining anticompetitive effect. Other factors which could be taken into account were any tendency towards concentration in the relevant market, the likely failure of the firm to be taken over, and the possible benefits of mergers among smaller firms in markets dominated by larger ones. The following year, in the *Philadelphia National Bank* case (1983), the Supreme Court reformulated its approach by promoting the market-share factor almost to a rule of law. The court confirmed that its role was not only to appraise the immediate impact of a merger, but also to predict its future impact, so that anticompetitive tendencies can be arrested in their incipiency. To be sound, such a prediction must be based on the market context in which the merger takes place. However, such an ideal was too elusive for the court: 'the relevant economic data are both complex and elusive ...[a]nd unless businessmen can assess the legal consequences of a merger with some confidence, sound business planning is retarded'. The court therefore prepared to manufacture what was effectively the first merger guideline, a test of illegality the simplicity of which was declared to be in the interests of sound and practical judicial administration. The court declared that:

a merger which produces a firm controlling an undue percentage share of the market, and results in a significant increase in the concentration of firms in that market is so inherently likely to lessen competition substantially that it must be enjoined in the absence of evidence clearly showing that the merger is not likely to have such anticompetitive effects.

Thus, a role of presumptive illegality was formulated, based on market share data. In the case itself a market share of 30 per cent was held to trigger the presumption. This structural approach to merger analysis dominated the judicial enforcement of section 7 until a reversal occurred in the *General Dynamics* case (1974), a case which continues to dominate judicial merger policy to date. In this case the court allowed evidence to rebut the presumption raised by a substantial market share. The court accepted that sustained market shares are often an indication of market power and of a power to dominate the market. However, on their own, market share data are not necessarily indicative of the ability to sustain power into the future. Other features of the market must be taken into account in order to assess the significance of market shares. In the *General Dynamics* case the market share of the merged enterprise did not give an indication of future ability because the real market power of the merging firms depended on the availability to them of uncommitted reserves. Without the ability to procure long-term contracts, a firm would be in a weak competitive position.

This approach to merger analysis signalled a new leniency to horizontal mergers in the courts; one commentator refers to this permissiveness as a 'judicial bias' against section 7 (Lipner, 1986). The presumption formulated in *Philadelphia National Bank* is still extant, but is now more easily rebutted by a variety of evidence relating to the relevant market. In the *Waste Management* case (1984) a combined market share of 48.8 per cent triggered the presumption, but the merger was permitted because extreme ease of entry into the market prevented firms with *apparent* market share from exercising that power to raise prices. The high market share figures simply did not accurately reflect future market power. Another way to analyse this situation would be to include within the definition of the relevant market those firms who would enter if price levels were attractive. The court declined to do this, but the Antitrust Division's Merger Guidelines do take such potential competition into account in defining the market. Although the presumption of illegality is often rebutted, it would be misleading to assume that all courts take such a line. There is still a conflict between those courts which adopt this 'pro-merger' approach and those which give a great deal more weight to the presumption of illegality based on market share alone. Davis suggests that this uncertainty in the judicial approach to mergers will generate more private enforcement litigation (Davis, 1986). Indeed 95 per cent of merger cases are brought by private plaintiffs; in an atmosphere of judicial uncertainty, litigation can be used by unwilling targets or unhappy competitors as a 'wild card'. It is certainly true that merger litigation is more uncertain as a result of *General Dynamics* but it is equally true that courts are now more determined to assess the real impact of a merger rather than its supposed impact based on economic extrapolations from market share data. It may be that the courts' willingness to tackle economic concepts is more apparent than real (Hay, 1985), but their willingness to enter the debate will lead to a more satisfactory merger policy once sufficient precedent has established their likely approach to evidence on market features tendered by the parties.

Enforcement of policy

The Antitrust Division (AD) of the Department of Justice, and the Federal Trade Commission (FTC) have concurrent jurisdiction to enforce merger policy under section 7, in addition to enforcement actions brought by private individuals. The AD is a prosecuting arm of government and its nature and structure is described in Chapter 2. The FTC differs markedly from the AD; it is an independent administrative agency with a wide spectrum of functions in the field of consumer, corporate and competition affairs. It acts as investigator, prosecutor and adjudicator, subject to appeals on law to the ordinary courts. The FTC is closely described in Chapter 5. The concurrent jurisdiction of the two agencies has the potential for conflict and confusion, but the relationship is one of friendly competition rather than antagonism. There is an effective liaison procedure to ensure that both agencies do not pursue the same case. Where preliminary investigations have begun on the same matter, an allocation will be made on the basis of expertise and experience. However it is rarely necessary to do this since the agencies have agreed to divide the antitrust market according to industry sectors. Cooperation between the agencies is such that the FTC maintains a small staff in the AD's pre-merger notification office (McCarty, 1985). Although the concurrent jurisdiction of the two agencies does not produce great practical problems, it has been criticised as inefficient and irrational (Gellhorn, 1982). The dual role is certainly a surprisingly resilient feature, but is supported by many, on the basis of the FTC's independence from the President, and for the beneficial effects of competition between the agencies.

Both agencies will gather intelligence on proposed mergers through the financial news media as well as by informal approaches from firms or their legal advisors. In addition, in certain cases formal prior notification must be given to the AD and FTC. This requirement, which has no equivalent in UK law, was added to the Clayton Act in 1976.[21] It ensures that no significant merger will escape scrutiny through default, and it suspends any such transaction so that the agencies are able to formulate their policy towards it. Prior notification is required only in the case of mergers where one firm has assets or net annual sales of at least $100 million, and the other of at least $10 million; and further where the transaction would lead to the bidder holding at least $15 million worth, or 15 per cent of, the voting shares or assets of the target. Given the very wide definition of merger in section 7, certain transactions which are unlikely to have antitrust implications are exempted from the need to notify. Such exempt transactions include, for example, the purchase of property in the ordinary course of business, acquisitions by a parent company of further shares in its subsidiary; investment transactions; and certain share issues. Transactions of this nature are unlikely to be proceeded against and a requirement to notify would be a needlessly disruptive formality.

Where notification is made, the merger transaction may not proceed for thirty days, during which time it will be assessed by the appropriate agency. In all probability, the agency will require further information before it is able to assess the anticompetitive impact of the merger, and a request for further information may be submitted within the waiting period. In this case the period of suspension will be extended by twenty days. The waiting period is similar to the time taken by the OFT in determining whether to recommend that a merger be referred to the MMC, but the American agencies must undertake a more demanding analysis, akin to the role of the MMC. It is vital to the proper functioning of merger policy in the US that, given such a short time, sufficient resources and information are available to the agencies. In the FTC summary information sheets are prepared weekly by a specialist unit and these are placed before a merger screening committee. It is this committee which determines the recommendations as to FTC policy with regard to the merger—whether to permit it to proceed without further delay, to issue a 'second request letter' requiring further information, or to take powers to subpoena relevant persons in order to elicit further information. Formal decisions on action are taken by the commissioners. Scheffman has found that the commissioners have become more interested in the information on which recommendations are made and that as a result investigations have become more evidence-intensive (Scheffman, 1985). Because delay may be costly to bidding and target firms and disruptive to the market, the FTC maintains a flexible approach to expedite investigations. It will enter into negotiations to narrow the scope of the second request letter, or to terminate the waiting period early. McCarty has found that over 60 per cent of notifications to the FTC in 1984 were granted early termination (McCarty, 1985). Alternatively, the waiting period will be extended by negotiation if the firms wish to meet the Director of the Bureau of Competition or the commissioners themselves. Both agencies have a large staff of lawyers and economists. The FTC economists investigate and report on mergers separately from the lawyers but there is a great deal of cooperation, especially in relation to framing the second request letter (Scheffman, 1985). Pre-merger procedures in the AD are similar; information is collected by way of the original notification, a second request letter, and by compulsory process where necessary. This information is analysed in a relatively short period and decisions on agency policy are taken at the highest level on the basis of internal recommendations. The structure of the AD is more triangular and decisions are taken by one person, the Assistant Attorney General, rather than in a collegiate way. This structural difference between the agencies is minimised by Katzmann on the basis that the chairman of the FTC has strong *de facto* control over decision making (Katzmann, 1980). As with the FTC, the AD economists prepare independent reports but engage in a close cooperation with staff lawyers at certain critical stages in the investigation (Warren-Boulton, 1985).

The Merger Guidelines
The similarity in the processes of the FTC and AD are not entirely reflected in a similarity in their substantive analysis. Both agencies have issued guidelines on their merger policy for the benefit of firms and professional advisors. Those issued by the AD are the better known and, although substantially the same in approach as those issued by the FTC, some analytical differences in approach and emphasis do occur (Schwartz, 1983). The Guidelines issued by the AD in 1968 were substantially revised in 1982 to take account of the developments in case law and antitrust economics, and further revisions were made in 1984.[22] The practical operation of US merger policy is to be found in the Merger Guidelines; an indication from the enforcement agencies that a merger is to be opposed on the basis of the Guidelines will usually result in the transaction being abandoned or a settlement being negotiated (Clanton, 1984). However, even where the enforcement agencies are successful in 'clearing off' potentially troublesome mergers at an early stage, private plaintiffs may still start litigation.

The 1982 and 1984 Guidelines emphasise the departure of merger analysis from the blunt presumptions laid down in *Philadelphia National Bank* (1963). Merger policy as set out in the Guidelines seeks to prohibit only those mergers which are anticompetitive; the pro-competitive mergers will ideally be identified and permitted. However, a purpose of the Guidelines is to guide business and to this end they must be expressed in clear and workably precise terms. The need for precision, for practicality, may be met only at the expense of subtlety (this is what Clanton, 1983, refers to as the tradeoff between certainty and analytical completeness). The production of any guidelines involves the risks that in some cases they will produce the 'wrong' results. There is a need for sacrifice: mergers which appear innocuous on the basis of the Guidelines but which in fact are anticompetitive must either be permitted in the interests of consistency or disallowed on an ad hoc basis. Guidelines will either limit the freedom of action of the enforcing agency, or their credibility (and therefore their utility) will be diminished by actions being pursued outside their terms. The 1982 Guidelines attempted to achieve simplicity of approach in order to safeguard such utility. This is how they were described by a commentator:

They represent a new positivism; a reduction of legal principles to a simple, unitary, quasi-scientific, outcome-orientated economic model that, in a generalised sense, has been offered as the model for solving all antitrust problems. By enforcing only one substantive goal—allocative efficiency—the model offers the appearance of clarity, predictability, and reduced government intervention (Fox, 1983).

Although many would not accept that the 1982 Guidelines did create a simple model (Kauper, 1983), a criticism of the 1984 Guidelines is that the tradeoff has been altered so that certainty has been compromised in favour of a more thoroughgoing analysis of the competitive impact of each merger (Baker, 1984).

Greater complexity, or increased pragmatism, on the part of the Guidelines will limit their utility to business. It will also tend to defeat another, covert, purpose which many detect in the Guidelines. That purpose is a desire on the part of the AD to influence the courts in the development of judicial merger analysis (Areeda, 1983; Baker and Blumenthal, 1983; Schwartz, 1983). Schwartz (1983) sees the Guidelines as a vehicle for the imposition of Chicago School economics on judicial practice. In a passage which contrasts sharply with Fox's view, he describes the Guidelines as 'an elaborate and costly pretense of science masking an intuitional or philosophically biased discretionary judgement...[Evidence from small business competitors] should outweigh statistical mumbo-jumbo if the courts are not to accede to the Department's purpose to lead them by the nose to a regressive revision of the antitrust laws'. The guidelines certainly reflect the Reagan administration's desire for a more permissive merger policy (Brummer, 1981; Rhoades, 1983), but Schwartz's fears appear not to have been fulfilled; the courts continue to adopt disparate approaches to merger enforcement, and do depart from the Guidelines (Davis, 1986).

The crux of the Guidelines' approach lies in the theory that greater concentration leads to a likelihood of collusion and ultimately to control over market price. Concentration data may only be examined in the context of the relevant market. The definition of the relevant market is the first substantive passage in the Guidelines. It is also the most radical departure from the pre-existing case law, in that it seeks to establish a methodical and largely non-subjective analytical framework based on the concept of market power. It seeks to elicit the smallest product and geographic area that would allow a hypothetical pure monopolist to profitably impose a 'small but significant and nontransitory' price increase. This is essentially a test for demand substitution (will consumers respond by switching to products in other markets?) and supply substitution (will producers respond by switching to, or commencing, production of products in this market?). The mechanical test for determining the boundaries of this market takes the form of a series of progressively expanding definitions based on the 'five per cent test'. For each product of the merging firms, the AD posits a price increase, usually of 5 per cent lasting one year, at the firms' location. If available data suggest that such price increase will be unprofitable for the hypothetical monopolist then a larger product and geographic market will be chosen and the test will be repeated. The relevant market will be the smallest one in which the price increase would be profitable;[23] at that point demand and supply substitution would cease to diminish the market.

In order to determine a firm's share of the relevant market, the AD will include not only those firms which presently produce the relevant products, but also the likely market share of those firms which have existing facilities which could, within one year, be used to switch to the relevant products in response to the assumed price increase. Firms which have no such existing facilities, and firms with existing facilities which could not be usefully employed to effect a production substitution (for example, because of distribution or marketing barriers) will not be included in the calculation of market share. Even firms of this nature will impose some competitive pressure on the relevant market through threat of entry. Entry barriers are not considered by the Guidelines as part of the definition of the market,[24] but are considered at a later stage in assessing the significance of concentration data. The market definition provisions, first introduced in their present form in the 1982 Guidelines, have attracted a variety of responses. They have been supported as a departure from the pragmatic approach of the courts to market definition (Baxter, 1983), and criticised for an overly theoretical methodology not easily applicable to real-world markets and operators (Harris & Jorde, 1983). Many other criticisms, relating to the inflexibility of the provisions have been substantially met by the 1984 revisions. However, the utility of the definition in any one case will depend on the availability of sufficient data.

Horizontal mergers Horizontal mergers are assessed according to the degree of concentration of the relevant market and the increase in concentration brought about by the merger. This is a re-interpretation of the 'undue percentage' and 'significant increase' passages in *Philadelphia National Bank*. The formula used by the Guidelines for the measurement of concentration is the Herfindahl-Hirschman Index (HHI). This measures concentration by summing the squares of individual firms' market shares, and ranges from a maximum reading of 10,000 in the case of pure monopoly to just above zero in the case of an atomistic market.[25] The HHI is divided into three zones—unconcentrated (HHI below 1,000), moderately concentrated (HHI between 1,000 and 1,800), and highly concentrated (HHI above 1,800). Mergers in unconcentrated markets (which remain unconcentrated after the merger) are not likely to be challenged under section 7 of the Clayton Act because the risks of collusion are low. At the other extreme mergers in highly concentrated markets which increase the HHI by more than 100 points will almost certainly be challenged. Mergers in such a market which only increase the market share by 50 points are likely to be challenged unless a consideration of non-concentration factors persuades the AD not to do so. In the middle region, in moderately concentrated markets, mergers are only likely to be challenged where the increase exceeds 100 points, and even in these circumstances the AD will take account of the non-concentration factors described below. In all zones, mergers with leading firms will be regarded more strictly.

The non-concentration features of a market which are taken into account in order to assess the competitive impact of a merger are derived from the approach of *General Dynamics* (1974). Market share alone will not usually be taken to be sufficiently indicative of competitive impact. Changes in market conditions, the availability of new technology, and the financial condition of relevant firms may all influence the future significance of current market shares and will be taken into account. Barriers existing in the international markets, such as import taxes or quotas, will affect the calculation and will be given due weight.

Entry barriers are also considered at this stage. Where entry barriers are low, high market shares are unlikely to provide market power. The Guidelines do not specify what factors will be considered to be barriers. The provisions are expressed in terms of the likelihood of entry in response to the familiar price increase hypothesis over a two-year period. Special consideration is given to the nature of the assets required for entry, to the dynamic condition of the market, and to minimum efficient size. The likelihood of 'inside entry' is also considered—that is, production expansion by fringe firms in response to a price increase. But no mention is made in the Guidelines of government-sponsored barriers, which many regard as the only significant ones.[26] Baker (1984) has found that the AD treats easy entry as a 'trump card' even in the case of high concentration figures.

Product variation between firms in the market will influence the likelihood of successful collusion. Homogeneity will render price collusion more easy, whereas heterogeneity will make it more difficult. Where there are clear cases of these phenomena, they will influence the AD in deciding whether to challenge a merger. However in the usual case of moderate variation, this factor will not be influential.

The nature of the market definition will also be taken into account, in order to mitigate any artificialities that occur in that definition. As mentioned in relation to market definition in monopoly control,[27] the choice of where to break the chain of substitution is often arbitrary and may distort analysis. The Guidelines therefore require a consideration of the closeness to the defined market of excluded products and geographic areas. Where the next best substitutes or areas are very close to the defined ones, they will exert a stronger competitive influence and depress the apparent importance of market shares. Similarly, the market definition will not comprise exactly similar substitutions over the whole range of products included, and any 'cold spots' incorporated within the market can be taken into account when assessing the impact of a merger. Where, for example, the merging firms produce goods which, although in the same market, are not so closely substitutable as other goods on the market, then the impact of the merger will not be so great as if the firms' products were perfect substitutes. The same considerations will apply to the geographical locations of the firms' activities.

Other aspects of conduct and performance on the market will affect the chances of collusion: a history of horizontal collusion, or other anticompetitive behaviour, or the elimination through the merger of a previously disruptive and competitive firm, will alert the AD to the need for close scrutiny of the merger. So will uncompetitive performance where this can be identified. One means adopted by the AD to identify such performance is excessive profitability compared to industries with similar capital intensity and risk. Such a test is clearly fraught with difficulties.

There is an apparent change in the relevance of efficiencies. The 1982 Guidelines stated that specific efficiencies would only be taken into account in 'extraordinary circumstances'. The 1984 Guidelines clearly provide that efficiencies will be taken into account as a factor affecting the significance of statistical data, where established by 'clear and convincing evidence', and where they can be shown to be achievable only by way of merger.[28] There is no limit to the type of efficiencies which may be submitted, although there is a warning that the AD will be sceptical with regard to administrative or general efficiencies. However, it is not anticipated that efficiencies will be permitted to save a merger with significant anticompetitive impact. McGrath, as Assistant Attorney General in charge of the AD has stated:

> If we had evidence that a merger would result in supra-competitive profits, that it was anticompetitive, then efficiencies would not be taken into account. We have not adopted the approach that we will balance expected efficiencies against expected anticompetitive consequences, and I do not think we properly could under the language of Section 7 (Note, 1985).

Non-horizontal mergers The Guidelines do not use the familiar tripartite distinction between types of merger (horizontal, vertical, and conglomerate). As an indication of the emphasis on horizontal concerns, the division in the Guidelines is between horizontal and non-horizontal mergers. Further, it is the horizontal aspects of non-horizontal mergers which are examined.

The AD views the potential dangers of vertical and conglomerate mergers as the loss of potential competition, the creation of barriers to entry, the increased likelihood of collusion, and the evasion of profit regulation by public utilities. Potential competition, whether it actually exists or is simply perceived by firms on the market, will exert a limiting influence on price levels in the market. The freedom of firms to collusively raise prices is restricted by the threat of entry. The removal of that threat may facilitate collusion and lead to higher prices. Further, the entering firm may have chosen a more beneficial form of entry, such as independent entry or the acquisition of a small firm in the market. Barriers to entry will be created by vertical integration on a market, by making it necessary for firms to enter at both levels if they wish to compete effectively. If the market at either of the levels is currently concentrated, then this increased barrier may facilitate uncompetitive behaviour.

Defences In the 1982 Guidelines, the AD stated that it would consider two defences to otherwise objectionable mergers. One of those defences—efficiencies—has now been integrated into the body of the guidelines as a factor to be taken into account when assessing the significance of statistical data. That leaves only the 'failing firm' defence, which has now been bolstered by a 'failing division' adjunct.[29] Anticompetitive mergers may be permitted where it can be shown that one of the firms would otherwise have failed financially and could not save itself through a less anticompetitive merger. Similarly, where a diversified firm intends to liquidate a failing division, the sale of that division to a competitor may be permitted under this defence.

The effectiveness of the Guidelines will depend to a large extent on the ability of the AD to persuade the courts to adopt the policy they enshrine. Courts may prefer to adopt a more diverse analysis based on social and political values outside the scope of economic efficiency (Cann, 1985). They may also prefer a more instinctive approach to the complexity of the Guidelines' calculations. For the Guidelines to be truly effective in determining the nature of merger policy, the courts must be convinced of their correctness, not only in government suits, but also in the mass of private litigation.

The enforcement agencies are given the opportunity to publicise their policies. The FTC justifies its consent orders extensively (Clanton, 1984), and the AD is obliged to enter consent decrees for scrutiny by the court. The court will give approval only after a period for public comment has been allowed. This semi-formal alternative to full litigation provides a good opportunity for the development and dissemination of merger policy.

NOTES

1. The Director General of Fair Trading is not empowered to make merger references to the MMC.
2. Newspaper mergers are dealt with under separate provisions of the 1973 Act, and are not considered here.
3. The 1973 Act contains provisions, in section 67, which identify the assets to be valued and the methods of valuation.
4. See p. 25, above.
5. The *P&O/European Ferries* merger (1986) was an exception to this general rule.

6. *City Code on Takeovers and Mergers*, Rule 12 (Panel on Take-overs and Mergers, 1985).
7. In the *Lonrho/House of Fraser* merger (1985), the proposed bidder was legally prohibited from purchasing the target shares but the MMC still treated it as having a sufficient intention to bid.
8. *London Brick/Ibstock Johnsen* (1983).
9. *Sunlight Services/Initial/Johnson Group* (1983).
10. *GUS/Empire Stores* (1983).
11. *Linfood Holdings/Fitch Lovell* (1983).
12. *Nabisco/Huntley & Palmer* (1982).
13. See p. 209.
14. But see the *Anderson Strathclyde* case (1986) for an account of the Secretary of State not following the advice of the MMC.
15. See the *Camera Care* case (1980), and the Commission's Interim Measures Practice Note [1980] 2 CMLR 369.
16. 'Amendment to the Proposal for a Council Regulation on the Control of Concentrations between Undertakings', OJ 1984 C 51/8.
17. See p. 172, below.
18. Celler-Kefauver Act 1950.
19. Hart-Scott-Rodino Antitrust Improvement Act 1976.
20. Antitrust Improvements Act 1980.
21. Hart-Scott-Rodino Antitrust Improvement Act 1976.
22. Department of Justice, *Merger Guidelines 1984*, 49 Fed. Reg. 26823.
23. Baker (1984) criticises the choice of the smallest possible market as capable in some circumstances of producing an unrealistic definition.
24. This feature is criticised by Ordover and Willig, 'The 1982 Department of Justice Merger Guidelines: An Economic Assessment', 71 *California Law Review* 535 (1983).
25. A market with ten firms of equal size would return an HHI reading of 1,000 ($10^2 \times 10$). A market with ten firms of unequal size would produce a different reading to reflect the influence of the leading firms—e.g. $20^2 + 18^2 + 18^2 + 15^2 + 14^2 + 5^2 + 3^2 + 3^2 + 2^2 + 2^2 = 1,520$.
26. See p. 12, above.
27. See p. 16, above.
28. See Kwoka and Warren-Boulton, 'Efficiencies, Failing Firms, and Alternatives to Merger: A Policy Synthesis', 31 *Antitrust Bulletin* 431 (1986) for a discussion of an alternative approach to the consideration of efficiencies.
29. McChesney, 'Defending the Failing-Firm Defence', 65 *Nebraska Law Review* 1 (1985).

4 The Restraint of Trade Doctrine

ENGLISH COMMON LAW

The English common law doctrine of restraint of trade is an aspect of competition law which provides a useful introduction to the modern treatment of business activity. This doctrine provides an historical link between modern competition law and the earliest attempts to regulate internal trade. Its study demonstrates the evolutionary nature of the control of competition by law.

The earliest statute dealing with free competition was *Magna Carta* (1225). Later statutes, concerned mainly with the problem of 'forestallers, regrators and engrossers', have been identified as the origin of the doctrine of restraint of trade, but this has been doubted by more recent commentators (Letwin, 1967; Heydon, 1971) and it is clear that since the economic context in which these statutes operated was so wholly different to that pertaining in modern times, they cannot claim a great relevance to the current doctrine of restraint of trade.

Of perhaps greater relevance to the early development of the doctrine of restraint of trade were the restrictive rules of the guilds, and the by-laws of towns and cities. The combined effects of these were that no person could practise any guild-controlled trade or craft until he had served as an apprentice (usually for seven years) and no one could freely set up in a town or city other than his own. Thus, a person who agreed with another not to practise his own trade or craft for a certain period could seek neither an alternative craft (without undergoing a further apprenticeship) nor an alternative location. This background accounts for the vehement opposition of the common law during this period to agreements in restraint of trade. In the case of *John Dyer* (1414), two men agreed that one would not trade as a dyer in a certain town for a six-month period. The judge said of this: 'the condition is contrary to common law and by God if the plaintiff was here, he would go to prison until he had made an end with the King'.

Agreements in restraint of trade were usually confined to two situations: an agreement by an apprentice not to compete with his master on qualification; and an agreement by the seller of a business not to enter into competition with the purchaser after the sale. An agreement of the latter type was the subject of *Mitchel v. Reynolds* (1711), where the transferor of a bakery agreed not to trade as a baker within the same parish throughout the period of the transfer. By the date of this case, the power of the guilds had diminished; an agreement not to carry on a specified trade would not therefore prevent the promissor from seeking an alternative activity or location. In some circumstances, therefore, such agreements were permitted.

It was (and still is[1]) the policy of the law to balance the advantages and disadvantages of restraints by determining the relationship between two conflicting liberties: freedom to contract and freedom to trade. Freedom to contract comprises a person's liberty to enter into any contract without interference from the State. But if this freedom were limitless, it would permit people to agree to restrict their own freedom to trade, a liberty which the common law values equally. The resolution of this conflict in policy has been modified over time, to reflect, to a certain extent, the contemporary social and political environment. Thus, the early hostility of the courts to any infringement of the freedom to trade was influenced by the labour shortage caused by the Black Death. In times of high unemployment, this is obviously an inappropriate response.[2]

The *Nordenfelt* case (1894) forms the basis of the modern application of the doctrine. In this case the seller of a guns and ammunition business agreed not to compete with the purchaser for twenty five years. The business was of an international nature and, likewise, the agreed restriction was world-wide. Lord MacNaughten delivered what is still regarded as the classic statement of the law and policy concerning restraint of trade:

> The public have an interest in every person's carrying on his trade freely; so has the individual. All interference with individual liberty of action in trading, and all restraints of trade of themselves, if there is nothing more, are contrary to public policy, and therefore void. That is the general rule. But there are exceptions: restraints of trade and interference with individual liberty of action may be justified by the special circumstances of a particular case. It is a sufficient justification, and indeed it is the only justification, if the restraint is reasonable—reasonable, that is, in reference to the interests of the parties concerned and reasonable in reference to the interests of the public.

This, then, is the compromise between the two conflicting liberties. All contracts in restraint of trade are presumed to be void, unless the transaction is nonetheless reasonable having regard to the parties' interests *and* the public interest. The only recent contribution to the development of the doctrine was the *Esso* case (1968), which widened the scope of the doctrine. Hitherto, most cases had concerned the classic restraint of trade situations—agreements between employer and employee, or between the seller and purchaser of a business. The agreement in question in the *Esso* case was an exclusive purchase agreement; in return for financial assistance, the garage proprietors agreed to purchase no petrol for resale other than Esso's. The court confirmed that *any* type of contract may be assessed under the doctrine if it is in restraint of trade. Thus, the modern English common law doctrine is capable of applying to any type of contract, such as exclusive purchase, exclusive sales, tying and horizontal price-fixing agreements,[3] as well as the traditional employer/employee, and seller/purchaser agreements. The doctrine has, to a certain extent, been eclipsed by statutory competition law, but nevertheless remains an important aspect of competition law.

The limits to the modern doctrine

There must be some limit to the doctrine, since all commercial contracts are, in a sense, in restraint of trade. There is no unanimity among judges on what these limits should be

(Heydon, 1971, p. 53 *et seq*). One widely accepted view is that the doctrine will not apply unless someone has *given up* an existing freedom. Thus if a firm purchases, or takes a lease of, a shop subject to a condition that it may use it only for the resale of a certain range of products or certain brands of products, the doctrine of restraint of trade will not apply. Similarly, where an oil company lets a petrol station to a firm on the basis that it may sell only that company's products. In these cases, it is said, the firm does not restrict its freedom to trade, since before purchasing the land or taking the lease it had *no* right to trade at all from the shop or petrol station. The sale or lease therefore *increased* the firm's capacity to trade.

Another limitation is that the doctrine will not apply to contracts which 'under contemporary conditions ... have passed into the accepted and normal currency of commercial ... relations'. (*Deacons* v. *Bridge*, 1984). For example, an agreement between the seller and purchaser of a business under which the seller agrees not to compete will not *of itself* fall within the doctrine: this form of contract is, under current conditions, accepted as part of the structure of a trading society. Only where the contract contains some unreasonable or unusual restriction, will the doctrine apply. It is now likely that a petrol solus agreement will not, of itself, attract the doctrine; its reasonableness will only be tested if it contains unusual restrictions or is for an unreasonably long duration.[4] This limitation, however, will be disregarded where a transaction which, although not unusual, has been concluded between parties of unequal strength, such as a music publishing company and an unknown songwriter (*Shroeder Music* case, 1974). As far as exclusive agreements are concerned, the doctrine won't apply if the purpose of the exclusivity is to absorb one party's output (of goods or services) rather than simply to prevent that party working for a competitor.

It is not only the parties to an agreement who may use the restraint of trade doctrine. People who are restrained by an agreement even though not parties to it may also seek injunctions and declarations. The doctrine is not, however, a regulatory device available to central enforcing agencies. It forms no part of a central strategic control system, such as the

Fair Trading Act 1973, the Sherman Act or Article 85 of the Treaty of Rome. Moreover, the traditional restraint of trade situations are unlikely to be regulated by UK competition statutes. The Restrictive Trade Practices Act 1976 affects only those agreements where *at least two* parties are restricted in certain specified ways; this is unlikely to be the case in employment contracts and business sales agreements. Further, most solus agreements are specifically exempted from the 1976 Act. It is conceivable that the imposition of such restraints by a monopolist could be regarded as an abuse of its monopoly. Even in such a case, this could only result in a recommendation being made by the Monopolies and Mergers Commission, which might be ignored by the Secretary of State. It is more likely that the imposition of such restraints would constitute an anticompetitive practice under the Competition Act 1980. However, the most important regulator in this area continues to be the common law.

The 'reasonableness' of restraints
The very essence of the doctrine is the nature of the courts' assessment of 'reasonableness'. A restraint will generally be reasonable as between the parties if it is given in return for 'consideration' and does no more than protect the legitimate interests of the party enjoying the benefit. Each transaction will, of course, turn on its own particular facts, and its reasonableness will be determined by having regard to the interests which the 'enforcing' party is seeking to protect; to the legitimacy of those interests; and to the scope of the restraints.

The interests of a person purchasing a business are quite plain: to be free from competition from the seller. Thus the agreement for sale may prohibit the seller from competing in a certain geographical area and for a certain duration. This arrangement makes perfect sense: the seller will be anxious to receive the best payment for the business; and the business will be much more valuable to the purchaser if he can be assured that the seller will not reduce its value by competing with it. It is also in the interests of the public to encourage and facilitate the free transfer of businesses, so that they can be controlled by the most efficient owner; the fact that a bargain is struck for the sale of a business indicates that the purchaser values it more highly than the seller.[5] But the restraints must be *no more* than is necessary. If the restraint is unduly wide in the sense that it covers markets outside those traded in by the business sold, in product or geographical terms, or is for too long a duration, then it will not be enforced by the courts. It should be stressed, however, that the courts are very reluctant to interfere in an agreement concluded between firms negotiating on equal terms. In the *Esso* case, one of the judges warned of the 'danger in preferring the guidance of a general rule, founded on grounds of public policy many generations ago, to the guidance given by free and competent parties contracting at arm's length in the management of their own affairs'.

This approach, still enthusiastically adopted by the courts,[6] is typical of the laissez-faire attitude of the common law as interpreted by the courts: where there is no oppression, parties should be free to contract on any terms *they* consider reasonable. Of course, an agreement acceptable to the parties may very easily be injurious to the public, but the courts seem very reluctant to strike down an agreement through the public interest test.

The interests of an employer and employee are rather different to those of the purchaser and seller of a business. The employer requires the assurance that an employee will not divulge to a competitor the trade secrets and confidential information acquired during employment. The only practicable way of achieving this is by prohibiting the employee from taking up employment with, or setting up as, a competitor. Unless the employee has some unique skill,[7] society will not generally suffer from such a restriction, especially in times of high unemployment. However, the interference with the liberty of the employee is regarded with hostility. The situation differs from that existing on the sale of a business. First, the parties will not normally have equal bargaining power, and secondly the restriction is not a necessary adjunct to property sold for value.

It is axiomatic, therefore, that if the restriction placed on the employee is *merely* to prevent competition, it will be unenforceable. The only interest which the employer may legitimately protect is the security of trade secrets, confidential information, customer lists or some other interest which is so inherent to the employer's business that it may be regarded as the employer's 'property'.[8] Apart from this limitation, the employee may use all the skill and experience gained in the service of the employer in any manner he wishes. The reasonableness of each restriction, as between the parties, will therefore turn on the position of the employee, his access to confidential information or trade secrets, the transferability of such information to other employers, and the duration of the restriction. In its consideration of the *public* interest, the court will also have regard to the effect of the restriction on the liberty of the employee (Prentice, 1983).

The consideration of reasonableness with regard to the parties' interests is a fairly easy task for the courts. It revolves round the identification of legitimate interests and the degree of protection they require. In the case of agreements negotiated by equal parties, the court virtually abandons any enquiry in this regard. But the evaluation of a restraint in the context of the *public interest* is a much more difficult task, a fact which probably accounts for the apparent reluctance of courts to tackle it seriously.

The identification of the public interest was fully considered in the *Texaco* case (1972). This case concerned a petrol solus agreement, and a great deal of evidence was given as to the effect of the agreement in terms of the allocation of resources and other aspects of economic efficiency. However, the court rejected this evidence as being of no use in the consideration of the public interest in restraint of trade cases. Judgements based on such data were 'by their nature matters for policy decisions by business administration, government or parliament'. The doctrine was characterised as a device to secure the liberty of individuals 'and not the utmost economic advantage'. If the courts had to take account of social and economic data in their consideration of the public interest, the judge claimed that the courts' task 'might not only involve balancing a mass of conflicting economic, social and other interests which a court of law might be ill adapted to achieve; but, more important [such interests] would lack sufficient specific formulation to be capable of judicial ... decision and application'.

The court therefore rejected all such data as being

injusticiable, and decided the question of public interest solely on the basis of whether the restrained party's liberty to trade had been unduly fettered. The judge in this case had been a Labour Solicitor-General and was chief Opposition spokesman in the debates on the Restrictive Trade Practices Act 1956. In those debates he opposed the creation of the Restrictive Practices Court on the basis that the issues arising under the Act would not be justiciable. Such a court, he argued, would make decisions 'founded neither upon law nor upon fact', but which were political and economic in character. The legalistic approach adopted by Ungoed-Thomas has been criticised by many commentators (e.g. Prentice, 1983) and is in marked contrast to the role of the American courts in their evaluation of economic data in antitrust cases (Rostow, 1960, but cf. Hay 1985). Since the *Texaco* case, however, there has been no clear judicial statement on the place of economic data in the evaluation of the public interest in restraint of trade cases. In the *Esso* case (1968), Lord Reid did say that the application of the doctrine ought to depend on the practical effect of restraints, rather than on legal niceties and he went on to consider the likely strategic behaviour of the oil company which imposed the restrictions. However, it is clear that no real examination of the effect of solus agreements in the retail petrol market was carried out.

EEC LAW

There is no separate doctrine of restraint of trade in EEC competition law but, as will be seen in the next chapter, Article 85 is capable of dealing with all types of restrictive agreement where there is, or may be, an effect on trade between EEC Member States. The usual 'employee' clause is unlikely to have such inter-State significance, but restraints imposed on the sale of a business could easily have such effect, and a recent Commission decision sets out the Commission's treatment of such arrangements.

The *Nutricia* decision (1984) involved post-sale non-competition clauses lasting ten years and five years in different geographical markets. The Commission confirmed that such an arrangement was contrary to Article 85(1) because it prevented competition between the seller and the purchaser and between the seller and other undertakings in the same market. The Commission recognised that such arrangements are not *per se* violations of Article 85(1): such restrictions may be necessary in order to ensure that the 'full commercial value' of the business is transferred to the buyer—in other words to ensure that the goodwill is transferred intact. However, the Commission adopted the same position as English courts in insisting that the protection from competition must be kept to the minimum. The minimum in the context of EEC law is that which is objectively required for the purchaser to assume, by active competitive behaviour, the market position relinquished by the seller.

The scope of the protection, with regard both to activities and to geographical area, must also be no more than the minimum necessary. Similarly, the duration of the protection must be strictly limited. Although each case must be evaluated in its own context, the Commission has provided guidelines in its decisions as to the duration which will be objectively necessary. In calculating this, the Commission will have regard to:

(a) the time it will take the purchaser to build up a clientele;
(b) the degree of brand loyalty in the relevant market;
(c) the time taken for new products or trade marks to be accepted by consumers;
(d) the period, following the sale, during which the seller would be able to make a comeback and regain old customers; and
(e) the duration of any agreements accompanying the sale, providing, for example, for the use by the purchaser of the seller's trade marks.

The ECJ, in the subsequent *Nutricia* case (1987) regarded it as the proper function of the Commission to assess the complex economic arguments in determining the legality of the clause. It should be borne in mind that the principal purpose of Article 85 is to prevent any limitation on competition. A

non-competition clause is anathema to this objective and will
be rigorously limited to the minimum required to protect the
purchaser's property.[9] The subject matter of this
property—the goodwill of the business—must also be
protected by its new owner through active competition with
those competitors who seek to reduce its value by improving
their own market shares. The Commission will therefore have
regard to conditions on the market and the nature of any
barriers to entry in analysing the non-competition clause.
Protection against the seller can be justified by the seller's
special knowledge of the business sold.

As to the non-traditional restraint of trade situations, such
as solus agreements and exclusive service agreements,
specialised rules for the application of Article 85 have been
developed by the European Court of Justice and the
Commission, and these are discussed in a later chapter.

US LAW

The English common law doctrine of restraint of trade formed
the basis of modern American antitrust law. Congress
intended that the courts should administer the Sherman Act
on the basis of the common law tradition,[10] and even in recent
cases there are references to very old English cases on restraint
of trade.[11] Apart from federal antitrust statutes, the law on
traditional restraint of trade situations is enshrined in the
American Law Institute's Restatement of the Law of
Contracts (2d)[12] and in many state laws.

The Restatement is couched in similar, though not identical,
terms to current English law. Thus, under the Restatement a
restraint that is ancillary to an otherwise valid transaction or
relationship (such as the sale of a business or the hiring of an
employee) will be unreasonably in restraint of trade, unless (a)
the restraint is no greater than is needed to protect the
promisee's legitimate interests; *and* (b) the promisee's need is
not outweighed by the hardship to the promisor and the likely
injury to the public. This formulation of the law has been
criticised (Handler and Lazaroff, 1982) in that it appears to
promote hardship to the promisor and public injury to

independent criteria rather than regard them merely as factors in the general test of the reasonableness of the restraint.

The traditions which have shaped US law on employee and vendor restraints are the same as those which fashioned English law. The intractable policy choice between free trade and free contract is as active in American courts as elsewhere. A Georgian court expressed the problem thus: '[w]hile public policy forbids any agreement which unreasonably restrains a person from exercising his trade or business, it is equally true that public policy also recognises that the freedom of persons to enter into contracts shall not be lightly interfered with'. The justifications supporting the reasonable enforcement of non-competition restraints have been so well rehearsed, that many American courts regard them as 'by now beyond question.'[13] In relation to restraints following the sale of a business, the US Court of Appeals (7th Cir.) cited Bork with approval: '[t]he most valuable asset of a business might be the good will of the public toward its owner ... the owner could not get a price reflecting the ... true ... value of his business unless he could promise the purchaser not to return to compete with the business sold.'[14] There is clearly a public interest in facilitating the sale of businesses, not only to preserve liberty of action, but also to encourage the movement of businesses towards more efficient operators. In relation to employee restraints there is a public interest in promoting the 'optimum amount of entrusting' by the employer towards the employee in order that the business be run efficiently. However, the courts must measure this interest against the hardship which a restraint may inflict on *all* employees—for example, by dissuading honest employees from moving to more valuable employment with a competing business (Blake, 1960; Corbin, Kaufman supp. 1982, para. 1391B). American courts have shown the same tendency as English courts to gloss over the public interest test (Sullivan, 1977 I; Note, 1982). Also, there is some controversy as to the criteria against which to measure the 'reasonableness' of a restraint. In the *National Society of Professional Engineers* case (1978), a majority of the Supreme Court held that in analysing the reasonableness of restrictions on competition, courts should have regard *only* to the competitive impact of the restriction. The balance to be struck is therefore between the pro-competitive and anticompetitive effects of a restriction and should not take account of anything falling outside the sphere of competition. This approach has been vigorously criticised in relation to restraint of trade situations (Robinson, 1980 II; Handler and Lazaroff, 1982), where social and political values are as germane as economics.[15] It remains to be seen whether courts will rigidly apply the *Professional Engineers* formula in relation to restraint of trade or whether they will consider the wider implications such as the limitations imposed on individual liberty.

In English competition policy, statutory law has very little impact in the restraint of trade area. Similarly, US federal antitrust statutes are not widely used against employee and vendor restraints. There is no reason why the Sherman Act should not be used in these situations, if sufficient effect on inter-State commerce can be shown. It is widely believed that the Sherman Act *was* intended to render illegal those agreements which were unenforceable under the common law (Attorney General, 1955). However, in spite of repeated calls for federal law to be used in this context (Blake, 1960; Goldschmid, 1973; Sullivan, 1977 I; Note, 1982), it seems that 'ancillary' restraints are left to State law, both statutory and common.[16]

NOTES

1. See, for example, Ungoed-Thomas in *Texaco Ltd* v. *Mulberry Filling Stations Ltd* [1972] 1 All ER 513, 525, '[t]he doctrine of restraint of trade deals with the relationship of two ... liberties: to contract and to trade'.
2. See Note (1933) 49 LQR 465; and *Bull* v. *Pitney Bowes Ltd* (1967).
3. Examples of the application of the doctrine include: retail petrol sales agreement (*Esso Petroleum* v. *Harper's Garage*, 1968); exclusive sales agreement (*The Boat Showrooms of London Ltd* v. *Horne Brothers (Boat Builders)* Ltd, 1980, unreported); solicitors' partnership agreement (*Deacons* v. *Bridge,* 1984); exclusive services agreement (*A. Shroeder Music Publishing Co Ltd* v. *Macauley*, 1974); 'retain & transfer' system in Football League (*Eastham* v. *Newcastle United Football Club Ltd*, 1964); rules of the Jockey Club excluding women

trainers (*Nagle* v. *Feilden*, 1966); and rules of the International Cricket Conference (*Greig* v. *Insole*, 1978).

4. The maximum duration is now probably five years, following the *Esso* case. All the major oil companies have given undertakings to the Secretary of State that they will not impose longer agreements—see *Trade and Industry*, 13 August 1976, p. 439.

5. For an economic analysis of this type of agreement, see M. Trebilcock, 'Restrictive Covenants on the Sale of a Business: An Economic Perspective', (1984) 4 *International Review of Law and Economics*.

6. For example *Clubtwo Ltd* v. *Ongakusha Ltd* (Court of Appeal 1983, unreported).

7. Or a skill which has required a large amount of resources to acquire, such as that of a doctor or an aircraft pilot.

8. In *Faccenda Chicken Ltd* v. *Fowler* (1985), the judge held that information acquired by an employee fell into three categories: trivial or publicly accessible information, which the law will not protect; expressly or implicitly confidential information which is learned by the employee and thereafter becomes part of his skill and knowledge, which will only be protected after employment if the employer imposes restrictive covenants on the employee; and trade secrets, which law will protect even in the absence of restrictive covenants. An industrial tribunal upheld the dismissal of a women employee after she went to live with an employee of a rival firm. Her employer feared that talk between the couple 'might lead to trade secrets being given away', *The Times*, 21 August 1985.

9. See, however, the Commission decision on the *BPCL/ICI agreement* (1984), where a non-competition clause led to a reduction in surplus capacity and more efficient production. The Commission granted an exemption for a lengthy fifteen years.

10. See Judge Taft in *US* v. *Addyston Pipe and Steel Co* (1898).

11. See, for example, Justice Stevens in *National Society of Professional Engineers* v. *US* (1978).

12. American Law Institute, Restatement of the Law Second, Contracts 2d, 1982, 188 (the 'Restatement'). See also Corbin (1982).

13. *Lectro-Vend Corp.* v. *Vendo Co.* (1980).

14. See *Water Services, Inc* v. *Tesco Chemicals Inc* (1969).

15. But see the discussion of non-competition covenants in Robin, *Business Firms and the Common Law* (Praeger, 1983), pp. 63–84.

16. R. Bork, 'Ancillary restraints and the Sherman Act', 15 *ABA Section of Antitrust Law Proceedings* 211 (1959).

5 Restrictive Trade Practices

ENGLISH LAW

Historical introduction

Much of the early history on the legal control of restrictive practices is contained in the chapter on restraint of trade. The following section outlines the development in the twentieth century of a statutory control of business practices.

In a report carried out for the Ministry of Reconstruction in 1919, an ad hoc body called the Committee on Trusts found a tendency throughout British industry to form trade associations and combinations 'having for their purpose the restriction of competition and the control of prices' (Report, 1919). This tendency arose out of the general depression of industry and the special circumstances of the First World War. These cartels existed to control resale prices, administer market-sharing arrangements and regulate output. Competition from outsiders was often eliminated by the imposition of collective exclusive sales and purchase agreements whereby suppliers or purchasers were obliged to deal only with members of the cartel. Many of these arrangements achieved monopolistic proportions. Industry claimed that such arrangements were efficient: the maintenance of profits through the cartels was said to lead to increased investment and reduced costs, and the absence of price competition promoted an increase in quality. The price competition which would flow from the disappearance of such arrangements and the consequent loss of profits would, it was said, lead to increased costs and reduced quality.

Industry did not accept that the maintenance of trade associations and combinations would lead to abuse. The Committee was not so confident: 'it is obvious that a system which creates virtual monopolies and controls prices is always in danger of abuse' (Report, 1919). The Committee seems to have been impressed by the evidence of a distributor who described one trade association of a monopolistic character in the following terms: 'it starves its distributors, its huge profits are a heavy toll on the wages of the poor, and the public's necessity becomes their opportunity' (Report, 1919).

The Committee did not attempt to determine whether actual abuses existed, but was concerned with the rapid growth of trade associations and combines in British industry. It also recognised public disquiet: '[w]e are satisfied that considerable mistrust with regard to their activities exists in the public mind, and that the effect of such mistrust may be equally hurtful to the political and social stability of the State' (Report, 1919). The Committee recommended the establishment of a permanent commission or tribunal to investigate monopolies, trusts and combines. The Committee also favoured the publication of information concerning the activities of trade associations and cartels. In a paper annexed to the Report, MacDonell proposed the public registration of restrictive agreements: '[t]he requirement as to filling [sic] of agreements might often be futile unless some tribunal had power to find on evidence as a fact that an agreement existed' (MacDonell, 1919).

No action was taken on the report, in spite of its vigorous recommendations and the fact that the courts were supporting the anticompetitive practices of trade associations and combinations (Atiyah, 1979). However in a White Paper on Employment Policy in 1944, the government expressed unease about the continuing cartelisation of industry and a determination to establish investigatory machinery. The outcome was the Monopolies and Restrictive Practices (Inquiry and Control) Act 1948, which set up the Monopolies and Restrictive Practices Commission ('the Commission) to investigate any cartel which accounted for at least one-third of the goods on the relevant market. The Commission was also able to investigate the effect on the public interest of specified types of practice, and one such report was that on Collective Discrimination (Monopolies and Restrictive Practices Commission, 1955).

The Commission made a detailed study of various forms of collective discrimination, including collective exclusive dealing agreements, resale price maintenance enforcement and aggregated rebates. The Committee on Trusts had drawn attention to some of these practices; the Commission found that they all restricted competition and adversely affected the public interest to a greater or lesser degree, by imposing undue rigidity in the market, affecting market structure, trading methods and prices. The Commission did not go so far as to say that all such practices would *always* be against the public interest; in exceptional cases, it held, there may be justifications. Such exceptional circumstances were specified as those where restraints were necessary: (a) to avoid risks to consumers; (b) to protect strategic industries or those threatened by foreign 'dumping'; (c) where necessarily incidental to a common price agreement operating in the public interest; and (d) to enable smaller concerns to compete effectively with a large concern which is itself resorting to restrictive practices.

The Commission considered two possible methods for the control of collective discriminatory practices—an abuse system, whereby such agreements would be required to be registered and those not found (after individual examination) to be in the public interest would be prohibited; and a prohibitive system, whereby there would be a statutory prohibition of all such agreements, with the possibility of exemption in particular cases. Although the majority of the Commission considered that the abuse system would lead to the abandonment of the practices through adverse publicity, and would be a less drastic innovation, they concluded that such a system would be 'cumbersome, slow and unfair'. The majority therefore favoured a general prohibition of the practices:

A general prohibition would give industry clear and unequivocal guidance as to the Government's policy, and would avoid the uncertainty and waste involved in detailed inquiries in each individual case. It would be much more effective than placing any reliance on the voluntary abrogation of harmful agreements which might result from publicity following the registration of agreements. It would avoid ... unfairness (para. 247).

Moreover, the majority recommended that the prohibition be part of the criminal law, and not merely give rise to civil actions. The minority (which did not include any economists) did not consider the practices under review to be generally injurious to the public interest, and considered the recommendations of the majority to be too sweeping and too inflexible in changing economic circumstances. The minority therefore favoured a system of registration and the individual examination of agreements to determine whether they operated contrary to the public interest.

In the event, the Restrictive Trade Practices Act 1956 took elements from both the majority and the minority (and from the earlier report of the Committee on Trusts). Restrictive agreements were made registrable and, although not prohibited, were presumed to be contrary to the public interest. A new body, the Restrictive Practices Court, was established to determine whether, in individual cases, a restrictive agreement operated in the public interest. The 1956 Act firmly favoured the majority view on resale price maintenance: agreements for the collective enforcement of resale price maintenance (e.g. by withholding supplies from defaulters) were prohibited without the possibility of exemption.

A number of amendments were made to the 1956 Act, and these were consolidated in the Restrictive Trade Practices Act 1976. The 1976 Act (the RTPA), together with the Restrictive Practices Court Act 1976 and some modifications contained in the Restrictive Trade Practices Act 1977, comprises the current statutory policy on restrictive trade practices. The current Acts provide an administrative system for the detection and registration of restrictive agreements and a judicial system for the evaluation of the effect of individual agreements on the public interest.

The Restrictive Trade Practices Act in outline
The Restrictive Trade Practices Act 1976 requires 'registrable' agreements to be submitted to the Office of Fair Trading for

entry on a public register of restrictive trading agreements. If any such agreement is not submitted within the time limits imposed by the RTPA, the restrictions are automatically void and it is unlawful for any party to seek to enforce them. Where an agreement has been registered in a timely way, it is the duty of the Director General of Fair Trading[1] to proceed against it in the Restrictive Practices Court. The Director General is entirely independent of this court and appears before it as a litigant, rather than an officer. As an exception to the Director General's duty to proceed, the RTPA[2] permits him to advise the Secretary of State that the restrictions in the agreement 'are not of such significance as to call for investigation by the Court'. If the Secretary of State accepts such advice then no further proceedings will take place (unless the Secretary of State directs otherwise) and the agreement will be treated as valid. The Director General has used this power to negotiate with parties to agreements for the removal of significant restrictions. Once before the court, the restrictions in an agreement will be declared void as being contrary to the public interest *unless* the parties can convince the court that, within the meaning of the RTPA, the agreements will not operate contrary to the public interest. Such a test will only be satisfied if the parties can guide the agreement through one of the 'gateways' provided in the RTPA and also satisfy the 'tailpiece' test. Both these terms are fully explained below.

Restrictive agreements

The effectiveness of any legislative policy on restrictive agreements will be determined by the scope of the legislation and the operation of the legislation *within* its scope. Criticism has been levelled at the RTPA on both of these criteria.

The RTPA applies only to 'registrable' agreements. No agreement outside the meaning of this phrase will be regulated by the RTPA, however restrictive its effects, and whatever its impact on competition. In this respect, UK policy on restrictive trading agreements is strictly formal in its approach, and contrasts sharply with the respective policies of the EEC and the US. Under its formal requirements[3] the RTPA will apply only to agreements where at least two of the parties carry on business in the UK and under which certain specified restrictions are accepted by at least two parties. There are therefore *four* requirements: (i) there must be an 'agreement'; (ii) at least two of the parties to the agreement must carry on business in the UK; (iii) at least two of the parties (not necessarily the same ones as in the previous requirement) must accept restrictions; and (iv) the restrictions must be of a type specified in the RTPA.

The meaning of 'agreement' It is a common characteristic of the three legal systems under consideration that the concept of 'agreement' is not defined in a narrow legalistic way. There is no requirement that an 'agreement' must satisfy all the requirements of that system's contract law. Thus, even though the RTPA is very formal in its requirement as to the *content* of an agreement, it is flexible with regard to the *form* of the agreement. Under the RTPA an agreement includes 'any agreement or arrangement, whether or not it is, or is intended to be enforceable ... by legal proceedings'.[4] This definition would include so-called 'gentlemen's agreements'. Lord Denning, in the Court of Appeal, talked of traders making 'their own arrangements in the cellar where no one can see. They will not put anything into writing, nor even into words. A nod or a wink will do'.[5] Apart from the obvious difficulties of detection, the meaning of 'agreement' is wide enough to cope with such a transaction. All that is required is a meeting of minds and a mutuality, where 'each party, assuming he is a reasonable and conscientious man, would regard himself as being in some degree under a duty, whether moral or legal, to conduct himself in a particular way ... so long as the other party or parties conducted themselves in the way contemplated by the arrangement'.[6] The vagueness of this concept was criticised by an English judge as 'calculated to drive any accurately-minded lawyer to despair'.[7] This criticism may be levelled generally at any informal aspect of competition policy, but may be met by a counter-argument which would stress the importance of maintaining a flexible and open-ended approach. The merits of such an approach are, first, that its informality reflects the behaviour of many subject to the RTPA; and secondly that it makes avoidance of the law more difficult.

Restrictions Before describing the restrictions specified in the RTPA, it is necessary to point out one further formal requirement of the Act. The Act separates agreements relating to goods from those relating to services.[8] In order for a 'goods agreement' to come within the scope of the RTPA, the two (or more) parties who carry on business in the UK must do so 'in the production or supply of goods, or in the application to goods of any process of manufacture'. The only restrictions which will be relevant to such an agreement will be those relating to goods. In the same way, a 'services agreement' will be regulated by the Act only if the businesses concerned are in the supply of services *and* the restrictions relate to services. This watertight division between 'goods agreements' and 'services agreements' can lead to absurd results in the context of a useful competition policy. The Second Green Paper adverted to this possibility by demonstrating that

if a number of manufacturers of goods agree that none of them will pay to any haulier more than a certain mileage rate for the services of hauling their goods [i.e. a 'service restriction'], their agreement will fall outside the legislation. But an agreement by the hauliers not to charge any of the manufacturers less than a certain mileage rate for hauling their goods would, of course, be registrable (Second Green Paper, 1979).

A definition of 'restriction' in the *Oxford English Dictionary* is 'something that limits or prohibits or hampers action'. Thus, a provision in an agreement which prevents a party from doing something that was impossible or prohibited by law, would clearly not be a restriction. Less clear, however, is the situation where a party has no commercial desire to do what the agreement forbids. The Restrictive Practices Court considered this problem recently[9] but did not rule definitively on it. What is clear however, is that a restriction must 'close a door' to the party concerned in the sense of preventing an existing freedom. On this point the Restrictive Practices Court has followed the line taken by the House of Lords in relation to the common law doctrine of restraint of trade.[10] A restriction contained in a lease granted to a person will, therefore, hardly ever be relevant to the RTPA.[11]

The specified restrictions The relevant restrictions under the

RTPA are expressed in terms of their function in the agreement, rather than in terms of their economic effect. The restrictions must be in respect of any of the following:

(a) the prices to be charged, quoted or paid for goods supplied, offered or acquired, or for the application of any process of manufacture to goods;

(b) the prices to be recommended or suggested as the prices to be charged or quoted in respect of the resale of goods supplied;

(c) the terms or conditions on or subject to which goods are to be supplied or acquired or any such process is to be applied to goods;

(d) the quantities or descriptions of goods to be produced, supplied or acquired;

(e) the process of manufacture to be applied to any goods, or the quantities or descriptions of goods to which any such process is to be applied; or

(f) the persons or classes of persons to, for or from whom, or the areas or places in or from which, goods are to be supplied or acquired, or any such process applied.

Corresponding provisions apply in relation to services agreements.

The danger inherent in any attempt to define 'restrictions' is one of over-inclusion. Taken literally, the terms of the Act would include virtually every commercial contract, even those of the most innocent kind. An agreement by a farmer to sell a field of potatoes to a wholesaler at a certain price will involve restrictions on the price to be charged, the quantities to be supplied and the person to whom the goods will be supplied. A system which required every such contract to be specifically justified would, in the absence of unlimited resources, be unworkable and undesirable.

In order to avoid over-inclusion of this nature, the RTPA provides that in 'an agreement for the supply of goods' no account is to be taken of any term relating exclusively to the goods supplied. This takes normal sales agreement out of the terms of the Act, but it has implications far beyond this. For example, if A agrees to sell doobies to B at a price not to exceed £x for a period of five years and B agrees: to incorporate the doobies only in certain equipment; to resell only to certain customers; and only in certain packaging, then this agreement (however restrictive it may be) will be exempted from the Act because all the terms relate exclusively to the goods supplied.

Other terms which are ignored by the RTPA are those relating to standards approved by the British Standards Institution (the American equivalent is the American National Standards Institute), and those relating to employment. Restrictions of the latter kind are dealt with in more specialised legislation. Also excluded from the Act are transactions such as exclusive dealing agreements and intellectual property agreements.

The scheme described so far extends to bipartite or multipartite agreements, of a formal or an informal kind, under which restrictions are accepted and imposed. There are, however, ways in which firms could remove themselves from this scheme, whilst still maintaining restrictive behaviour. Two such ways would be: (i) to delegate the subject matter of the restrictions to a trade association which could unilaterally lay down trading rules or recommendations; or (ii) simply to exchange information on prices etc., in order to avoid the uncertainties of competition. The two techniques are related in that a common method for the exchange of information is through the offices of a trade association.

The Act copes with both such activities. Agreements made by trade associations are taken to be the agreement of each of its members. Further, where a trade association makes recommendations to its members in respect of any matter covered by the specified restrictions (see above), then the Act makes the constitution of the association subject to registration as if it had contained an agreement by each member to be bound by the recommendations of the association. It should be noted that the Restrictive Trade Practices Act 1956 (the forerunner of the present Act) was enacted partly as a result of public concern over the restrictive activities of trade associations. These mainly consisted in the imposition of swingeing penalties on members who, for example, attempted to sell below the price imposed by the association (Richardson, 1969). The minority in the Collective Discrimination report recognised that '[m]uch of the public unease on this matter arises from a feeling that the recalcitrant trader is made the subject of some sinister "Star Chamber" procedure' (Monopolies and Restrictive Practices Commission, 1955).

The technique of exchanging information is a potentially more serious problem for competition policy. There is a conundrum: one of the conditions assumed to exist in a state of 'perfect' competition is that of perfect knowledge of market conditions, both current and future (i.e. 'market transparency'), and yet the broadcasting of such information may have an anticompetitive effect. Scherer has expressed this well. After characterising perfect market knowledge as one of the least important assumptions for perfect competition, he states that '[i]t might seem paradoxical that there could be anything harmful about information dissemination activities, which at first glance appear only to perfect the market. However, perfect information is unanimously beneficial only in the context of purely competitive markets' (Scherer, 1980). In oligopolistic markets a price-cutter will wish to keep its price secret from the other market participants for fear of retaliation. A system of information dissemination will ensure that such retaliation will be swift and certain. There will therefore be a deterrent to depart from the original price structure, and an incentive to pursue a consciously parallel price policy. An international enquiry into information agreements also suggested that market transparency in a polypolistic market *may* result in the market becoming oligopolistic through increased interdependence between firms (OECD, 1966).

The Report following such enquiry set out the arguments that had been put in favour of price information agreements. These included the assertions that such agreements help achieve effective competition by allowing comparisons between prices, discounts, terms of sale and production costs; that they allow market participants to assess the significance of price cuts and therefore maintain price stability and 'undue' price-cutting through the avoidance of 'undesirable' price wars; and that they prevent unfair competition whereby buyers could play sellers against each other through misrepresenting business terms. Most commentators, however, would argue that price information agreements whereby identifiable information is exchanged has a collusive rather than a competitive effect.[12] There is evidence that, in several countries, the use of information agreements as a business practice emerged as a response to legislation outlawing openly collusive agreements (O'Brien and Swann, 1968). The dissemination of anonymous statistical business data, however, will usually have a *beneficial* effect, and there would be little economic benefit in outlawing this type of agreement.

The RTPA brings information agreements under control in its usual formal manner. Thus there must be an agreement between two or more persons carrying on business in the United Kingdom in a goods industry, under which provision is made 'for or in relation to' the furnishing by two or more parties of certain information to each other, to other parties, or to persons not party to the agreement. Any such agreement must be registered in the same way as a restrictive agreement. The Act lays down the types of information which will be relevant, but leaves it to the Secretary of State to bring this section of the Act into force. The Secretary of State has done so,[13] but only in respect of information relating to prices charged, quoted or to be charged or quoted; and to the terms or conditions under which goods have been or are to be supplied. It was (and remains) open to the Secretary of State to include information relating to a host of other items, such as recommended prices, quantities or descriptions of goods supplied, costs of production etc.

An important feature of these provisions is that the Act will only apply to an *exchange* of information or at least a dissemination from more than one source, in the same way as it insists on a *mutuality* of restrictions under its definition of restrictive agreements. There are no provisions concerning information agreements relating to services.

Registration
Where a restrictive or information agreement is registrable, it[14] must be submitted for registration *before* the date on which any restriction or information provision takes effect, and in

any case within three months of the date of the agreement. The opportunity to register is limited to that period. Failure to register on time cannot be rectified, and if the severe consequences of non-registration are to be avoided, it will be necessary to abandon the agreement and start again. This contrasts very sharply with EEC policy, whereby failure to notify does not *of itself* affect the validity of an agreement, but lays the parties open to the possibility of fines in respect of any period before notification takes place. It also contrasts with US policy, where no registration is possible.

The consequences of non-registration are severe because it is only by way of submission for registration that the competitive effect of an agreement can be evaluated. Thus, a registrable but unregistered agreement is void in respect of all restrictions and information provisions. Further, it is 'unlawful' for any UK party[15] to the agreement to give effect to, to enforce, or purport to enforce, any of the restrictions or information provisions. 'Unlawful' in this context does not mean illegal in a criminal sense; the Act merely gives a right to anyone who may be 'affected' by the operation or enforcement of an unregistered agreement to bring a civil action for an injunction and/or damages.

It is not clear who may be considered to be 'affected' by the operation of a restrictive agreement for the purposes of bringing legal proceedings. Clearly other market participants, at the same level and at different levels, could be so affected. However, ultimate consumers of the goods and services will usually be the group to whom any detrimental effect will be passed. The difficulty and expense of mounting an action for breach of statutory duty has had the result that an action will be likely only where the consumer is in an exceptionally strong market position or where the damage suffered is of a considerable magnitude. The only publicised successful claim—which was settled out of court—was brought by the Post Office (now British Telecom) against a number of cable-makers in respect of unregistered restrictive agreements concerning the supply of cables. The Post Office recovered £9 million.[16]

A system which partly relies for its enforcement policy on private actions but which makes such actions so hard to bring, will clearly not be fully effective. Two writers suggest that 'there is little reason to believe that the cartel arrangements governed by the RTPA often cause individual, as opposed to collective, loss . . .' (Merkin and Williams, 1984, p. 444). There does not appear to be convincing evidence to support this view. Indeed, the Second Green Paper characterised the treble-damage action available for private enforcement in the United States as 'a notably powerful provision' (Second Green Paper, 1979).

An alternative course of action will be for the affected party to bring the unregistered agreement to the attention of the Director General, who *may* investigate the matter. In most cases this will be sufficient to cause the parties to the agreement to abandon the restrictions. While this will not compensate the consumer or other market participants for the damage suffered, it will offer some reassurance with regard to future conduct. Unfortunately, the investigative powers of the Director General may be exercised only where objectively there is reasonable cause to believe that an unregistered restrictive agreement has been made;[17] that is, reasonable cause must exist *in fact* and not just in the mind of the Director General. This provision prohibits 'fishing expeditions', but will also prevent more justifiable investigations. The Director General has described the limitations on his powers of investigation as a 'catch 22 situation' (Borrie, 1986). The restrictions are sometimes reflected in the heavy onus which the Director General places on complainants. Thus, in one instance in which a complainant asked the OFT to consider bringing an action against a number of manufacturers thought to be engaged in a price-fixing agreement, the OFT told the complainant that it would have to provide detailed factual evidence on product costs, prices, profitability, technology and varying levels of demand. Additionally the complainant was asked to produce an assessment by knowledgeable persons of the changes in the circumstances since the last case against the manufacturers.[18] The complainant viewed this as a 'very considerable task indeed' and was unable to commit itself to the research effort required.

In addition to the possibility of a private action by an 'affected' person, the Director General also has power to seek a court order prohibiting UK parties from operating an unregistered agreement. Defiance of such a court order could lead to criminal proceedings.

The stark formal remedies available for the enforcement of the legislation are underpinned by an informal system for the negotiated 'purifying' of agreements. Firms are encouraged to submit details of proposed agreements to the OFT as a 'fail-safe' procedure to ensure that the agreements will not lapse through failure to register in time. The OFT will then examine each agreement to see if it can be exempted from Court proceedings under section 21(2) (which concerns agreements which are not of such significance as to call for investigations by the Court).[19] In this regard, the OFT will analyse the agreement to determine whether it 'is likely to reduce competition where such competition would be advantageous to users or consumers, or whether [it] is likely to give rise to discriminatory or other unfair results to firms or consumers' (OFT, 1976). The OFT will enter into discussions with the parties to attempt a modification to an agreement in order to render it 'insignificant'. In other cases, the OFT may enter into discussions the result of which will be the abandonment of the agreement, or the 'filleting' of the agreement to eliminate restrictions. Through these informal methods, the vast bulk of registered agreements need not be considered by the Restrictive Practices Court.[20] The Director General attributes the sharp reduction in the workload of the Restrictive Practices Court to the success of the informal procedures, with 732 agreements having been dealt with under section 21(2) by the end of 1985 (Borrie, 1986). Agreements dealt with under this procedure mainly comprise restraints of trade on the sale of a business, franchise agreements and trade association codes of practice. Borrie (1986) provides details of the process and the criteria used in determining the 'significance' of agreements.

However, the small number of agreements coming before the Court may not be an indication of the success or efficiency of the legislation. To illustrate this point it is necessary to consider the possible courses of action open to a member of a cartel. These are threefold: (i) to leave the cartel if it is no longer operating (or never did operate) to its advantage; (ii) to seek to defend the cartel agreement before the Restrictive Practices Court as not being contrary to the public interest; or (iii) to maintain the cartel in a clandestine manner in order to avoid regulation. The first course of conduct may be attractive to small firms 'forced' into restrictive agreements with more powerful firms. In such a case the small firm could seek a declaration that the restrictions are void for non-registration, and an injunction to prevent the other party or parties from operating the restrictions. However, a small firm is unlikely to take such a precipious step against a powerful firm unless such action would be beneficial in the long term. This is most likely where the existence of the firm is being threatened by the operation of the restrictions. In any event, the RTPA, in its insistence on mutuality, will not apply where only the weaker party has accepted a restriction.

The second possibility—the defence of the agreement before the Court—has proved very difficult in practice. Once an agreement has been placed on the Register it may be years before it is dealt with by the Court. The expense incurred in such proceedings may also be considerable, and will usually 'run into tens of thousands of pounds, and . . . may approach a quarter of a million pounds' (Second Green Paper, 1979). In addition, the Court has imposed a very heavy burden on firms and is seldom convinced that an agreement should be permitted. The practical result is that most agreements—including those which do not in fact operate against the public interest—will be abandoned before the Court hearing.[21]

In view of these difficulties, cartel members may be most likely to adopt the third course of conduct—the clandestine maintenance of the cartel—in the hope that failure to register will prevent the OFT learning of the cartel's existence. The Second Green Paper recognised the possibility of such a tactic: '[u]ntil fairly recently the problem of unregistered agreements had not been thought to be serious, but the number of unregistered agreements . . . which have come to light in recent years . . . has thrown doubts on this supposition' (Second Green Paper, para. 5.47). After an extensive empirical study of the effectiveness of the Restrictive Trade Practices Acts 1956–1968, Swann came to the conclusion that the legislation was 'significantly inadequate to deal with evasion of the law'

(Swann, 1974). Writing at a much earlier date, Hilton found that what is notable about British restrictive agreements 'is not their rarity or weakness so much as their unobtrusiveness' (Hilton, 1919). The obvious drawback of clandestine operation is one of enforcement by participants, since disaffected members may withdraw and bring the cartel to the notice of the OFT. The instability of cartels through divergence in views between members has long been recognised (Hilton, 1919; Posner, 1977; Scherer 1980).[22] Even in the absence of treachery, the existence of the cartel may come to light through its effects on others, or simply through carelessness. Indeed, unregistered restrictive agreements are mainly discovered by the OFT through 'whistle-blowing' by previous parties or by persons affected (Borrie, 1986).[23] Research conducted into the impact and effectiveness of the RTPA has necessarily concentrated on the fate of *registered* agreements (e.g. Swann, 1973), and the Second Green Paper assessed the RTPA on this basis. However, the incidence and importance of unregistered agreements, though not capable of proper assessment, must at least be recognised in a consideration of the RTPA.

The evaluation of agreements

The Restrictive Practices Court After an agreement has been submitted for registration, and where no exemption or filleting has proved possible, the Director General is under a duty to refer the agreement to the Restrictive Practices Court (RPC) and to proceed against the agreement as a litigant. The procedural rules of the RPC are very similar to those existing for the settlement of disputes between ordinary litigants in ordinary courts. The RPC is not, however, an ordinary court. It has a specialised jurisdiction covering the evaluation of agreements registered under the RTPA, the enforcement and administration of the RTPA[24] and matters arising under other competition legislation.[25] The composition of the RPC is also different from other courts; it combines legal expertise with commercial and business acumen. Thus, it comprises three High Court judges, a judge from the Scottish Court of Session, and a judge from the Supreme Court of Northern Ireland; in addition, up to ten lay members may be appointed by virtue of their 'knowledge of or experience in industry, commerce or public affairs'.[26] At present there are six lay members. The whole court does not convene to hear cases; instead, one judge will sit with two lay members. The power to split into 'chambers' in this way was given to the RPC because it was thought that its workload would require simultaneous hearings. In fact, this has not proved to be the case; the RPC is virtually redundant in terms of substantive cases. If the judge and members cannot all agree on a matter, the majority view will prevail unless it is a matter of law, in which case the judge alone may rule definitively.

On the basis of the composition of the RPC in 1985, it appears that the role of the lay members is not to enable the RPC to generate economic theory for the assessment of agreements brought before it.[27] Of the six lay members serving in 1985, only two were professionally involved in accountancy or economics (one of these had been an expert economics witness in previous hearings of the RPC). The common characteristic of RPC lay members is extensive experience in industry at the highest level and previous service on public bodies. In response to a questionnaire, all lay members ranked commercial and industrial experience as being of at least equal importance to service as a lay member as academic quali-fications.[28] Indeed, most members discounted the latter as being of any importance to their role.

The RPC may therefore be characterised as a judicial body which convenes only occasionally, presided over by a non-specialist judge (the judge presiding in 1985 previously sat in the Family Division of the High Court) assisted by members who are highly experienced industrial managers but who, generally, are not economists. In the usual adversarial process characteristic of the English court system, all expert economics input comes from the witnesses presented by the litigating parties. The RPC must evaluate the complex economic data and conflicting arguments on economic theory and prediction.

The creation of the RPC by the Restrictive Trade Practices Act 1956 was a novel step; previously all competition matters had been dealt with by the Monopolies and Restrictive Practices Commission, an administrative body reporting to government. At the time of the introduction of the 1956 Act, industry, whilst accepting the inevitability of the statutory control of restrictive practices, was determined to avoid such control falling within the ambit of the Commission. The judicial process—open, clinical and adversarial—was preferred to the administrative procedure, regarded as secretive, bureaucratic and removed from commercial reality.

The Conservative government yielded to the pressure brought to bear by industry and opted for the judicial RPC rather than an administrative body such as the Commission (Stevens and Yamey, 1965; George and Joll, 1975). Richardson records that '[t]he most significant proposal as regards conforming with the view of industry was the decision to set up a court' (Richardson, 1969, p. 78). (In the early years of the RPC's operation, industry was to regret this move, as almost all agreements were found by the RPC to be contrary to the public interest.) Industry's original views were not surprising, given that the courts had traditionally supported the right of traders to enter into agreements of the most restrictive nature. Analysing the policy of English courts in the inter-war period, Atiyah found that it was 'plain that judicial sympathies were entirely on the side of freedom of contract, no matter how anti-competitive the arrangements might be ... it is quite plain that the judges' sympathies were enlisted on the side of the businessmen who were making such efforts to restrict competition.' (Atiyah, 1979).

The creation of this new judicial body gave rise to great controversy both in the parliamentary debates on the 1956 Bill and amongst commentators outside Parliament. The argument concerned the ability of such a body to apply legal criteria to essentially economic, political and social matters. This is the question of 'justiciability', and the Opposition (Labour) opposed the creation of the RPC on this basis. Their chief spokesman was Ungoed-Thomas,[29] who stated during the parliamentary debates: '[w]hat we are doing here is to drag the judges into the vast field of political and economic matters' (quoted by Stevens and Yamey, 1965. This book contains a very full study of the parliamentary history of the RPC, and remains the most comprehensive study of the nature of the RPC). Stevens and Yamey found that, whilst the control of restrictive trade practices is a policy area which courts *are* able to administer, the policy of the 1956 Act was not made sufficiently clear to the RPC and the criteria for determining the public interest were imprecise (Stevens and Yamey, 1965). They conclude:

The failure to appreciate the nature of the judicial process led Parliament in 1956 to commit to the judges the type of tasks which even American judges, far more accustomed to handling matters of an economic and political nature, would assume were beyond their competence. The Restrictive Practices Court is called upon to make the type of decisions the [US] Supreme Court has insisted are 'value choice(s) of such magnitude' that they are 'beyond the ordinary limits of judicial competence'. The Restrictive Practices Court is required to indulge in 'some ultimate reckoning of social or economic debits and credits' to determine which agreements are 'beneficial'. It is left to the Court to distinguish between the 'benign' and the 'malignant'. In achieving these ends the Restrictive Practices Court is required to involve itself in a process of evaluation and decision-making which does not appear to be peculiarly suited to the judicial process or causally related to the peculiarities of legal logic or legal relevance. [The quotation marks relate to remarks of Justice Brennan in the US Supreme Court decisions in *US* v. *Philadelphia National Bank* (1963).]

Cunningham agrees that the legislation was insufficiently thought through for its efficient administration by the RPC (Cunningham, 1974). Wilberforce, however, concluded that the RPC found little difficulty in reaching the conclusions required of it, and pointed to the fact that common law courts dealing with restraints of trade were involved in making judgments on matters of social and economic significance (Wilberforce *et al.*, 1966). However, see *supra* p. 112 for the very restricted nature of the courts' functions in restraint of trade cases, and especially the failure or reluctance of the courts to take account of economic and social data.

The Second Green Paper acknowledged the force of the arguments against justiciability, but concluded that the procedures and composition of the RPC enabled it to carry out its tasks: '[t]he complexity of the economic judgments required arises from the nature of the problems themselves rather than from the nature of the criteria, and we consider that equal difficulty would arise in any alternative evaluation procedure'.

In his first reported judgment, the current President of the

RPC (Anthony Lincoln J) seemed to accept an essentially judicial role for the RPC, as an interpreter of legislative policy rather than a policy-creating body. Thus, in his judgment in the *ABTA* case (1984), the President stated:

Counsel for the Director General of Fair Trading was concerned during the course of his submissions to steer the court away from any temptation to enunciate its own policy or its own conception to what is in the public interest. He urged on us that Parliament has laid down its policy with regard to restrictions and that the court has no positive role in deciding what the public interest is. They are deemed to be contrary to the public interest unless the specific circumstances are established and the court is confined to the role of finding whether those circumstances exist. At first sight it would seem curious that a tribunal which is given jurisdiction by Parliament under section 1(3) of the Act 'to declare whether or not any restrictions ... are contrary to the public interest' can be said to have no positive role or, as also submitted, no role at all in deciding what the public interest is.

The public interest test It is now necessary to turn to the means by which the RPC evaluates registered agreements in the context of the public interest. The RTPA lays down that, in order for a registered agreement to survive, the parties to it must satisfy the RPC that the agreement may pass through one or more of the 'gateways' provided in section 10 (goods agreements) and section 19 (services agreements). In addition, the RPC must be satisfied that the balancing provisions contained in the 'tailpiece' to each of those sections favour the agreement. The gateways are as follows (for goods agreements):

(*a*) that the restriction or information provision is reasonably necessary to protect the public against injury;

(*b*) that the removal of the restriction or information provision would deny to the public as purchasers, consumers or users of any goods other specific and substantial benefits or advantages enjoyed or likely to be enjoyed by them as such.

(*c*) that the restriction or information provision is reasonably necessary to counteract anticompetitive measures taken by anyone not party to the agreement;

(*d*) that the restriction or information provision is reasonably necessary to enable the parties to the agreement to negotiate fair terms for the supply of goods to, or the acquisition of goods from, any other person who dominates the input or output market;

(*e*) that the removal of the restriction or information provision would be likely to have a serious and persistent adverse effect on the general level of unemployment in areas in which a substantial proportion of the trade or industry to which the agreement relates is situated;

(*f*) that the removal of the restriction or information provision would be likely to cause a reduction in the volume or earnings of export business which is substantial either in relation to the whole export business of the United Kingdom or in relation to the whole business (including export business) of the said relevant industry;

(*g*) that the restriction or information provision is reasonably required to support any other restriction which has been permitted under the gateways or;

(*h*) that the restriction or information provision does not directly or indirectly restrict or discourage competition to any material degree in any relevant trade or industry and is not likely to do so.

The 'tailpiece' requires the RPC to further satisfy itself that the restriction or information provision is 'not unreasonable having regard to the balance between those circumstances [i.e. in the gateways] and any detriment to the public or to persons not parties to the agreement ... resulting or likely to result from the operation of the restriction or the information provision'. The group of 'persons not parties to the agreement' includes persons engaged in the same market at the same or different stages and also persons 'seeking to become engaged in the trade or business of selling such goods or of producing or selling similar goods'.

It will be immediately apparent that the gateways do *not* relate exclusively to competition. There is no single, pro-competitive policy underlying the RTPA. Instead, the legislation presents the RPC with a number of policy alternatives; this is a paradigm illustration of the interplay between competition policy and other aspects of governmental economic and social policy. Thus (disregarding gateway (*g*), which is merely ancillary), only three of the gateways—(*c*), (*d*), and (*h*)—are concerned with maintaining competition; others are concerned with the effect of the restrictions on the public: (*a*) and (*b*); with local employment (*e*); and with export earnings (*f*).

Table 3 sets out details of the cases in which parties have sought to defend a restrictive agreement under the gateways.[30] The table shows that: (i) very few agreements have been defended before the RPC; (ii) of those agreements which have been defended, few have been upheld; and (iii) the most common gateway pleaded is paragraph (b). A number of other trends may be discerned from the judgements of the RPC; it is convenient to deal with these by reference to the individual gateways.

Gateway (a) has been pleaded on three occasions (see Table 3), none of which were successful. The parties must convince the RPC that a risk of injury would exist in the absence of the restrictions and that the restrictions provide *proper* protection. The Collective Discrimination report[31] had recommended the inclusion of such a gateway, but pointed out that general legislation, rather than competition law, would usually ensure public safety. The report envisaged that such a gateway would be used only in 'rare cases in which there is no legislation and it is more convenient *temporarily at any rate*, that there should be restrictive arrangements so that it is not left only to the discretion of individual manufacturers or traders to decide on the standards of safety'. The growth of protective legislation has made gateway (a) even more redundant; it was last pleaded in 1963. It should also be noted that the restrictions relating to certain safety standards are not registrable under the RTPA.[32]

Gateway (b) is the most commonly pleaded of all the gateways, mainly because its extremely vague language would appear to be applicable to most situations. It has been pleaded successfully in nine cases, the great majority of occasions on which the RPC has upheld agreements. The class of persons to whom this gateway is directed is '*the public* as purchasers, consumers or users . . .'; the phrase refers to all purchasers or all consumers or all users, taken together. It must be shown that, within the relevant class, a sufficiently important part will be denied a benefit or advantage by the removal of the restriction. The benefit or advantage claimed must not only be

Table 3:
'Gateway' decisions of the Restrictive Practices Court

Case	Type of Agreement	Gateway and main justifications pleaded	Observations of RPC
Chemists Federation Agreement (1958)	Collective exclusive dealing agreement between manufacturing, wholesaling and retailing members of assoc. Quality control agreement.	(a) and (b) Public assured of qualified advice at pharmacies, and benefited from quality control.	Restrictions too wide to achieve objective; risk of injury too remote to justify restrictions; quality control existed even in absence of restrictions.
Yarn Spinners Assoc.'s Agreement (1959)	Horizontal price-fixing agreement.	(b) and (e) Removal of restriction would lead to cut-throat competition, detrimental to public, and would produce high local unemployment.	price stability *not* preferable to free market conditions. Removal of restriction would not lead to monopoly. Argument on unemployment accepted, but advantage was outweighed by detriment of maintaining excess capacity in industry.
Blanket Manufacturers' Agreement (1959)	Horizontal agreement restricting price, minimum quality and other conditions of sale.	(b) Price restrictions ensure quality and investment in industry; other restrictions operated in public interest.	Economic conditions did not warrant price restrictions. Minimum quality restrictions upheld. Other restrictions of no substantial benefit to public.

Case	Type of Agreement	Gateway and main justifications pleaded	Observations of RPC
Water-Tube Boiler Makers Assoc. (1959)	Tendering restrictions.	*(b)*, *(d)* and *(f)* Restrictions permitted manufacturers to survive recession, exercise countervailing power to preponderant purchaser and maintain level of exports.	No evidence that public would be disadvantaged by removal of restrictions. 'Fair terms' under para. (d) defined as those 'upon which an efficient manufacturer could make and sell his goods at a reasonable, but no more than a reasonable, profit'. Argument not accepted on facts. Export justification accepted; detriment to purchasers (higher prices) outweighed by export advantages. *Agreement upheld*
Scottish Bakers' Agreement (1959)	Horizontal price-fixing agreement.	*(b)* Price-fixing lead to stability and lower prices, halted concentration and maintained quality.	Price stability no alternative to free market. Other arguments rejected on facts.

Bakers' Agreement (1959)	Horizontal price-fixing agreement.	(b) Agreement specified 'maximum prices' and therefore kept prices down.	Classification of prices as 'maximum' was masquerade; they were really fixed prices. Prices would be lower in competitive conditions. Manufacturers high profits militated against claim that restrictions protected consumers.
British Carpet Manufacturers' Agreement (1960)	Horizontal and vertical price-fixing agreements. Exclusive dealing agreement.	(b) and (f) Fixed prices were beneficial to public; quality was maintained.	Price stability no alternative to free market. Prices were fixed arbitrarily. Public had too little information to make use of quality restrictions. Exclusive dealing unjustifiable.
Phenol Producers' Agreement (1960)	Horizontal price-fixing agreement.	(b) Price stability; maintenance of prices to prevent diversion of raw material to less efficient use.	Fixed prices higher than competitive prices would be; excessive price disadvantageous to public. Other arguments rejected on facts.

Case	Type of Agreement	Gateway and main justifications pleaded	Observations of RPC
Black Bolt and Nut Assoc.'s Agreement (1960)	Horizontal price-fixing agreement.	(b) and (g) Fixed prices covered vast range of types—removed need for purchasers to 'shop around'.	Prices fixed at reasonable rates. Argument on 'shopping around' accepted—kept down administrative costs of purchasers. Absence of price competition had increased technical development of industry. Benefit to purchasers outweighed detriment of higher prices. *Agreement upheld*
Doncaster and Retford Cooperatives (1960)	Geographical market-sharing agreement.	(b) Prevented overlapping services which would lead to decrease in profit and dividend.	Overlapping would not affect pattern of trade.
Wholesale Confectioners' Agreement (1960)	Horizontal sale and purchase price-fixing agreement.	(b) Wholesalers able to supply uniformly in all areas; consumer price kept down; retailers didn't need to 'shop around' for wholesale price.	Wholesale profits were large enough to ensure supply to all areas. Need to 'shop around' not unduly burdensome on retailers.

Agreement	Type	Arguments	Decision
Motor Vehicle Distribution Scheme (1960)	Vertical price-fixing agreement; agreement on preferential discounts and minimum standard for distributors.	(a) and (b) Retail price not prescribed, merely published. Public provided with network of efficient distributors and local after-sales service. Entry of new models facilitated.	True intention of agreement was to *fix* prices. Other claimed advantages would exist even in absence of scheme.
Cement Makers Federation's Agreement (1961)	Horizontal price-fixing agreement. Geographical market-sharing agreement.	(b) and (g) Price competition would lead to price increase, since increased risks of competition would require greater return on capital.	Court accepted arguments. *Agreement upheld.*
Associated Transformer Manufacturers' Agreement (1961)	Horizontal price-fixing agreement.	(b), (d) and (f) Price war would lead to decrease in research and development and consequent loss of quality. Restrictions provided countervailing power against preponderant purchaser. Removal would lead to loss of exports.	All arguments rejected on facts. 'Fair terms' under para.(d) defined as in *Water-Tube Manufs* but better test thought to be a comparison of terms offered by preponderant and non-preponderant purchasers.
British Bottle Assoc.'s Agreement (1961)	Horizontal price-fixing agreement.	(b) Price war would lead to instability, loss of quality and concentration.	Price war unlikely to occur. Any price reductions would not prejudice industry or customers.

Case	Type of Agreement	Gateway and main justifications pleaded	Observations of RPC
Lino Manufacturers Assoc.'s Agreement (1961)	Horizontal price-fixing agreement.	(b) and (f) Price war would lead to loss of quality, low stockholding, instability and loss of exports.	Price war unlikely (little surplus capacity); other arguments rejected on facts.
Newspaper Proprietors Assoc.'s Agreement (1961)	Exclusive dealing agreement (restricting entry at retail level)	(b) Influx of entry would lead to low profits, cessation of home delivery and restricted choice.	Arguments rejected on facts—there would not be a significant influx because of need to establish delivery service.
Permanent Magnet Assoc. Agreement (1962)	Horizontal price-fixing agreement	(b), (f) and (g) Price competition would lead to loss of technical cooperation; exports would suffer.	Technical development of substantial benefit to public—could not exist in conditions of price competition. *Agreement upheld.*

Standard Metal Windows Group (1962)	Horizontal and vertical agreements	(b) and (g) Prices would rise; quality would decrease; industry would become more concentrated.	Agreement had facilitated high level of exchange of costing and technical information. Prices had been kept down—made members more effective competitors with non-members. *Agreement upheld*
Net Book Agreement (1962)	Vertical price-fixing agreement.	(b) and (f) loss of price guarantee would lead to fewer book retailers, higher prices and restricted choice.	Removal of price guarantee would cause bookshops to lose out to non-specialised retailers. Higher costs would result in non-publication of marginal books. *Agreement upheld*
Tyre Trade Register (1963)	Collective exclusive dealing	(a) public protected by scheme which required presence of qualified person at point of sale.	Buyer's market was highly competitive—purchasers would require good service. No evidence that agreement affected competence of retailers.
British Jute Trade Agreement (1963)	Horizontal price-fixing agreement	(e) Restrictions required to complement government intervention to protect local employment from threat of cheap imports.	Existing government intervention machinery was adequate, without need for restrictions.

Case	Type of Agreement	Gateway and main justifications pleaded	Observations of RPC
Birmingham Building Trades Agreement (1963)	Horizontal agreement on trading terms.	(b) Requirement to use standard term contracts reduced risk to building owner of technical and legal default.	Standard-form agreement could be used in absence of restrictions.
British Paper and Board Makers' Agreement (1963)	Horizontal purchase price-fixing agreement.	(b) Minimum purchase price restrictions assured steady supply of raw material from suppliers. Loss of supply would lead to increased prices to public.	Raw material was of such importance that individual manufacturers would take steps to ensure supply, even in absence of restrictions.

National Sulphuric Acid Assoc. Agreement (1963)	Joint purchasing agreement.	(d) and (g) Restrictions necessary to exact fair terms from preponderant seller. Restrictions on use and resale necessary to main purpose of agreement.	Common purchasing agreement necessary in this case because preponderant seller had shown disposition to force unreasonable terms. Other restrictions accepted as necessary to this purpose. 'Fair terms' defined as those which would apply if the market did not contain a preponderant seller.
Glazed and Floor Tile Home Trade Assoc. Agreement (1964)	Horizontal price-fixing agreement.	(b) Agreement discouraged production of non-standard tiles. Loss of standardisation would lead to higher costs and prices, loss of technical cooperation, and requirement for purchasers to 'shop around'.	Agreement had promoted standardisation; erosion would lead to higher prices. Other arguments not accepted. Advantages outweighed detriments (smaller choice) *Agreement upheld.*
British Iron and Steel Federation Agreement (1964)	Vertical price-fixing agreement.	(b) and (g) Removal of restriction would lead to higher costs.	Agreement did keep down prices. *Agreement upheld.*

Case	Type of Agreement	Gateway and main justifications pleaded	Observations of RPC
British Heavy Steel Makers' Agreement (1964)	Horizontal price-fixing agreement.	*(b)* Price war would arrest modernisation and expansion, leading to future loss of output and quality, and increased prices.	Arguments rejected on facts.
Locked-Coil Rope Makers Assoc. Agreement (1964)	Horizontal agreement for common sales price between members and common sales price to preponderant purchaser.	*(b)*, *(d)* and *(f)* Restrictions necessary to exact fair terms from preponderant purchaser.	Arguments rejected on facts.
Finance Houses Assoc. Agreement (1965)	Horizontal agreement on terms of trade.	*(b)* Restrictions kept down prices and protected public from entering into imprudent financial arrangements.	Prices would not rise if restrictions removed, especially because of increased price consciousness of public. Prevention of imprudent commitments was in any event in the interests of Finance Houses, without need for restrictions.

Black Bolt and Nut Assoc. Agreement (1965)	Horizontal price-fixing agreement.	(g) Restrictions required to maintain price agreement already approved by RPC.	Necessity of new restrictions (widening class of purchaser affected) accepted. *Variation of agreement upheld.*
Distant Water Vessels Development Scheme (1966)	Horizontal price-fixing agreement; minimum quality restrictions.	(b) lower prices, inelastic demand conditions, would lead to lower returns, arrested modernisation, higher long-term prices.	Court accepted arguments. *Agreement upheld.*
National Federation of Retail Newsagents (1969)	Trade boycott.	(d) Boycott necessary to exact fair terms from preponderant supplier.	Arguments rejected on facts.
Mallaig and N.W. Fishermen's Assoc. Agreement (1970)	Quota restrictions.	(b) Restrictions necessary to conserve fish and ensure continued supply.	Adequate government measures existed to conserve fish.

Case	Type of Agreement	Gateway and main justifications pleaded	Observations of RPC
Scottish Daily Newspaper Society's Agreement (1972)	Horizontal agreement to restrict sales.	(h) Restrictions were temporary and designed to render market more competitive (by ending labour dispute).	Arguments accepted. Temporary loss of papers outweighed by advantage of maintained higher choice. *Agreement upheld.*
Association of British Travel Agents' Agreement (1984)	Exclusive dealing agreement; restrictions on retail premises and other trading terms.	(b) Removal would expose public to financial instability of operators and reduce standard of service.	Exclusive dealing gave rise to financial stability and was of benefit to public. Restrictions on premises hindered entry of new competition. *Agreement upheld in part.*

'specific', it must also be 'substantial'. The substantiality will be judged on a predictive basis, having regard to the probable future effects of the restrictions. It can be seen from Table 3 that the RPC has accepted the following as specific and substantial benefits or advantages:

(i) the removal of the need to 'shop around' where this would cause a disproportionate increase in the administrative costs of purchasers;

(ii) technical development and cooperation in the industry;

(iii) the maintenance of prices at lower than competitive levels;

(iv) the maintenance of choice and/or outlets;

(v) the preservation of quality.

In most of the cases in which the RPC has rejected arguments based on gateway (*b*), it did so because the evidence was unconvincing. It should be noted, however, that even where it *can* be shown that the restrictive agreement has given rise to price stability, this will not *in itself* satisfy gateway (*b*): the RPC has clearly stated on a number of occasions that price stability is no alternative to free price competition.

Gateways (*c*) and (*d*) reflect the fact that a degree of market power may be a natural and efficient response to the exercise of power by another market participant: a powerful purchaser may best be controlled by a powerful supplier or group (or *vice versa*). In a seminal work, Galbraith developed the theory of countervailing power (Galbraith, 1952) and the Collective Discrimination Report (Monopolies and Restrictive Practices Commission, 1955) recommended the inclusion of a gateway which would permit such an arrangement. Gateway (*c*) has, in fact, never been considered by the RPC. The gateway permits traders to protect themselves against the anticompetitive activities of 'any one person'. The risk of injury to the public's interests arising as a result of such agreement will be avoided through use of the tailpiece. However, a policy of permitting restrictive agreements in these circumstances seems to be less preferable than regulating the person carrying on the anticompetitive practices, either through monopolies legislation or under the Competition Act 1980.

This comment may also be made in relation to gateway (*d*), which is concerned with restrictions which enable traders to secure 'fair terms' from preponderant suppliers or purchasers. However, in these circumstances it may be more effective to enable traders to exercise control over the preponderant party (through operation of their countervailing power) rather than to regulate that party through the 'external' controls available in the monopolies legislation and the 1980 Act. Traders threatened by the preponderance of a dominant firm may be in the best position to decide the nature and extent of any measures required to counteract such threat, and when to adapt such measures to changing market conditions. If such measures can be justified as being no more than necessary, and are not unduly injurious to the wider public, then they are likely to be preferable to conditions imposed by government on the recommendation of the Monopolies and Mergers Commission or the Director General of Fair Trading. The gateway has been considered by the RPC in five cases but has succeeded only in one. It may seem from Table 3 that the RPC has adopted different approaches to the meaning of 'fair terms'. In the *National Sulphuric Acid* case (1963) it seemed to settle on a definition: fair terms are those which would have obtained in similar market conditions but where there was no preponderant seller (or purchaser). The requirement to define 'fair terms' is probably the task of the RPC which is the furthest removed from the traditional functions of a court; the issue of justiciability occurs most acutely in this context.

Gateway (*e*), which relates to the protection of local employment, has been considered twice; in one case the agreement satisfied the gateway, but failed to satisfy the tailpiece. The policy underlying the gateway is not 'competition' policy; indeed it is an example of competition policy giving way to other economic considerations. In times of high unemployment the need to protect local communities from social and economic depression is a pressing one; the tailpiece will, however, ensure that such a need will not be permitted to override the detriment to the public consequent on the restrictive agreement. Gateway (*f*), which relates to export earnings, has been considered on seven occasions but has succeeded only once. This was the only gateway to which the Second Green Paper recommended an amendment. The gateway, as presently expressed, permits restrictions which increase the volume of exports, but does not permit those which lead to a decrease in imports. There would appear to be no sound policy basis for this anomaly, other than the obligation imposed under the EEC Treaty not to impede the free movement of goods across national frontiers. The Second Green Paper therefore recommended that the gateway be widened to allow restrictions which, *through increased efficiency*, lead to a reduction in imports.

Gateway (*g*) does not provide an independent justification for a restrictive agreement; it permits restrictions which underpin *other* restrictions which have themselves been approved by the RPC.

The final gateway, (*h*), was added to the 1956 Act by the Restrictive Trade Practices Act 1968, which brought information agreements under legal control. It was anticipated that gateway (*h*) would be used in those cases where information exchange has no adverse effects on competition.[33] In fact the gateway has been pleaded only once, and in relation to a restrictive, rather than an information, agreement. In that case, several newspaper publishers agreed not to produce newspapers during the continuance of a strike. The publishers pleaded that the stoppage was intended to be temporary and was designed to bring the strike to a speedy conclusion and thereby restore competition between the publishers. The RPC accepted these arguments and upheld the agreement. In considering this gateway, reference must always be made to the power of the Director General in relation to 'insignificant' agreements. The exercise of this power will relieve many parties from the necessity of proceeding to the RPC on the basis of gateway (*h*).

As mentioned above, a successful claim under a gateway may be struck down when the RPC considers the agreement under the 'tailpiece'. In fact this has only happened once, in the *Yarnspinners* case (1959). Here, the RPC considered that the detriment to the public from maintaining excess capacity in the relevant industry outweighed the advantage of preventing local unemployment. The Second Green Paper reported that the RPC's function with respect to the tailpiece involved it in 'the most complicated economic questions' but did not consider that the lack of legislative guidance had caused any difficulty.

Shortcomings of UK law
The Second Green Paper, whilst recognising the shortcomings of the RTPA, considered that, on balance, it had contributed to economic efficiency. However, the impact of *unregistered* agreements must form an important caveat to any such statement. There is no reliable evidence on the extent of such impact; as Lord Denning has said, the parties to such agreements 'do not shout it from the housetops. They keep it quiet'.[34] The major drawbacks of the legislation are threefold: its formal nature; the registration procedure; and the formulation and exercise of the public interest test.

The formal nature of the RTPA has the result that the legislation impinges only on those agreements which demonstrate the required formal characteristics. The applicability of the RTPA will therefore depend on the manner in which an agreement is drafted rather than its intended or actual effect. The purported advantage of a formal sytem is that firms may obtain clear advice as to whether a given agreement will be caught by the legislation (Korah, 1975).

However, the complexity of the RTPA largely negates this. The Second Green Paper admitted that 'the expenditure of scarce legal and administrative resources on sorting out the ... question of registrability could be considered wasteful'. In any event, the other side of the 'certainty' coin is that firms will 'devote their energies and the ingenuity of their advisors to the discovery of forms of agreement or varieties of procedure which on technical grounds they can assert to fall outside [the legislation]' (Rogers, 1963).

Secondly, restrictive or information agreements must be submitted for registration *before* the relevant provisions take effect. Failure to register on time will render the provisions incurably void, and the parties will be exposed to the risk of a civil suit by anyone affected by the agreement. This scheme gives rise to the ludicrous and artificial procedure whereby the parties must abandon the unregistered restrictions, register them and then bring them back into force. The legislation does not seem to take account of the fact that commercial agreements are often entered into urgently or on the basis of rapidly changing drafts. In addition, where an agreement has not been registered, it may be difficult or impossible for a party enjoying the benefit of a restriction to persuade the parties accepting the restrictions to partake in the procedure described above without offering them some fresh consideration in return.

The registration procedure has disadvantages not only for the parties to registrable agreements, but also for the enforcement authorities. This springs from the fact that there are no financial penalties for non-registration. Apart from the risk of civil suit by 'affected' persons, the only practical consequence of non-registration is that the Director General may obtain an order from the RPC that the parties cease to operate such agreement, or any other to like effect. As shown above, the restricted nature of the Director General's investigatory powers renders such a course of action unlikely. In view of the fact that the RPC is unlikely to uphold registered agreements brought before it, the incentive to register is not great.

Finally, the evaluation procedure, designed as it is to be justiciable, has proved cumbersome, slow and expensive. Of the cases on Table 3, the average period between the agreement being referred to the RPC and the judgment being delivered was over thirty-two months. The delay between registration and referral can be considerably longer than this. These factors, combined with the very strict line taken by the RPC, dissuade most parties from taking the trouble and expense to defend registered agreements before the RPC. The practical effect is twofold: first, all but a few registered agreements will be prohibited *per se* without any evaluation of their effects on competition or the public interest. Secondly, short-term agreements, which expire before the RPC has had a chance to declare them invalid, may exist and operate outside the law's control. The need for the radical revision of restrictive trade practices policy is widely recognised. The review of competition policy commenced by the Department of Trade in 1986 is expected to look at the problems closely.

The most attractive reform would be to do away with the Restrictive Practices Court, which has been singularly unsuccessful, and to replace the justiciable system with a more flexible effects-level system along the lines of Article 85 of the Treaty of Rome.

EEC LAW

Article 85 in outline
The basic EEC law on restrictive trade practices is contained in Article 85 of the EEC Treaty. Procedural and other details are provided in Regulation 17.[35] Decisions of the Commission of the European Communities (the Commission) and judgments of the European Court of Justice (ECJ) apply and develop the statutory law.

Article 85 is short and may be reproduced in full:

ARTICLE 85

1. The following shall be prohibited as incompatible with the common market: all agreements between undertakings, decisions by associations of undertakings and concerted practices which may affect trade between Member States and which have as their object or effect the prevention, restriction or distortion of competition within the common market, and in particular those which:
(a)   directly or indirectly fix purchase or selling prices or any other trading conditions;
(b)   limit or control production, markets, technical development, or investment;
(c)   share markets or sources of supply;
(d)   apply dissimilar conditions to equivalent transactions with other trading parties, thereby placing them at a competitive disadvantage;
(e)   make the conclusion of contracts subject to acceptance by the other parties of supplementary obligations which, by their nature or according to commercial usage, have no connection with the subject of such contracts.
2. Any agreements or decisions prohibited pursuant to this Article shall be automatically void.
3. The provisions of paragraph 1 may, however, be declared inapplicable in the case of:
—any agreement or category of agreements between undertakings;
—any decision or category of decisions by associations of undertakings;

—any concerted practice or category of concerted practices; which contributes to improving the production or distribution of goods or to promoting technical or economic progress, while allowing consumers a fair share of the resulting benefit, and which does not:

(a)   impose on the undertakings concerned restrictions which are not indispensable to the attainment of these objectives;

(b)   afford such undertakings the possibility of eliminating competition in respect of a substantial part of the products in question.

The purport of Article 85 is therefore as follows. All restrictive agreements which have any inter-State significance are prohibited under the Treaty and, as such, are void; however, the prohibition may be lifted where it can be shown that a restrictive agreement has certain (specified) counter-vailing advantages.

Agreements between undertakings, decisions by associations of undertakings and concerted practices

Unlike UK law, Article 85 does not impose any formal limitations on the type of agreement which may be regulated. However, in common with UK law, the concept of 'agreement' is extremely wide and flexible. The term is not restricted to those arrangements which satisfy technical legal rules on contracts (*FEDETAB* case, 1980); it simply has to be shown that one party has voluntarily undertaken 'to limit its freedom of action with regard to the other' (*Japanese Ball-Bearings Agreement*, 1975). In spite of the very wide meaning given to 'agreement', certain trading behaviour may be impossible to classify as such. For this reason, Article 85 also applies to 'concerted practices', defined by the ECJ as a form of collusion between firms 'which, without having been taken to the stage where an agreement properly so-called has been concluded, knowingly substitutes for the risks of competition, practical cooperation between them which leads to conditions of competition which do not correspond to the normal conditions of the market' (*Sugar* case, 1975). Conscious parallelism of this nature usually occurs only in oligopoly conditions, where oligopolists are trying to secure collectively the benefits of joint profit maximisation, by coordinating their behaviour to mimic monopoly. The object of such collusion is to maintain prices at a super-competitive level; firms in an oligopoly market can achieve this without the need to resort to agreements, 'in the sense that each firm makes its own price and output decisions without consulting the others in a smoke-filled room' (Scherer, 1980).

For the purposes of applying Article 85, the 'normal conditions' of the market will be found by having regard to the nature of the products, the size and importance of the firms involved, and the size and nature of the market. Conscious parallelism *of itself* will not give rise to Article 85 liability: firms in an oligopoly remain free to respond to competitors' actual and anticipated conduct. However, where such behaviour results in the distortion of competitive conditions on the market (e.g. by bringing about price equilibrium at a higher level than would have resulted from competition between the firms), it will be taken to be a strong indication of a concerted practice. In these conditions, evidence of contact between competitors to facilitate coordination (such as exchanges of information—*Gerhard Zuchner* case, 1982) will be sufficient to amount to a concerted practice.

In the *Dyestuffs* case (1972), the evidence of the concerted practice consisted of three uniform price increases on close or identical dates. It appeared from the evidence that the price leader gave notice of proposed price increases, and these were brought into force by all firms. Where a competitor did not agree to the increase, the other firms did not put it into operation. In the *BP Kemi* decision (1979), the Commission confronted the application of identical prices by firms which had previously been bound by an express price agreement and which continued to exchange detailed information. The Commission took cognizance of these circumstances and ruled that an 'application of identical prices may not by itself prove a concerted practice, but it may amount to strong evidence of such in practice when it is unlikely to occur in the normal conditions of the market'. Taking particular account of the information exchange: '[i]t does not seem possible that the exchange of sensitive information of such kind could take place without the coordination of the behaviour of the parties'. The Commission will be searching for more than 'barometric price leadership' in an oligopoly; it will look for parallel price increases in conjunction with other indications of collusion, such as contacts between firms on projected price changes (*Zinc Producer Group* decision, 1985).

The final category of transactions caught by Article 85 are 'decisions by associations of undertakings'. This phrase is aimed at the activities of trade associations. As seen under the discussion of UK law, trade association activities may be efficiency-producing but they may also facilitate cartelisation. Thus, the constitution of a trade association which restricts new entry, or indeed any recommendation which members regard as binding, will be caught by Article 85, whenever the object or effect is anticompetitive. It will be recalled that UK law also deals specifically with trade association activities.[36]

All the transactions caught by Article 85 involve the presence of 'undertakings'. The meaning of this word owes more to the *economic* identity of a market participant than to its *legal* personality. Undertakings are not defined in the Treaty, but the ECJ has developed its own interpretation. Article 85 is directed at independent decision-making centres which are involved in economic activity; the definition of 'undertaking' is the same as that of 'firm' in economic terminology. An undertaking may be an individual carrying on business as a sole proprietor, a partnership, a limited company, or any of the other corporate and non-corporate enterprises that have developed in the national legal systems. The important characteristic of an 'undertaking' is not its legal independence (such as a company's independence from its shareholders) but its *economic* independence. Economic and legal independence do not always exist together. A subsidiary company will have another company (the 'parent company') as its sole or major shareholder. Under company law, the two will be separate legal persons but in most cases, especially where the subsidiary is wholly owned by the parent, the subsidiary will have no economic independence: it will not be a decision-making centre separate from its parent.

An agreement between parent and subsidiary company will not, therefore, be an agreement *between undertakings* for the purposes of Article 85, unless it is an unusual example of a subsidiary with real freedom to determine its course of action on the market. The same considerations will apply in the context of an agreement between 'sibling' subsidiaries. Because of the

ECJ's insistence on real economic autonomy in its definition of 'undertaking', EEC law does not have the concept of 'intra-enterprise conspiracy' which has been the subject of recent debate in the American legal system.[37]

Agreements between an enterprise and an employee will not be an agreement *between undertakings*. Nor will an agreement between a principal and an agent, where the agent merely carries out instructions and does not have an independent role on the market. In practice of course, the term 'agency' may be applied to a number of different types of commercial relationship, each with a different significance for Article 85. In order to give firms some guidance on the impact of Article 85 on agency agreements, the Commission has issued a Notice known as the *Christmas Communiqué*.[38] Here the Commission distinguished between agents and independent undertakings respectively according to the distribution of financial risk between the parties. It is not the function of an agent to accept any such risks; if he does he will be classified as an independent undertaking. In more recent individual decisions of the Commission, it appears that the criteria set out in the *Christmas Communiqué* are not the only ones which will be taken into account in determining whether or not an agency relationship exists (Leigh and Guy, 1976). Other matters taken into account will be the degree to which the agent is economically dependent on the principal; whether the agent performs a merely 'auxiliary' function; and whether the agent is fully integrated into the distribution network of the principal.

The international significance of agreements
The transactions mentioned in the preceding section—agreements, decisions and concerted practices—will only be liable to regulation under Article 85 if they have some significance for the EEC. Article 85 measures such significance by dealing only with agreements etc. *which may affect trade between Member States*. The examination of an agreement for such a characteristic is not carried out for the purposes of evaluating its merits or demerits, but simply to determine whether the EEC has jurisdiction to deal with it. The enquiry is positive rather than normative. The information sought is whether the

agreement is *likely* to alter the pattern of trade between Member States. Such alteration may take the form of an increase or decrease in the volume of trade or a change in the identity or number of the undertakings engaged in it. What is to be excluded, therefore, are agreements with purely domestic effects; these will fall to be considered, if at all, under the national competition policy of the relevant Member State. It is important to note that it only has to be shown that an agreement is *likely* to affect inter-State trade in the sense that it is capable of so doing; it need not be shown that such trade actually has been affected.

It should also be appreciated that an agreement where all the parties are from the same Member State may still be capable of affecting trade Member States; 'narrow-minded lawyers' must beware of the economic effects of apparently domestic agreements (de Jong, 1975). Thus, an agreement which maintains prices at a high level in one Member State may have such effect by encouraging traders in other Member States to export to the high-price area. Agreements which would have a more obvious effect on inter-State trade are those which contain an import or export ban: if A sells doobies to B on the condition that B does not resell them outside the country, the agreement will have an obvious significance for the EEC. Again, if M, a UK manufacturer, decides to sever links with his retail distributors in France and instead appoints D as his exclusive French distributor, there may be no change in the *volume* of trade between the UK and France but the pattern of trade has certainly changed—previously there were many export contracts, now there is only one.

Since the examination of an agreement's effect on inter-State trade is carried out to determine its significance for the EEC, it follows that such effect or potential effect should not be merely negligible. Some guidance is given to firms as to whether their agreements may be considered negligible. This is contained in another Commission Notice, the *Notice on Agreements of Minor Importance*.[39] The terms of this Notice will be discussed in the next section.

The anticompetitive object or effect of agreements
Here lies the greatest difference between UK competition

policy and that of the EEC. In UK policy, the RTPA applies only to agreements under which certain specified restrictions are accepted by parties with certain specified characteristics. But in EEC law, Article 85 is concerned only with the *economic effect* of an agreement, and not with its formal characteristics. So long as there are at least two undertakings party, there is no limit to the type of agreement to which Article 85 may apply. All that must be shown is that the effect will or may be anticompetitive: the Article applies to transactions *which have as their object or effect the prevention, restriction or distortion of competition.*

It is not necessary to show that an agreement was intended to and actually does prevent competition, it is enough if *either* its object is anticompetitive *or*, whatever its object, its effect or potential effect is anticompetitive. By the extension of the scope of Article 85 to the objects of an agreement, EEC competition law has the ability to act prophylactically: there is no need to wait until it can be shown that the agreement has produced actual repercussions on the market. Conversely, it is not open to the parties to an agreement to plead that the anticompetitive objects of their agreement had not succeeded in practice. However, the objects of an agreement will not be evaluated in an entirely unrealistic manner: the economic context of the agreement will also be examined to determine whether the agreement will at least be *capable* of an appreciable anticompetitive effect. The enforcement authorities do not wish to waste resources 'tilting at windmills': the *probable* effects of an agreement must be taken into account when evaluating the significance of its objects.

Even where no anticompetitive objects can be shown, the agreement will be examined as to its probable effects on competition. Article 85 will apply only where the probable effects on competition are of an appreciable nature. The Commission has issued a Notice to give some guidance as to the meaning of this requirement: the *Notice . . . on Agreements of Minor Importance*,[40] which applies also in the consideration of an agreement's effect on inter-State trade.

The Notice recites the Commission's policy of promoting the interests of small and medium-sized undertakings as long as competition is not harmed to too great an extent. Agreements between undertakings engaged in the production or distribution of goods or services will, in the Commission's opinion, not fall within Article 85 where two criteria are fulfilled: (i) the products which are the subject of the agreement together with all similar products of the 'participating undertakings' do not represent in a substantial part of the common market more than 5 per cent of the total market for such products; *and* (ii) the aggregate annual turnover of the 'participating undertakings' does not exceed 200 million (approx 138 million). The 'participating undertakings' referred to include not only the parties to the agreement but also their subsidiary and parent companies. When measuring the market share, the similarity of products is judged from the consumers' viewpoint, having regard to characteristics, price or use.

The usefulness of the Notice to firms is limited in that it may be difficult to measure the relevant market share, either because no reliable figures exist for the market (especially where there is no trade association which carries out statistical surveys) or because there is doubt over the definition of the relevant market.

Where cases come before it, the ECJ will also excuse agreements of a negligible nature. In making such assessment, the ECJ will have regard to all the factual, legal and economic circumstances surrounding the agreement. This is best illustrated by reference to the *Brasserie de Haecht* case (No.1) (1967). The proprietors of a small Belgian café entered into a solus agreement with a brewery whereby, in return for financial assistance, the proprietors promised to purchase all their drinks from the brewery. When sued for a breach of the agreement, the proprietors claimed that the agreement was invalid under Article 85. The brewery countered that such a small agreement could not possibly have an appreciable effect on competition or on trade between Member States. The ECJ ruled that the agreement must be examined in the context of the market, which was characterised by the existence of a very large number of similar solus agreements concluded between Belgian brewers and retailers. Although when viewed in isolation such contracts were insignificant, their collective effect was appreciable.

In assessing the economic context of an agreement it is of course vital to determine the relevant market. The reader is referred to the discussion of the this aspect in relation to monopoly policy.[41]

Two remarks must be made about the location of an agreement's anticompetitive effects. First, Article 85 seeks to protect competition within the Common Market and not just competition between the parties to the agreement. A horizontal price-fixing agreement between firms in the same market, or a specialisation agreement, will clearly affect competition between the parties. But a vertical agreement such as an exclusive distribution agreement, although having an impact on competitive conditions in the market, will not affect competition *between the parties*, since they are not competitors. In its consideration of an exclusive dealing agreement, the ECJ in the *Consten and Grundig* case (1966) held that

Article 85 refers in a general way to all agreements which distort competition within the Common Market and does not lay down any distinction between those agreements based on whether they are made between competitors operating at the same level in the economic process or between non-competing persons operating at different levels ... Competition may be distorted within the meaning of Article 85(1) not only by agreements which limit it as between the parties, but also by agreements which prevent or restrict the competition which might take place between one of them and third parties.

Secondly, the effects of the anticompetitive behaviour must be felt (or be capable of being felt) 'within the Common Market'. This aspect will be discussed more fully in Chapter 7, but it should be noted at this point that the location of the firms carrying on the anticompetitive agreement is not of importance. Theoretically, the significant feature will be the location of the *effects* of the agreement. Thus the Commission has stated '[t]he fact that the head offices of several or all the participant undertakings are outside the Community does not prevent [Article 85(1)] from being applied, as long as the results of the agreements ... spread to the territory of the common market ...'.[42] As will be seen in Chapter 7, however, the ECJ has not applied a full-blooded effects doctrine in practice. On the other hand, where the undertakings are located inside the Common Market and the effect of their agreement is felt only outside it, then Article 85 will clearly have no application.

Alternatives to orthodox agreements—information exchange

As pointed out in the discussion on UK law, the alternatives to bipartite or multipartite agreements are the delegation of functions to a trade association and the adoption of information exchange agreements. We have seen that Article 85 deals expressly with trade association activities; it also covers, by implication, anticompetitive information agreements. The ECJ has not rule definitively on information agreements but the Commission has, on several occasions. In its *Notice on Cooperation between Undertakings* (1968) the Commission stated that agreements providing for the exchange of opinions or experience; joint marketing research; joint comparative studies; or joint statistical exercises would not be contrary to Article 85. The purpose of such agreements is to enable the parties 'to determine their future market behaviour freely and independently.' However, where the parties' freedom of action is limited or their market behaviour is coordinated, this may well restrict competition. From Commission decisions taken subsequent to the Notice it is clear that the *exchange* of individualised information on prices will be prohibited under Article 85 (Toepke, 1982). However, the Commission does not appear to object to a firm obtaining details of a competitor's prices, say through a third party (*Vegetable Parchment* decision, 1977). Non-individualised information may be exchanged, that is 'a purely statistical arrangement with a breakdown of data by product, country and period of time which is not conducive to collusion' (*Seventh Report on Competition Policy*, 1977). Information exchanges which take place in the context of an oligopoly will be critically examined by the Commission, and will be prohibited if the effect is to facilitate a concerted practice (*Peroxygen Products* decision, 1985).

Notification

It will be recalled that under UK law it is necessary to register a restrictive agreement in order *both* to preserve its legality and to commence the procedure whereby it may be justified before the Restrictive Practices Court. EEC law adopts a different position. There is no compulsion to register all restrictive agreements, and failure to register has no effect on the legal status of the agreement. Article 85(2) states that agreements which violate Article 85(1) are *automatically* void; it is substance rather than process which nullifies the agreement.

Nevertheless, there is a system (set up under Regulation 17) whereby agreements may be notified to the Commission, and there are good reasons for so doing. First, firms may be unsure as to whether their agreement violates Article 85(1) or not. Although they may seek advice from lawyers and economists, in many cases it will not be possible to determine the question with certainty. In these circumstances the parties may apply to the Commission for 'negative clearance', that is, a certificate by the Commission that on the available facts there are no grounds for action under Article 85(1). Such certification by the Commission does not change the legal effect of the agreement—it does not go so far as to declare that Article 85 does not apply, but that is its practical effect.

Secondly, the parties to an agreement may know, or suspect, that it contravenes Article 85(1) but may wish to secure an exemption under Article 85(3) on the basis that the agreement has countervailing advantages. Such exemptions may be granted by the Commission either in individual cases or to entire categories of agreements. Where individual exemption is sought then, subject to a few exceptions, the only way in which this may be done is by notifying the agreement to the Commission in the required manner. Whereas any ordinary court in a Member State may examine an agreement to see if it contravenes Article 85(1), only the Commission may grant an exemption under Article 85(3).

Notification is therefore an essential prerequisite to exemption. The Commission has issued a number of 'block exemptions' whereby agreements are exempted by category, without the need for individual exemption. The use of block exemptions by the Commission considerably reduces its workload by removing the requirement for individual notification. The Commission has retained the right to examine agreements even when they are covered by block exemptions, and to remove such exemption in individual cases where appropriate. Block exemptions have so far been issued for agreements dealing with exclusive distribution;[43] exclusive purchase;[44] specialisation;[45] patent licensing;[46] motor vehicle distribution;[47] and research and development.[48] The essence of block exemptions is that they grant exemption under Article 85(3) for agreements which contravene Article 85(1). They differ, therefore, from section 9 and Schedule 3 of the Restrictive Trade Practices Act 1976 which remove certain agreements from the entire scope of legislative control. Some firms may wish to apply both for negative clearance and for an individual exemption, on the basis that if the Commission refuses a negative clearance it may then proceed immediately to consider the possibility of an exemption. This is facilitated by the fact that the same form (Form A/B) is used for both types of notification.

There is a third reason to notify an agreement: it provides immunity from fines. Where the Commission finds that an agreement contravenes Article 85(1) and may not be exempted under Articles 85(3), it may impose swingeing fines on the firms. However, no fines may be imposed in respect of the firms' activities in the period between notification and the Commission's final decision, so long as the activities accord with the notified agreement. There is therefore a great incentive for firms to notify agreements promptly, especially where they judge the chances of negative clearance or exemption to be slim. Such a system is open to abuse: firms could conclude plainly restrictive agreements, notify them immediately and then, in time, abandon them if required to do so by the Commission, without financial penalty. In order to reduce the chances of such abuse, Article 15(6) of Regulation 17 permits the Commission to inform the firms that, after a preliminary examination of the agreement, it is of the opinion that the agreement contravenes Article 85(1) and could not be exempted under Article 85(3). The immunity from fines ceases on the delivery of an 'Article 15(6) Notice'. Unfortunately the usefulness to the Commission of this device was cut down by a decision of the ECJ which requires the Commission to observe the same procedures when formulating an Article 15(6) notice as it does when formulating a final decision. As a result, very little use has been made by the Commission of this procedure.

It was originally thought that notification would also confer a status of 'provisional validity' on an agreement, but this is not longer the case. It therefore remains open to any person affected by an agreement to seek a declaration from a national court that it is void through contravention of Article 85(1), and to seek an injunction and/or damages. Alternatively, a person affected by an agreement may complain to the Commission, who may then take up the matter. The Commission is under no obligation to pursue such a complaint, although it may be called on to give reasons if it decides not to proceed with it (Temple Lang, 1981). If it does decide to proceed, or if it initiates its own procedure, the Commission has considerable powers to demand evidence and to examine books and business records on firms' premises.[49]

In common with the practice of the OFT, the Commission will enter into informal negotiations with firms either after notification, or where firms approach the Commission before their agreement has been completed. Indeed, an average of over 200 notifications are disposed of informally by the Commission each year. This leaves a relatively small number of agreements to be dealt with by way of final decision.[50] The Commission announced in 1983 that it intended to make greater use of informal procedures leading to the issue of 'comfort letters' rather than formal decisions. Temple Lang has found that in selecting cases to be dealt with by way of formal decision the Commission has given more importance to establishing legal principles than to producing economic results in the market under review, a fact he attributes to the preponderance of lawyers in the relevant section of the Commission (Temple Lang, 1981). The increased use by the Commission of informal methods of settlement injects a degree of flexibility into antitrust procedures, but does carry some risks with regard to legal certainty and protection (Van Bael, 1985; Waelbroeck, 1986; Claydon, 1986).

It is now necessary to consider the choices open to a member of a cartel in the context of EEC law. These are the same three choices as are available under UK law:[51] (i) leave the cartel; (ii) seek to defend it; or (iii) maintain it in a clandestine manner. If a party chooses to leave a cartel, any commercial retaliations, or the effect of the continued operation of the cartel, may be countered by an action in the *national* courts for an injunction and/or damages, on the basis of Article 85. In addition, or as an alternative, a complaint may be made to the Commission, which will then investigate and may initiate action.

Where firms seek to defend their agreement, by way of notification to the Commission, there remains the possibility of an action in a national court at the suit of someone adversely affected by the agreement: notification does *not* confer provisional validity. In addition, the exemption process is slow; the average annual number of new notifications is over 170, but the Commission only disposes of about seven cases per year by way of formal decision. The cost of such application will also be considerable, taking into account the professional fees of lawyers, accountants and economists.

However, the third possible choice—the clandestine maintenance of the cartel—is fraught with danger: members are exposed to the risk of actions in national courts, complaints to the Commission and consequent Commission investigations. The latter may lead to a decision that the cartel is contrary to Article 85(1); not having notified the agreement, the Commission will not consider the possibility of exemption and there will be no immunity from fines.

The evaluation of agreements
Where informal negotiation has not been successful, the Commission will proceed to a formal investigation and evaluation of the agreement. This will lead to a decision stating whether or not the agreement contravenes Article 85(1). If it does the decision may also contain a cease-and-desist order and possibly a fine. If the decision follows a notification for exemption, then it will also determine whether or not Article 85(3) applies to the agreement. Any decision of the Commission may be appealed to the European Court of Justice.

The Commission examines restrictive agreements in the context of the public interest, as defined by Article 85(3); in this respect it performs a similar function to the Restrictive Practices Court. However, the two bodies are greatly dissimilar in character. Whereas the RPC is a judicial body, the Commission is an administrative regulatory body.[52]

The public interest test In order for an agreement to be given
exemption from Article 85(1), the Commission must be
satisfied that *all* the four requirements of Article 85(3) apply,
viz that (i) the agreement contributes to improving the
production or distribution of goods *or* to promoting technical
or economic progress; (ii) consumers are allowed a fair share
of the resulting benefit; (iii) the undertakings are not subject to
restrictions which are not indispensable to the attainment of
such objectives; and (iv) the undertakings are not afforded the
possibility of eliminating competition in respect of a substantial part of the products in question.

In examining these requirements in relation to an
agreement, the Commission will not rely exclusively on the
submissions of the parties but will deploy its own resources to
collate information on the relevant market and the
participants. Nonetheless, the Commission is not entitled to
consider the applicability of Article 85(3) on its own initiative:
the parties must have properly notified the agreement for
exemption. Of the fourteen decisions taken by the Commission
in 1983 and 1984 in which exemption was refused, nine were
based on the purely formal ground that the parties had not
notified the agreement.[53] In the same period twelve decisions
granted exemption. In any case, where exemption is refused the
parties have a right to appeal to the ECJ, and since 1966 individual firms have made use of such appeals procedure. The ECJ will
not attempt to substitute its own economic judgment for that of
the Commission, but will limit itself to 'an examination of the
materiality of the facts and legal descriptions which the
Commission deduces there from' (*Consten and Grundig* case,
1966).

As the supreme court of the Common Market, the ECJ
deals with the full range of Community legal topics. It is a non-
specialist court comprised of judges appointed by the Member
States. The same questions of justiciability arise in relation to
the ECJ's function under Article 85 as arise in relation to the
functions of the RPC. However, unlike the formalism of the
UK legislation, Article 85 embraces an 'effects' approach. It is
the function of the ECJ, therefore, to examine an agreement in

the light of all its repercussions on the market; it is inevitable that it will impose its own understanding of economic theory on any such evaluation.

It is difficult to make general comments on the application of Article 85(3), but it seems that the Commission will deal favourably with joint ventures,[54] specialisation agreements[55] and agreements for the reduction of surplus capacity.[56] Agreements which are unlikely to obtain exemption are those incorporating price-fixing,[57] export and import bans,[58] or market sharing.[59]

Many of the shortcomings of the UK law on restrictive trading agreements are avoided in the EEC through the adoption of the effects approach as opposed to the formalism of the Restrictive Trade Practices Act (RTPA). Article 85 may apply to *any* form of business conduct which has an anti-competitive object or effect. This may increase uncertainty for firms wishing to operate within the law, but the increasing case law of the Commission and the ECJ enables more confident legal advice to be given to firms. In addition, the willingness of the Commission to enter into informal negotiations reduces the risk of law-breaking.

The necessity to notify an agreement in order to obtain exemption should not be equated with the destructive provisions of the RTPA which require registration at a precise time in order to preserve the lawfulness of the agreement; an agreement does not become unlawful under Article 85 merely though non-registration. On the other hand, the enforcement of Article 85 is rendered very much more effective by the ability of the Commission to levy substantial fines—up to 10 per cent of a firm's turnover—a power which the Commission has exercised enthusiastically.[60] In addition, the Commission can levy default penalties for refusal to comply with orders to permit the Commission to inspect a firm's files, or for deliberate or negligent misstatements in a notification. Although these powers will not result in all restrictive agreements being duly notified to the Commission, they must influence the decision to notify or not.

US LAW

Historical introduction[61]

In the early years, US law on restrictive practices consisted of the English common law on monopolies and restraints of trade. A dislike and mistrust of monopoly was well suited to the American culture, and an anti-monopoly, anti-combination tradition was soon firmly established. However, in the second half of the nineteenth century, the new technology available to manufacturing industry brought about a change in the size of manufacturing units and in the legal entities by which manufacture was carried on. The corporation emerged as an important new phenomenon; and the common law often proved inadequate to cope with many of its activities.

The politically influential farmers were the first group to call for a strengthening of the law on monopolies and restrictive practices. Grouped together within the Granger Movement, the farmers' lobby was especially powerful.[62] Their complaints centred on their deteriorating economic position caused, as they perceived, by combinations and price-fixing cartels amongst manufacturing industries and the railroad companies in particular. The latter were the main target for the farmers' hostility; particularly egregious was the railroad companies' practice of price discrimination in favour of the vast steel-manufacturing combines. The Granger Movement declined after the passage of the Interstate Commerce Act 1887, which regulated the railroads, but the public antipathy to monopolise and combinations did not decline. The increased use of the 'trust' was simply a legal device to combine firms within a tightly controlled cartel, closely resembling monopoly. Although it was only one of many similar devices, it became the object of public hostility, and any anticompetitive combination became known in popular parlance as a 'trust'. Hence the use of the expression 'antitrust' for the laws which eventually emerged to deal with all cartels.

The portrayal of the movement against the restrictive practices of industry in the years leading up to the Sherman Act as a popular clamour or crusade is one that has entered American legislative mythology. Legal historians, however, are more cautious. Letwin, while acknowledging that there was 'real public feeling' against the trusts, feels that the intensity of such feeling is now hard to judge, and has found some evidence to suggest that, then as now, the media were responsible for inflaming public feeling (Letwin, 1967). Thorelli describes the public concern as serious enough to make federal action a 'clear desideratum, if not an absolute necessity' (Thorelli, 1954). Certainly the popular movement was important enough for both political parties to ensure that their platform contained promises of action against the trusts, promises which eventually led to the passage of the Sherman Act 1890.

In the years leading up to the passage of the Act, the common law was successfully used to destroy many trusts; but many still remained. A popular notion was that the new Act was simply a device to restate the common law in statutory form, and thereby strengthen it. Senator Sherman's many statements in Congress to this effect were received without demurrer. The nature of the relationship between the common law and the Act was to become critically important in the early cases in which the Supreme Court interpreted the Act's meaning and scope. However, one influential commentator has characterised the senator's definitions of the relevant common law as 'an artificial construct, made up for the occasion out of a careful selection of recent decisions ... plus a liberal admixture of the senator's own policy prescriptions' (Bork, 1966). Whether or not the Sherman Act replaced or merely restated the common law, popular opinion was not quieted by either its terms or its interpretation by the Supreme Court. As Letwin has said, the Act was regarded by many as a 'law that does not tell the public exactly what it may do and does not tell judges exactly what they must do' (Letwin, 1967).

Congress had enacted a statute with very broad terms in order to cover every possible form of anticompetitive combination or contract. Article 85 and 86 of the Treaty of Rome adopted the same approach over half a century later. But in the 1890s many interest groups were unhappy with the broad discretion given to the courts and there emerged a call for the Sherman Act to be supplemented by a new law which would particularise all the activities which were considered to be illegal. Further, there was a call for an administrative commission to be created to enforce the policy in accordance with strict instructions, rather than on a discretionary basis. This movement therefore supported the idea that the law should be administered by an expert administrative commission rather than by the normal courts. It will be recalled that in the UK, on the passage of the Restrictive Trade Practices Act 1956, exactly the opposite call was made—business interests were anxious to remove jurisdiction from an expert commission (the Monopolies and Restrictive Practices Commission) in favour of a court staffed, at least partly, by ordinary judges.

Public confidence in the judicial administration of the Sherman Act underwent a 'crisis'[63] when the Supreme Court, in the *Standard Oil* case (1911), interpreted the Act in accordance with the 'rule of reason'. Essentially the Court held that the Act, like the common law, did not seek to condemn *all* contracts in restraint of trade, but only those which *unreasonably* restrained trade. The importance of this decision lay not only in its fundamental implications for antitrust enforcement, but also in the public perception that the Supreme Court had taken sides in an active public debate (Letwin, 1967).

The laws which emerged from this debate were the Clayton Act and the Federal Trade Commission Act, both enacted in 1914. The Clayton Act proscribed a number of activities—price discrimination, tying and exclusive contracts, and anticompetitive mergers. These proscriptions were, however, strongly qualified by the statutory language. Mergers and exclusive contracts, for example, were prohibited only insofar as their effect may be to substantially lessen competition or tend to create a monopoly.

The Federal Trade Commission Act established the Federal Trade Commission (FTC) as an independent administrative agency and charged it with a number of functions. The bedrock of the FTC's powers were contained in section 5, which declared unlawful 'unfair methods of competition'. Congress had rediscovered the impossibility of framing precise definitions in effective antitrust statutes. It was hoped that the FTC would somehow translate the general language of the Act into practicable rules for the business community: 'no businessman reading the Act would come any closer to finding the line between lawful and unlawful conduct' (Letwin, 1967). But the apparently unlimited scope of the law and the lack of policy guidance given to the FTC placed intolerable strains on the agency and contributed to its failure as an effective anti-trust enforcer, at least until the early 1970s.

The Sherman Act

'Every contract, combination ... or conspiracy' The statutory prohibition of restrictive agreements is contained in section 1 of the Sherman Act:

Every contract, combination in the form of trust or otherwise, or conspiracy in restraint of trade or commerce among the several States, or with foreign nations, is hereby declared to be illegal.

The section goes on to impose *criminal* sanctions for any violation of the prohibition. It will be noticed immediately that the section contains no provision similar to Article 85(3) of the Treaty of Rome or the 'gateways' of the UK legislation for the exemption of 'beneficial' agreements. By its terms, therefore, it appears to condemn out of hand *all* restrictive agreements without further consideration. The problem with such an approach is that it renders the prohibition absurdly wide. All commercial contracts will restrain the parties to a certain extent: a simple contract for the sale of goods prevents the seller from selling those goods to another person or at a different price, and the purchaser is similarly restrained. Indeed 'every agreement concerning trade, every regulation of trade, restrains. To bind, to restrain, is of their very essence' (Justice Brandeis in the *Chicago Board of Trade* case, 1918). It became a question of great controversy as to whether the Sherman Act intended to, or should, prohibit *all* contracts which restrain trade.

The difficulty springs from the very general language of section 1. As the Supreme Court has said, '[o]ne problem presented by the language of s.1 of the Sherman Act is that it cannot mean what it says' (*National Society of Professional Engineers* case, 1978). A prohibition of all contracts in restraint of trade 'served to indicate strong moral reprobation'

(Henderson, 1924) but is difficult to apply in practice. Doubly difficult because the term 'restraint of trade' was used as a term of art in the common law.[64] It was unclear whether the use of these words was intended to indicate that the Sherman Act was no more than a statutory restatement of the common law (which, as stated in Chapter 4, only condemned *unreasonably* restrictive agreements), or whether the inclusion of the phrase *'every* contract, combination ... or conspiracy' was intended to cast a wider net. Henderson believes that Congress did not use the words in their common law meaning but in their political context: '[w]as Congress to admit that a trust or monopoly could ever be reasonable? ... Any qualification or definition or exception tended to weaken the apparently sweeping and inclusive range of the statute, and hence its rhetorical value' (Henderson, 1924).

It was left to the courts to decide whether the law prohibited every contract in restraint of trade or only those which unreasonably restrained trade. The early judgments of the Supreme Court firmly supported the literal interpretation: the plain and ordinary meaning of the Act was that 'every' such contract was prohibited. So held the majority of the Supreme Court in the *Trans-Missouri* case (1897). In the *Addyston Pipe* case (1899) the Supreme Court again rejected the common law distinction between reasonable and unreasonable restraints as having any relevance to the Act; all contracts whose direct and immediate effect was to restrain trade were condemned.

But the decision of the Supreme Court in the *Standard Oil* case (1911) reversed this interpretation. In this case, the court reviewed the common law which existed when the Act came into force, and supported the principle that where the Act used the same language as the common law, it should be given the same meaning. The broad language of the Act was used in order to catch all forms of restrictive practice, and 'to protect ... commerce from being restrained by methods, whether old or new, which would constitute an interference,—that is, an undue restraint'. Such language rendered the possible scope of the section so wide that some judgement was necessary to apply it in practice; that standard should be the standard of reason applied at common law.

Henceforth only those contracts which *unreasonably*

restrained trade would be held to be contrary to the Sherman Act. The gloss so applied to the plain words of the Act became known as the 'rule of reason'. The classic restatement of this form of analysis was contained in the judgment in the *Chicago Board of Trade* case (1918).[65]

The true test of legality is whether the restraint imposed is such as merely regulates and perhaps thereby promotes competition or whether it is such as may suppress or even destroy competition. To determine that question the court must ordinarily consider the facts peculiar to the business to which the restraint is applied; its condition before and after the restraint was imposed; the nature of the restraint and its effect, actual or probable. The history of the restraint, the evil believed to exist, the reason for adopting the particular remedy, the purpose or end sought to be attained, are all relevant facts. This is not because a good intention will save an otherwise objectionable regulation or the reverse; but because knowledge of intent may help the court to interpret facts and to predict consequences.

Under the rule of reason, as originally expressed, the words of the Sherman Act were judicially interpreted to cover only those restraints which unreasonably restrain trade. The influence of the common law, which formulated this approach, is as relevant today as it was in the *Standard Oil* case.[66] In the more modern cases, however, the meaning of 'rule of reason' is slightly different. It is now spoken of in contrast to the analytical approach, 'per se' illegality. It is important to appreciate that *both* per se and rule of reason analyses take place within the confines of the interpretation laid down in *Standard Oil*.

The rule of reason approach is the norm; under this approach the competitive impact of an agreement—and therefore its legality—can only be evaluated by analysing the facts peculiar to the business, the history of the restraint, and the reasons why it was imposed.[67] Such an exercise is, of course, costly; both sides in the dispute must undertake a complex and prolonged economic investigation into the entire history of the industry involved[68]—and the court must analyse this 'in an effort to determine at large whether a particular restraint has been unreasonable—an enquiry so often wholly fruitless when undertaken'.[69] In addition to these explicit costs to the enforcement and adjudication authorities and litigants, the relative inexpertise of many judges with regard to economic theory and prediction gives rise to a risk that erroneous decisions will be made (Scherer, 1980).[70]

In deference to these costs and in order to promote certainty in business, certain practices will be regarded by the courts as 'per se' illegal. In relation to these activities, all that need be shown is that they took place; no extensive investigation into their precise competitive impact will be carried out. This per se approach, being a departure from the norm, will only be used where the courts have had considerable experience of the activity in question. Indeed, the approach will only be utilised where the activity threatens the proper operation of the economy by always or almost always tending to restrict competition and decrease output.[71] Per se illegal activities will demonstrate this 'pernicious' effect and will lack any redeeming virtues.

Such practices currently include horizontal price-fixing or market division agreements, group boycotts, vertical resale price maintenance and tie-in sales. The purpose of all such activities is manifestly anticompetitive, and a detailed investigation into their precise impact will almost always reveal them as being unduly restrictive, and hence illegal. An inflexible rule outlawing them will therefore achieve substantial savings at the cost of sacrificing those few agreements which, on a rule of reason analysis, may have been shown to have no substantial competitive impact.

Thus, once the court is satisfied that the activities actually do fall within a 'per se illegal' category, the parties are not permitted to show that, in the particular case, pro-competitive results will flow. For example, in the *Socony-Vacuum* case (1940) the court said: '[w]hatever economic justification particular price-fixing agreements may be thought to have, the law does not permit an enquiry into their reasonableness. They are all banned because of their actual or potential threat to the central nervous system of the economy'.

It should be stressed that these two different analytical approaches do have a common purpose; they both seek to measure the competitive impact of the challenged activity. Rule of reason analysis will *not* take account of matters falling outside such test. No enquiry will be undertaken into the reasonableness of fixed prices or the advantages of monopoly as opposed to competition in certain industries. The policy of the Sherman Act is to favour free competition, and the Supreme Court has consistently categorised any submission which derogates from this as being a matter for Congress rather than the courts. This approach contrasts sharply with the approach taken by UK legislation. Many of the 'gateways' in the Restrictive Trade Practices Act expressly subvert competition in favour of other policy objectives, such as public safety, employment and export earnings. But in the *National Society of Professional Engineers* case (1978), where the defendants argued that free competition amongst engineers might compromise public safety, the Supreme Court described the argument as 'nothing less than a frontal assault on the basic policy of the Sherman Act'. The Court went on to say:

> The assumption that competition is the best method of allocating resources in a free market recognises that all elements of a bargain—quality, service, safety and durability—and not just the immediate cost, are favourably affected by the free opportunity to select among alternative offers ... the statutory policy precludes inquiry into the question whether competition is good or bad.'

Weaver has found that the lawyers at the Antitrust Division, who are responsible for the initiation of prosecutions for Sherman Act offences, enthusiastically adopt this analytical approach:

> [they] strongly oppose any attempts to balance the value of competition against that of other economic or social goals. They do not accept that major conflicts among these goals exist in the long run, and they accept neither general arguments in favour of more economic planning nor more specific arguments suggesting that some desired social goal will not be well served by maximum competition (Weaver, 1977).

Seen in this light, the rule of reason approach does not differ fundamentally from the per se approach. Indeed the latter could be regarded as merely a truncated rule of reason analysis, the unreasonableness of the activity being measured by reference to data collected by the courts through many years' experience of the challenged activity. The similarity between the approaches is even more marked when the court has to review the challenged activity in order to be satisfied that it has been properly 'labelled' as per se illegal. This has prompted some commentators to describe per se and rule of reason not as separate analytical approaches, but as part of one continuum, or sliding scale, of analysis (Reich, 1980; Sullivan, 1980).

The phrase 'contract combination ... or conspiracy' in section 1 of the Sherman Act is intended to cover all the varieties of cooperation covered by the word 'agreement' in the UK Restrictive Trade Practices Act and the phrase 'agreements between undertakings, decisions by associations of undertakings and concerted practices' in Article 85 of the Treaty of Rome. As mentioned in relation to UK and EEC law, restrictive agreements may take many forms, not limited to express contracts. The Supreme Court stated very clearly in the *Paramount Pictures* case (1948) that 'it is not necessary to find an express agreement. It is enough that a concert of action is contemplated and ... conformed to'. The court will therefore look to see what the parties actually did rather than what they said, if indeed there is a record of anything they did say.

In common with EEC law, section 1 of the Sherman Act will apply to concerted behaviour even in the absence of an identifiable agreement. But like EEC law, consciously parallel behaviour will not, of itself, be sufficient to found liability. The behaviour of the parties or the circumstances of the market must indicate that the activities of the firms resulted from a conspiracy and not, for example, from identical cost structures. Consciously parallel behaviour without conspiracy will not found liability (*Theatre Enterprises* case, 1954; Attorney General's Report, 1955). Posner has argued that economic data may be used to show that tacit collusion must have taken place in an oligopolistic market, without the need to show actual collusion (Posner 1976), but the weight of academic opinion, both legal and economic, is sceptical of this approach (Scherer, 1977), and the clear requirement of section 1 for a contract, combination or conspiracy would seem to reject Posner's approach. The character of the Sherman Act as a *criminal* statute should not be overlooked; circumstantial evidence of criminal conduct should be treated cautiously.

Even in the context of oligopoly, therefore, the Sherman Act requires some 'agreement' between the actors, that is to say 'a unity of purpose or a common design and understanding or a meeting of minds' (*Paramount Pictures* case, 1948). A contract between a parent company and its wholly owned subsidiary will not amount to such an 'agreement', because there is a constant unity of purpose between them as a result of their common ownership.

The relationship between a parent company and its subsidiary is also relevant to another requirement of section 1—that there should be at least two persons acting in concert. The distinction between section 1 and section 2, which is concerned with monopoly, is that unilateral action can only be attacked under section 2, and never under section 1. Section 2, however, may be used only where a firm is in a monopoly position or when it is actively acquiring monopoly. This immunity enjoyed by firms engaging in unilateral action outside section 2 is said to 'reduce . . . the risk that the antitrust laws will dampen the competitive zeal of a single aggressive entrepreneur' (*Copperweld* case, 1984). Until recently, it was thought that an anticompetitive agreement between a parent company and its wholly owned subsidiary could be illegal under section 1. However, in the *Copperweld* case the Supreme Court rejected the concept of 'intra-enterprise conspiracy' in that context. The rationale for treating concerted activity differently (and more harshly) than unilateral activity is that concerted activity reduces the effective number of independent centres of decision-making and thereby reduces the diversity of economic power.[72] This phenomenon does not occur in the context of unilateral activity. An agreement between a parent and its wholly owned subsidiary is closely analagous to unilateral activity; it concerns the internal organisation of the firm rather than its external relations. Even where the subsidiary has some autonomy on the market, the parent company could impose its will at any time. The court will not therefore enquire whether any apparent autonomy exists. However, in the case of a subsidiary which is not wholly owned, the court will enquire into the 'separateness' of the subsidiary from its parent(s). If a degree of autonomy does exist, then the concerted activity of the two firms could attract section 1 liability.

There is therefore a gap in the Sherman Act through which

the anticompetitive activity of a single firm may pass. As we shall see in Chapter 6, this gap is plugged by section 5 of the Federal Trade Commission Act, which regulates unfair methods of competition. A similar gap in the UK restrictive practices legislation is also plugged by a catch-all provision in the Competition Act 1980. However, in EEC law the gap remains unplugged.

Interstate significance of agreements

Like Article 85 of the Treaty of Rome, the Sherman Act is a federal law and is concerned only with restrictive agreements which have a significance in a federal context. Section 1 is directed against 'restraint[s] of trade or commerce *among the several States ...*'. Restrictive agreements which do not have such significance will be regulated by the respective State laws. In common with Articles 85, the 'interstate commerce' test is carried out to determine the jurisdiction of the federal courts, rather than to analyse the competitive impact—and hence the legality—of the challenged agreements. Even an increase in inter-State trade could therefore attract liability under the Act.

Sullivan has grouped the relevant cases into two categories: (i) those where the activity of the parties is 'in' or 'in the flow of' inter-State commerce; and (ii) those which do not fall into the first category but which materially affect inter-State commerce (Sullivan, 1977 II). The first category will fall within section 1 even though the actual effect on inter-State commerce may be minimal. Activity falling within the second category will be covered by the Act only if the effect on trade is substantial.

Information agreements

As mentioned earlier in this chapter, restrictive practices may sometimes not take the form of simple agreements or conscious parallelism between firms but may operate within a trade association or as reciprocal information exchange agreements. Unlike the Restrictive Trade Practices Act and Article 85, section 1 of the Sherman Act does not *expressly* cover trade associations' activities. However, it is clear that unreasonable restraints of trade will not escape Sherman Act liability simply because they are carried on by or through a trade association.

Trade associations are unlikely to impose express price agreements, but services provided by them may facilitate price collusion among their members. More easily identifiable practices would include group boycotts and, in some circumstances, contract standardisation (Malin and Lawniczak, 1982). Perhaps the most significant of the 'non-orthodox' agreements are those relating to the exchange of information on price and other terms of trade. These are covered by the broad terms of section 1 of the Sherman Act. However, although the exchange of price information is usually carried out as a substitute for express price-fixing arrangements, American courts have not treated the two as being necessarily analogous. Thus, the per se standard applied to overt price-fixing agreements is commuted to a rule of reason analysis in relation to price (and other data) information exchange. The court will enquire into the purpose and effect of the arrangement in order to determine whether it was intended to, or did, facilitate collusion rather than competition (*United States Gypsum Co.* case, 1978).

Clearly, in oligopolistic markets where the product is fungible, price exchange is more likely to be a collusive exercise, but this is not inevitably so (Scherer, 1980).

The administration of section 1 of the Sherman Act
The administration of US antitrust law is characterised by the dual role of the Antitrust Division of the Department of Justice and the Federal Trade Commission (FTC). In addition, private individuals have considerable access to anti-trust statutes and may bring civil actions for damages and injunctions. The structure and organisation of the Antitrust Division is examined in Chapter 2. The FTC has a remit extending over the whole of antitrust policy, but it is convenient to examine its nature and structure in the context of restrictive trade practices policy.

The Federal Trade Commission As mentioned in the historical introduction to American law, the FTC was created as a result of the Supreme Court interpreting the Sherman Act by reference to the rule of reason. The public saw this as a 'softening' of the law by the courts. The idea behind the

186 Monopoly, Competition and the Law

creation of the FTC was that it would enforce the new antitrust statutes as an administrative agency, away from the
influences of the judiciary. It was also expected to give
guidance to business as to the meaning and scope of the new
laws. It shares jurisdiction with the Antitrust Division (AD) in
relation to mergers, but has exclusive jurisdiction to enforce
section 5 of the Federal Trade Commission Act, which (in its
present form) prohibits 'unfair methods of competition in or
affecting commerce, and unfair or deceptive acts or practices
in or affecting commerce'. Subsequent judicial interpretation
of this section has determined that its scope covers any activity
which is contrary to any of the antitrust statutes as well as any
activity which violates their spirit or purpose. In practical
terms therefore, the FTC and the AD have simultaneous jurisdiction over the entire scope of antitrust law. As we shall see,
however, the enforcement techniques of the two agencies are
markedly different. In addition to its antitrust jurisdiction, the
FTC also administers and enforces federal consumer
protection legislation. This dual role likens it to the British
Office of Fair Trading.

Two highly critical reports on the FTC in the late 1960s
highlighted bureaucratic inefficiency and ineffectiveness within
the agency. As a result, major organisational and procedural
changes were made in an effort to make the FTC a major and
effective antitrust enforcer. Most commentators agree that the
agency is much improved, though critics continue to call for its
abolition and the transfer of its functions to the AD (Gellhorn,
1982).

The FTC is composed of four commissioners and a
chairman, all appointed by the President on political grounds.
The political affiliations of the appointees have possibly been
of more importance than their suitability for the post
(Katzmann, 1980). As a reflection of this, the FTC Act
specifies that not more than three of the five-person
Commission may be from the same political party.

The Commissioners head a complex staff structure; two
components of that structure are the Bureau of Competition and
the Bureau of Economics. The Bureau of Competition, staffed by
attorneys, is the section responsible for overseeing compliance
with the antitrust laws, by gathering intelligence and

commencing actions against allegedly anti competitive activity. The Bureau of Economics, housed away from the Bureau of Competition, advises and coordinates with the staff attorneys, especially in relation to the choice of cases to be pursued.

The Chairman of the FTC has a considerable influence over the agency, and the Director of the Bureau of Competition is also a key figure. However, the selection of cases to be pursued is substantially the product of rivalry and competition between the staff lawyers and economists (Katzmann, 1980; Clarkson and Muris, 1981). Katzmann sees this relationship as 'institutionalized conflict'. Like their colleagues in the Antitrust Division, the lawyers in the FTC are keen on litigating cases and are much more disposed to press for cases to be initiated than the more conservative economists. The latter perceive their role as being a counterweight to the Bureau of Competition; Katzmann quotes one young economist: 'we are saviours of the free market, contending against forces bent on government intervention' (Katzmann, 1980). The enthusiasm of the attorneys to litigate cases springs mainly from the fact that a position at the FTC is seen as a means of gaining early litigation experience and thereafter joining a private law firm. Most attorneys at the FTC join with the intention of moving on after two to five years (Katzmann, 1980; Clarkson and Muris, 1981).

The creative tension between the lawyers and economists is mirrored by a debate on the proper way in which FTC resources should be deployed. This is the debate between a reactive and a proactive approach. A reactive approach consists of an FTC response on a case-by-case basis to those agreements or activities which come to its notice either through the 'mailbag' or as a result of investigations. This approach discounts the importance of planning the agency's activities on a strategic basis as a way of maximising its long-term effectiveness. A proactive approach gives greater emphasis to bringing about long-term structural changes in industry in order to create an atmosphere for competition by removing imperfections.

The attorneys favour a reactive approach, which leads to shorter, easier cases and more frequent litigation. The economists, who generally regard anticompetitive conduct as a product rather than a cause of market imperfections (Katzmann, 1980), favour the longer and more complex structural cases. The views of the economists cannot be ignored since they take part in the evaluation committee meetings which advise the Director of the Bureau of Competition on whether to initiate proceedings. However, it appears that the approach of the FTC is still mainly a reactive one (Clarkson and Muris, 1981). The economists have, however, persuaded the FTC largely to abandon cases on price discrimination under the Robinson-Patman Act, by demonstrating that these cases had the effect of protecting small businesses at the expense of efficiency.

Mailbag complaints remain the FTC's most important source of intelligence. Where these show a likely anti-competitive activity, a preliminary investigation will be carried out. If this confirms the original suspicions, the commissioners may sanction the opening of a formal investigation. During this investigation, the FTC may gather intelligence through a 'civil investigative demand' process in the same way as the Antitrust Division. It also has a right of access to, and the right to copy, any documentary evidence, but this does not amount to a power of search and seizure (Oppenheim, Weston and McCarthy, 1981). In addition, the FTC has the right to demand from almost any firm, whether under investigation or not, an annual or special report dealing with any questions raised by the FTC in relation to the firm's conduct, organisation and business. This is a spectacularly comprehensive and potent power.

Enforcement of antitrust policy—judicial and administrative alternatives From the above description it can be seen that investigative powers and case-selection procedures of the FTC and Antitrust Division are similar. However, once a decision has been made to proceed with a case, the procedures of the two agencies are markedly different. The Antitrust Division will bring a prosecution and/or civil action in an ordinary court. The process will thereafter follow the normal rules of criminal and civil procedure. A successful prosecution will result in a fine or imprisonment, and the civil action may give rise to injunctions and orders affecting the firm's structure.

Appeals from such verdicts or decisions will follow the normal judicial route.

The procedures of the FTC reflect a doubt in the justiciability of antitrust issues.[73] Criticism of the judicial enforcement of antitrust policy may be based on several grounds. First, that the legal process is too slow, especially in relation to antitrust suits which can drag on for more than ten years. Secondly, that ordinary judges are not generally competent to deal with complex economic issues. Thirdly, that the legal method—which relies on precedent and doctrine—is not suited to achieve economically efficient results because economic theory will be inadmissible unless it complies with previous judicial precedent (Katzmann, 1980). The force of these last two criticisms depends, of course, on the view taken of the place of *non*economic objectives in antitrust enforcement. And fourthly, that criminal procedures and penalties are unsuitable for antitrust enforcement. In this view, antitrust cases are not conflicts between 'right and wrong' but conflicts between different interest groups. Such conflicts ought to be resolved by adjustment rather than punishment (Henderson, 1924). This view ignores the enormous weight of evidence that certain economic activities are so clearly against the public interest, whether on economic, political or social terms, that they are properly viewed as 'wrong'.

On the basis of these and other criticisms, the FTC adopted a non-judicial enforcement method. Thus, where the FTC decides to proceed with a case, it issues a complaint to the firm(s) involved. The firm then has the right to a hearing before the administrative law judge, who is an employee of the FTC but who operates separately from the Bureau of Competition. At the hearing, the Bureau of Competition's attorneys will put the case against the firm. The firm, through its attorneys, will put forward a 'defence'. The administrative law judge will issue an initial decision which must then be endorsed by the Commissioners. If the decision is against the firm, the order of the FTC will take the form of a cease-and-desist order or other corrective measure; no further penalties ensue unless the order is not complied with. Failure to comply can attract civil penalties of up to $10,000 per day. The FTC procedure does not exist wholly outside the judicial system, in that orders of the FTC can be appealed to a federal court of appeals.

As in the UK and EEC systems, the formal enforcement of antitrust in the USA is supplemented by an informal settlement procedure. Indeed, the vast majority of AD and FTC cases are settled by consent. Perhaps because of its practical importance, some procedural limitations have been imposed on this process. Where a firm negotiates a consent decree with the Antitrust Division, the firm will, without admitting liability, agree not to engage in certain activity (e.g. the operation of a restrictive cartel) and the AD will agree not to prosecute. This negotiated settlement, or 'consent decree', must then be submitted to the court along with a statement by the AD known as a 'competitive impact statement'. The proposed settlement must also be published to allow for comments by interested persons. The court will only sanction the settlement if it regards it as being in the public interest.

This system involves more formality and publicity than the corresponding practices of the UK and EEC authorities, but by forcing the parties to consider the impact of the settlement in the light of any alternatives, the consent decree system creates a particularly useful and effective enforcement process.[74] Its popularity with business springs from the fact that it avoids litigation, with its attendant delays, costs and publicity. More importantly, where litigation by the AD results in judgment against a firm, this is *prima facie* proof that the firm carried on the illegal activities. Such proof would facilitate a private action for treble damages against the firm. A negotiated consent decree avoids this disadvantage.

The FTC has a similar consent order system. Consent orders may be negotiated before a formal complaint is issued, or during the hearing of the case before the administrative law judge. Again, the proposed order will be published for comment before it is finally confirmed by the FTC.

Consent decrees may not be negotiated where the AD is considering a criminal prosecution, rather than a civil action. However, where a prosecution is commenced a firm may apply to the court to enter a special plea, known as *nolo contendere*. This plea really means 'I don't want to argue whether I am innocent or guilty; treat me *as if* I am guilty'. Where such pleas are accepted, the defendant firm will be punished as if it had been found guilty after presentation of evidence. The advantage of such a plea is that the legal process is expedited considerably and, as with a consent decree, pleas of *nolo contendere* cannot be used by private litigants as proof of guilt. Consent decrees and orders, and pleas of *nolo contendere* are settlements which are negotiated in the context of impending or actual litigation. However, just as the UK system permits 'fail-safe' applications to the Office of Fair Trading, and the EEC system permits applications for 'negative clearance' and the issue of 'comfort letters', the US system permits firms to *initiate* contact with the antitrust authorities in order to avoid antitrust liability arising at all.

The Antitrust Division will, if requested, issue a business review letter which states that, on the basis of evidence presented to it, it has no present intention of proceeding against the agreement or activity reported. This is not a very valuable assurance since the AD can change its mind at will. However, it is unlikely that the AD would bring a criminal prosecution after having issued a business review letter (Sullivan, 1977 II). The fact that the procedure offers no real immunity from civil actions by the AD has resulted in its being little used by business. It is also FTC policy to issue 'advisory opinions' stating its views on *proposed* activity. A favourable opinion may be withdrawn at will but the FTC will give notice to the firms in order to allow them to discontinue the restrictive agreement or practice. However, a favourable advisory opinion does not give immunity against action by the Antitrust Division.

We are now in a position to summarise the choices open to a member of a cartel, under the US antitrust system. The three-fold choice is the same as under the other two systems: to report the cartel to the antitrust authorities; to operate the cartel in a clandestine manner; or to leave the cartel. The first choice comprises the business letter review and advisory opinion procedures. As mentioned above, the lack of practical immunity provided by these procedures has resulted in little use being made of them. A clandestine cartel may be kept from the attention of the authorities, but there is always the danger of a complaint being made by a competitor, consumer or dis-affected cartel member. In such a case, or where the cartel comes to light through other means, the AD or FTC may initiate a criminal, civil or administrative action. (There is no danger however that *both* the FTC and the AD will commence proceedings; a sophisticated liaison system between the agencies prevents them both proceeding against the same activity or agreement.) Even at this stage, however, all is not lost; a proposed civil action by the AD or administrative action by the FTC may be avoided through a negotiated settlement. A proposed criminal action is more serious because it can result in very heavy fines (up to $1 million for a corporation or $100,000 for a person) and even imprisonment. Moreover, a guilty verdict in a criminal trial will facilitate a private civil action brought against the firms by persons injured by the restrictive practice. Successful civil plaintiffs are entitled to treble damages.

The third choice, leaving the cartel, may attract commercial retaliation by 'loyal' members, but if this injures the leaving party, the cartel members may lay themselves open to a risk of private action or a complaint to the authorities. The leaving party may also have criminal liability for the past activities while a member of the cartel.

Except in cases where the cartel falls into a per se illegal category—and is therefore likely to be subject to *criminal* action if discovered—the US system favours the clandestine maintenance of a cartel. Firms have very little to gain from revealing their cartel to the authorities but, on discovery, still have the chance to negotiate a settlement. Unlike the UK and EEC systems, the US system does not penalise firms merely for keeping the cartel secret. A system which effectively favours noncompliance in this way must constantly undermine its own effectiveness.

The US antitrust system

It will be apparent from the description of the US antitrust system that there are features which distinguish it from the EEC and UK systems. The overriding characteristic of the US system is its 'purity' in terms of competition, and this sets it aside from the other two systems. Congress determined, through the Sherman Act, that the benefits of a determined pursuit of competition outweighed any disadvantage that might be encountered. The opening paragraph of the Attorney General's report on the antitrust laws described the 'opportunity for market access and fostering of market rivalry [as] basic tenets of our faith in competition as a form of economic organisation' (Attorney General's Report, 1955). Thus, no other social or political objective may be pleaded as an alternative to competition. The task of the courts does not therefore involve the balancing of different objectives; it simply consists in measuring the *competitive impact* of the restrictive agreement. Of course this is not a simple task, but it does not involve the courts in creative policy-making.

Unlike the UK and EEC systems, therefore, there is no specific public interest test against which to measure a restrictive agreement—no equivalent of the 'gateways' or Article 85(3).

This purity of approach explains why the ordinary court system is used to administer much of the antitrust laws. Collusive behaviour was regarded by the framers of the Sherman Act as being of a criminal nature, and therefore a matter for the ordinary judiciary. It is true that the role of the FTC in antitrust enforcement does dilute the judicial approach with an administrative one, but ultimately the decisions of the FTC are appealable to the courts.

The overlapping jurisdiction of two agencies at federal level is also a feature unique to the American system, and even now is not uncontroversial. But perhaps the greatest difference between the American system and the other two is that it does nothing to encourage or compel the registration of restrictive agreements with the enforcing authorities.

NOTES

1. RTPA s.1(2)(c).
2. *Ibid.*, s.21(2).
3. *Ibid.*, ss.6 and 11.
4. *Ibid.*, s.43(1).
5. *Registrar of Restrictive Trading Agreements* v. *W H Smith* (1969).
6. Lord Justice Diplock in *British Basic Slag Ltd* v. *Registrar of Restrictive Trading Agreements*, LR 4 RP 116, 154 (1963).

7. Lord Justice Danckwerts, *ibid.*, p. 149.
8. Services agreements were not brought under legal control until 1973.
9. *Diazo Copying Materials* (1984).
10. See *Esso* v. *Harper's Garage* (1968).
11. *Ravenseft Properties Ltd* v. *Director General of Fair Trading* (1977).
12. See, to the contrary, A.J. Eddey, *The New Competition*, 4th edn. (1917).
13. Restrictive Trade Practices (Information Agreements) Order 1969, enacted under the Restrictive Trade Practices Act 1968.
14. I.e. two copies of the entire agreement or, where the agreement was not fully committed to writing, of a memorandum setting out its terms. For futher details, see the Registration of Restrictive Trade Agreements Regulations 1984, SI 1984 No. 392.
15. I.e. any party who carries on business in the UK.
16. *Annual Report of the Director General of Fair Trading 1979*, p. 37.
17. *W.H. Smith* case, *supra*, n.5.
18. Confidential letter to author.
19. See p. 123 above. The corresponding provision in the Restrictive Trade Practices Act 1956 spoke of agreements which were 'of no substantial *economic* significance' but the disappearance of the word in s.21(2) of the RTPA does not appear to have affected the operation of the law.
20. The workload of the RPC has been cut down to such an extent by these informal methods that it no longer publishes its own series of law reports. Cases of the RPC are now reported in another, wider, series—*Industrial Law Reports*.
21. The Court may still pronounce on the abandoned agreement in order to prevent the parties from reviving it or entering into similar agreements in the future. Since the agreement will be undefended, the 'pronouncement' will be a formal declaration of invalidity.
22. For an account of one unstable cartel, see *Finance Houses Associations Agreement* (1965).
23. Or through investigations by outsiders—e.g. the press: the lead story in the *Sunday Times* 9 December 1984 concerned the exposure of a cartel in the professional boxing market.
24. The RPC has the following powers under the RTPA: (i) to make orders prohibiting the operation of restrictions which have been declared contrary to the public interest, either because of an unsuccessful defence, or because no defence was entered; (ii) to make orders prohibiting the parties from entering into agreements 'to the like effect' as prohibited agreements; (iii) to make interim orders prohibiting the operation of restrictions pending final evaluation; (iv) to declare whether or not an agreement is subject to registration, and to rectify the register; (v) to make orders prohibiting the operation of an unregistered agreement (where it should have been registered); (vi) to order persons to appear before it to be examined by the Director General; (vii) to levy penalties for contempt of any of its orders.

25. The RPC may order persons to desist from carrying on a course of conduct detrimental to the interests of consumers (Fair Trading Act 1973, s.35 *et seq.*); it may also exempt classes of goods from the provisions of the resale price maintenance legislation (Resale Price Act 1976, s.14 *et seq.*).
26. S.3 Restrictive Practices Courts Act 1976.
27. Speaking in the parliamentary debates on the Restrictive Trade Practices Act 1956, the Lord Chancellor said that he expected that 'the expertise and experience of practical affairs of the lay members will contribute to [The RPC's] judgments' (see Stevens and Yamey, 1965, p. 33).
28. One member did not respond directly to this question.
29. Ungoed-Thomas later became a High Court judge. He gave a significant judgment in the *Texaco* case (see above p. 112).
30. For more detailed synopses of the earlier cases, see Wilberforce *et al.* (1966); see also Stevens and Yamey (1965). For full reports of the cases, see the citations in the Table of Cases.
31. See above, p. 121.
32. See above, p. 127.
33. See above, p. 129.
34. *Registrar of Restrictive Trading Agreements* v. *W H Smith* (1969).
35. Council Regulation (EEC) 17/62 (1962).
36. See above, p. 127.
37. See p. 183. For an alternative view, see van Rijn (1983).
38. *Official Notice on Contracts for Exclusive Representation Concluded with Commercial Agents* (1962).
39. *Commission Notice of 3 September 1986 Concerning Agreements of Minor Importance Which Do Not Fall Under Article 85(1)*, OJ 1986, C231/2.
40. *Ibid.*
41. See *above*, p. 13.
42. EEC Commission, *Notice on Japanese Imports*, 1972 OJ C111/13.
43. Reg. (EEC) No. 1983/83.
44. Reg. (EEC) No. 1984/83.
45. Reg. (EEC) No. 417/85.
46. Reg. (EEC) No. 2349/84.
47. Reg. (EEC) No. 123/85.
48. Reg. (EEC) No. 418/85.
49. It also has the power to mount 'dawn raids' on the premises of firms. See above p. 46.
50. Approximately 90 per cent of cases are settled by the Commission without a formal decision or fine—Temple Lang, 'EEC Competition Policies: A Status Report', in *Enterprise Law of the 80s*, ed. F.M. Rowe *et al.* (ABA Press, 1980).
51. See the discussion of these choices on p. 132, above.
52. For a description of the Commission, see above p. 45.
53. See Editorial, *European Law Review* 293 (1984).

54. *Carbon Gas* (1984); *Carlsberg* (1985); *Rockwell-Iveco* (1983); *Uniform Eurocheques,* (1985).
55. *VW/Man,* (1984); *Synthetic Fibres* (1985); *BPCL/ICI* (1984).
56. *Synthetic Fibres, supra, BPCL/ICI supra.*
57. *Vimpolto* (1983); *Cast Iron & Steel Rolls* (1984).
58. *Polistil/Arbois* (1984); *Peroxygen Products* (1985); *John Deere* (1985).
59. *Benelux Flat Glass* (1984).
60. For example in *AKZO* (1985), the Commission levied fines totalling 10 million ECU (approx. £7.4million).
61. See Thorelli (1954) and Letwin (1967), on which much of this section is based.
62. By 1875, 10 per cent of farmers were grouped together in the Granger Movement (Letwin, 1967).
63. *Ibid.,* p. 253.
64. See Chapter 4.
65. *Chicago Board of Trade* v. *US* (1918).
66. For example, Mr Justice Stevens in the *National Society of Professional Engineers* case traced the rule of reason under the Sherman Act to the English case of *Mitchel* v. *Reynolds* (1711). See p. 107 above for a description of this case.
67. *National Society of Professional Engineers* (1978).
68. *Northern Pacific Railroad Co.* v. *United States* (1958) p. 5.
69. *Ibid.*
70. This risk is readily acknowledged by the courts—e.g. '[o]ur inability to weigh, in any meaningful sense, destruction of competition in one sector of the economy against promotion of competition in another sector is one important reason [why] we have formulated per se rules' (*United States* v. *Topco Associates* (1972) p. 609–10); '[j]udges often lack the expert understanding of industrial market structures and behaviour to determine with any confidence a practice's effect on competition' (*Arizona* v. *Maricopa County Medical Society* (1981).
71. *Broadcast Music* v. *Columbia Broadcasting System* (1979).
72. See Areeda, 'Intraenterprise Conspiracy in Decline', 97 *Harvard Law Review,* 451 (1985).
73. See the discussion on justiciability in relation to UK law, p. 136, above.
74. For a discussion of the consent decree procedure, see Boyer (1983).

6 Anticompetitive Practices

The regulation of anticompetitive practices cannot be undertaken solely through monopoly control or the control of restrictive trading agreements. Both policies have limitations which may make them unable to cope with certain commercial behaviour which damages the competitive equilibrium. In monopoly policy, there is the need to show the existence of a dominant position, in either structural or effective terms. In the control of restrictive trade practices, there is the need to show the existence of an agreement, even though the concept of agreement is loosely defined. In UK and US policy there is therefore legislation which fills in the gaps left by other aspects of competition law, and which underpins policy generally through the use of sweeping terms. In the UK, such control of anticompetitive practices is provided by the terms of the Competition Act 1980; in the US, section 5 of the Federal Trade Commission Act gives the FTC comprehensive power to control anticompetitive practices of all kinds. The EEC has no such 'background' legislation, but Article 85 has been interpreted in ways which stretch its use beyond orthodox restrictive trade practices control.

This chapter will examine the processes used in the three legal systems to control anticompetitive practices. In addition, it will examine the attitude of the legal systems to particular trading practices, insofar as this has not already been done in the context of monopoly, merger, or restrictive trade practices policy.

UK POLICY

Prior to 1980, there was no provision in UK law for the control of individual cases of unilateral anticompetitive behaviour except in the context of an investigation by the Monopolies and Mergers Commission. Instances of refusal to deal (including those amounting to selective dealing arrangements), tying practices and discriminatory pricing escaped investigation or control unless carried on by a monopolist. The Competition Act 1980 was enacted to remedy that situation; it is a radical law in two ways. First it seeks to control anticompetitive practices for the first time, and secondly, it abandons the 'form' approach of the restrictive practices legislation for one based on effects, and inspired by the wording of Article 85 of the Treaty of Rome.[1] The adoption of the 1980 Act was a direct result of the recommendations of the First and Second Green Papers.

The First Green Paper considered that monopoly investigations were inadequate to control many instances of anticompetitive practices. Of particular concern were restrictions on the sale of competing products, certain discount practices, tying and full line forcing. Monopoly investigations were thought to be inadequate to control such practices because the firms which carry them on may have dominance only in a highly localised geographic market. It would be inefficient to bring the MMC procedure to bear in these cases, since the process would take an unduly long time, and the small firm might have inadequate resources to respond to the MMC's investigation. The resources of the MMC would be better used in cases of more general concern. In keeping with the general nature of UK competition policy, the First Green Paper recommended that any new legislation should specify the practices which were to be covered by a new system of investigation. The Second Green Paper departed from this in recommending that, except for certain egregious cases, anticompetitive practices should not be specifically prohibited since the anticompetitive nature of any behaviour is largely determined by market conditions and the economic strength of the relevant firm. The Second Green Paper went on to recommend a procedure for the investigation and control of anticompetitive practices and these proposals were largely adopted in the 1980 Act.

The heart of the 1980 Act is section 2 which provides a wide, effects-based definition of an anticompetitive practice. Such a practice is defined as a course of conduct pursued by a person in the course of business which has or is intended to have or is likely to have the effect of restricting, distorting or preventing competition in connection with the supply or acquisition of goods or services in the UK or any part of it. The definition is free of the formal characteristics of the Restrictive Trade Practices Act and the Fair Trading Act, and is apparently wide enough to include all forms of anticompetitive behaviour affecting UK markets. It is clear that the section is not restricted to situations where competition is adversely affected in the market in which the relevant firm operates. The conduct of a firm may affect competition only in a contiguous or associated market, and conduct of this nature will be capable of examination under the 1980 Act. In the *Holmes McDougall* report (1985), for example, a magazine publisher refused to accept advertisements which included a reference to the price of the advertised product. This conduct restricted competition in the product markets, but not in the relevant magazine market. There have also been a number of investigations of exclusive franchise arrangements, where the franchisee and franchisor operated within different markets.

It was argued by one firm investigated under the Act that section 2 covered only 'misconduct'. Any wider interpretation, it was argued, would include pro-competitive conduct which led to the disappearance of a competitor. This was a reflection of a general concern voiced at the enactment of the 1980 Act that the Act would be interpreted in a way which protected competitors rather than competition. This argument was rejected by the MMC in *Sheffield Newspapers* (Cmnd. 8864, 1982). It considered that the Act should not be interpreted as protecting competitors, since the failure of an unsuccessful competitor was a feature of competition. However, the MMC cautioned that 'to fail in competition is not the same thing as to be excluded from competing because competition is restricted, distorted or prevented'. It ruled that anticompetitive practices under the 1980 Act were not limited to illegal conduct, nor confined to 'irregular' or 'unacceptable' conduct, but were defined purely in terms of their effect on competition, without exclusions. Another interpretation of the Act, similarly rejected in the same report, was that the Act would only enable a practice to be examined for its effect on the public interest where it was unreasonable as between the parties concerned. This interpretation, borrowed from the common law on restraints of trade,[2] was clearly unsupportable on the wording of section 2.

The apparent breadth of section 2 is, however, cut down in many particulars. Section 2 (2) provides that any course of conduct envisaged or required by a restriction in an agreement registrable under the Restrictive Trade Practices Act 1976 will not count as an anticompetitive practice under the 1980 Act. This is the case even in respect of registrable agreements which are unlawfully unregistered, and means that the 1980 Act is unable to prop up the weaknesses of restrictive trade practices policy. Under section 2 (3), the Secretary of State is empowered to exclude any course of conduct from the provisions of the Act. This power has been used liberally and three broad classes of conduct are presently excluded from control.

First, a whole range of topical areas are excluded, relating to transport by air[3] and sea;[4] certain building society agreements, agreements of agriculture and fisheries associations, and others.[5] Secondly, the inclusion of contractual conditions in an agreement relating solely to the supply of goods outside the UK is similarly excluded.[6] Third, and most significant, *any* conduct of a firm with a UK turnover of less than £5 million and with a turnover of less than 25 per cent of the relevant market, will be excluded.[7] The provisions of the Act were intended to be a departure from the statutory definition of monopoly, with all its attendant difficulties. However, there remained a need for some standard of dominance to be stated. There would be little point in including the conduct of all firms within the ambit of the Act. Conduct of itself will rarely give rise to concern; it must be related to the economic position of the firm carrying it on. Thus, only where a firm has some dominance will its conduct have any competitive significance. A firm with a market share of less than 25 per cent will rarely have market power, unless its competitors have only tiny market shares, but such a firm may still fall within the Act where its turnover is greater than £5 million (a fairly modest figure when compared to the £30 million threshold value of target assets required by UK mergers legislation).

The significant difference between this definition of market power and that provided for monopoly control under the Fair Trading Act is that the 1980 Act is intended to be applied even where the market power is enjoyed at a very local level. Because the procedures under the 1980 Act are swifter and cheaper than monopoly control procedures, it is possible to examine the conduct of firms which enjoy only local power but which are utilising that power in a way detrimental to the competitive process. The definition of the relevant market will be conducted in the same way as for monopoly control, on the basis of substitutability, but the geographic aspect of that definition will be more readily restricted to a part only of the UK. Of the investigations already undertaken by the Director General of Fair Trading under the 1980 Act, several have concerned markets at a local level. Three investigations concerned the distribution areas of certain local newspapers (*Sheffield Newspapers*, 1981; *Scottish and Universal Newspapers*, 1983; and *Essex County Newspapers*, 1983). These cases in particular demonstrate the differences between the firms' considerable market strength within a small geographical area and their insignificant share outside the local market. Their strong local position enabled them to carry on conduct of a potentially damaging nature which would have been effectively unchecked but for the terms of the 1980 Act. Two other investigations have concerned the local franchising arrangements of national transport concerns (*British Railways Board—Brighton Central Station*, 1982; and *British Airports Authority—Gatwick Airport*, 1984), and two others, services provided only in the London area (*London Electricity Board*, 1982; and *Thames Television*, 1984). In one investigation, the Director General had regard to the effects of a practice at both national and local levels (*Arthur Sanderson*, 1981).

Investigation by the Director General
Where the Director General of Fair Trading is of the opinion that a firm may be engaged in a course of conduct which may

amount to an anticompetitive practice, he is able to commence an investigation to determine whether such is the case. The nature of the legislation means that the investigation process will usually be initiated through complaints received rather than through the monitoring functions of the OFT (Office of Fair Trading, 1986).

Informal contact between the OFT and the 'suspected' firm may often dispose of the matter without the need for a formal investigation.

Table 4:
Competition reports of the Director General of Fair Trading

Arthur Sanderson	27 August 1981
Petter Refrigeration	29 May 1981
Sheffield Newspapers	27 October 1981
Raleigh Bicycles	27 February 1981
London Electricity Board	29 April 1982
Wm Still & Sons	22 July 1982
British Rail—Brighton Station	24 November 1982
Scottish and Universal Newspapers	11 January 1983
British Rail—Motorail	9 February 1983
British Rail—Godfrey Davis	18 May 1983
Essex County Newspapers	14 July 1983
Thames Television	3 February 1984
British Airports Authority—Gatwick	22 February 1984
Ford Motor Co.	21 March 1984
British Telecom	10 October 1984
BBC/ITP	13 November 1984
Holmes McDougall	3 October 1985

The Director General's Report for 1985 gives three examples of firms agreeing to modify their behaviour in response to preliminary contacts by the OFT (Director General, 1985). Once an investigation has been commenced, the Director General is under a duty to proceed with it as expeditiously as possible. The average time taken from the publication of the notice indicating an intention to carry out an investigation to the publication of the report is around eight months, which is considerably more speedy than a full-scale monopoly enquiry, but perhaps longer than would be ideal. The investigation involves the collation of material on the relevant market, the firms involved and the nature and effect of the conduct under review. In order to evince as much evidence as possible, the Director General publishes notices of the investigation at an early stage in publications that are likely to come to the attention of those affected by the conduct. Further, the Director General has powers to call for documents or other evidence; there is no power, however, to mount 'dawn raids' on the premises of firms to secure evidence of a course of conduct.

The Director General's report will present information on the market and the principal participants, will describe the course of conduct, if it is found to exist, and will assess whether such conduct is anticompetitive within the meaning of the Act. It is not the function of the Director General's report to rule on any matters of public interest which may arise in connection with such anticompetitive practices. This first-stage report is restricted to fact-finding and assessment on purely competition grounds, without consideration of the wider issues. For example, in the *British Airports Authority—Gatwick Airport* report (1984), the Director General expressly excluded a consideration of the possible benefits of franchising agreements relating to quality control and operational efficiencies, and restricted his analysis to the circumstances in which franchising arrangements may be anticompetitive.

With this complaints-led, reactive, system of work allocation, the types of conduct covered by reports tend to be haphazard rather than planned. In the first four years of operation under the Act, the Director General published fifteen reports. Only one report was published in each of the years 1985 and 1986, which *may* indicate that the earlier reports have had a modifying effect on the bahaviour of UK firms, or that informal processes are proving successful. It may equally be a reflection of choice with respect to resource allocation within the OFT generally. Where the Director General does find anticompetitive practices, he must consider whether any public interest issues are raised. If they are, then it is open to the Director General to refer the matter to a second investigation, by the Monopolies and Mergers Commission. This second-stage investigation will recover the ground covered in the Director General's report, and then go on to assess the public interest issues. However, before this second-stage process is embarked on, the firm involved is given an opportunity to give appropriate undertakings to the Director General with regard to its future conduct. The onus is on the firm involved—it must come forward with suitable undertakings for the Director General to consider. Where the Director General receives these, they will be published, and the conduct of the firm will be monitored to ensure compliance with the undertakings. In these circumstances there is no need for the matter to proceed to the MMC, unless the undertakings become inadequate over time and are not replaced, or the firm is found not to have complied with them.

Competition references to the Monopolies and Mergers Commission

Where the Director General has found that a firm has engaged in an anticompetitive practice and he has not accepted undertakings from it, then, if public policy issues may be raised by the matter, a reference may be mde to the MMC for a second-stage investigation to take place. The mere finding of an anticompetitive practice will not automatically lead to such a reference, even in the absence of suitable undertakings. In the *British Railways Board—Motorail* report (1983) and the *British Railways Board—Godfrey Davis* report (1983), the Director General found that the behaviour of the firms, whilst anticompetitive, was not of significant effect and the matter did not proceed. In *Holmes McDougall* (1985), the Director General found that many other firms in the market were engaging in the same type of anticompetitive behaviour as the firm under investigation, and for that reason a reference to the MMC restricted to that firm alone would not have restored competitiveness to the market.

Only the Director General may make a competition reference to the MMC (subject to a power of veto in the Secretary of State), and where a reference is made it must be restricted to the firms, products, and practices investigated in the Director General's report. It is the task of the MMC to confirm whether or not the specified course of conduct (or similar conduct) had been carried on by the firm within the preceding twelve months, whether such conduct thereby amounted to an anticompetitive practice, and whether such practice operated or may be expected to operate against the public interest. Clearly the last item will be the MMC's major contribution to the process. Although the first two items will already have been investigated by the Director General, the intention of the 1980 Act is that the MMC will have a completely free hand, within the terms of the reference, and will not be bound by the findings of the Director General. The MMC has disagreed with the findings of the Director General on the existence of an anticompetitive practice on only one occasion.

The MMC must fulfil its functions within a six-month period, with a possible three-month extension. The subsequent report is formally made to the Secretary of State, but delivered also to the Director General. Where the MMC report is that the public interest has been or may be compromised, the Secretary of State will take account of any recommendations for action included in the report or given by the Director General. Where the situation can be remedied through modifying the behaviour of the firm involved, the usual course of action will be for the Secretary of State to request the Director General to seek appropriate undertakings from the firm. The difference between these undertakings and those following the first-stage report of the Director General is that at this later stage the initiative will come from the enforcing authorities rather than from the firm. There is a great incentive for the firm to agree to give undertakings, since the alternative would be for the Secretary of State to make an order regulating the firm's behaviour. There is a very wide range of orders open to the Secretary of State in order to counteract the damage or potential damage done to the public interest. The Secretary of State has not yet had to exercise these powers to impose regulatory orders following an MMC competition report. Undertakings have been accepted in all three cases in which the MMC has so far found that anticompetitive practices have operated against the public interest, (*Bicycles*, HC 67, 1981–82; *Sheffield Newspapers*, Cmnd 8664, 1982; and *Ford Motor Co.*, Cmnd 9437, 1980). In the *Ford* report, the MMC recommended that the situation be remedied by a change in the law, together with an expression of hope that the firm would restrain its (lawful) behaviour. In the end, the firm agreed to give undertakings.[8]

Table 5:
Competition reports of the MMC

Bicycles	HC 67 (1981)
Sheffield Newspapers	Cmnd 8664
London Electricity Board	Cmnd 8812
Ford Motor Co.	Cmnd 9437
BBC/ITP	Cmnd 9614

The processes laid down in the 1980 Act are characterised by a high degree of publicity. The texts of all references, reports and undertakings are published, as are any variations in them. However, commercial confidentiality and personal privacy are maintained by excluding from the public reports any matter which may prejudice these interests. The adoption of a system comprising a discretionary power of investigation, rather than a prohibition coupled with a power to exempt, means that the earliest date on which firms may feel obliged to refrain from pursuing a course of conduct will be the publication of the Director General's report. In common with UK monopoly policy, the 1980 Act does not give individuals any enforceable rights against firms who injure them through anticompetitive means. The pragmatic approach of the Act makes this inevitable at least in the period before the Director General has reported.

The public interest The criteria against which the MMC are to assess the public interest issues of an anticompetitive practice are exactly the same as for monopoly and merger control, and are laid down in section 84 of the Fair Trading Act 1973. It will be recalled[9] that this section provides for an open-ended assessment of the public interest, with a list of minimum criteria which the MMC are bound to consider. The function of the MMC under section 5 of the 1980 Act is a modified version of its function in monopoly and merger references; it must inform itself of the factual situation and assess those facts in the light of the public interest, with no effective restrictions or guidance as to how it is to fulfil its task. The fluid and comprehensive nature of the definition of anticompetitive practices and the pragmatic approach adopted with relation to the meaning of public interest make the MMC the natural choice of body for the task assigned to it under the 1980 Act. The two-part process also separates the administrative role of the OFT from the expert role of the MMC. This is not to suggest that the OFT does not require a high degree of expertise to carry out its own investigations, but the MMC fulfils the 'wise men' approach to regulation, characteristic of UK practice.

The MMC has only made five reports under these provisions of the 1980 Act, three of which found a practice to be against the public interest. These reports will now be considered in the context of all the reports published by the Dirctor General on the existence of anticompetitive practices.

Distribution systems
Selective systems for distribution or servicing have been investigated by the Director General on three occasions, and found to be anticompetitive where the firm was dominant or was able to exclude firms from an area of the market (*Bicycles*, 1981; *Still & Sons*, 1982). However, selective distribution systems of themselves are not regarded as neccessarily anticompetitive. In *Arthur Sanderson* (1981) the market was found to include sufficient substitutes to negate the system's adverse effect on excluded dealers. In addition, the grounds on which dealers were selected were mainly reasonable, relating to minimum turnover requirements. The OFT was less clear in its attitude to a geographical basis for selection, but in view of the strength of competition, took no action on it. The MMC examined a selective distribution system in *Bicycles* (1981). The criteria imposed by the firm for the selection of distributors related both to geographical location and to a collection of other factors, such as technical expertise and servicing facilities, which were designed to exclude discount stores from the distribution network. The MMC regarded geographical criteria as tending to restrict competition and possibly to lead to local monopoly. However, it accepted the firm's arguments that such restrictions were necessary in order

to preserve dealer loyalty and a chain of viable dealers. Since it found that the criterion did not in practice materially restrict competition, the MMC found its imposition to be justified. However, the other criteria were found to have the effect of preventing price competition at retail level, and thereby led to higher prices and a restriction in consumer choice. The MMC accepted the argument that certain products require a minimum level of technical expertise in their distribution, and it recommended that the firm be required to supply its products only to those applicant retailers who could demonstrate a level of skill similar to existing dealers. In addition, because the firm's reputation may have been harmed by the distribution of its products through discount stores, it was not required to supply products under its leading brand name.

Exclusive dealing arrangements, whereby suppliers agree to supply only on the basis that the dealer does not sell competing products, have been examined in two cases. In both cases, the practice was found to be anticompetitive because of its effect on excluded market participants. The possible benefits of exclusive dealing agreements, which are explored in relation to EEC law below, were not considered by the Director General because the balancing of costs and benefits is the task of the MMC. In one case the firm gave undertakings to abandon the practice, and in the other, *Sheffield Newspapers* (1982), the MMC had an opportunity to examine the public policy issues. This report concerned the obligation imposed by a newspaper publisher on its retail distributors that they should not distribute a competing publication. The MMC stated expressly that the purely competitive effects of this practice would not be dispositive of the matter; the public interest test under the 1980 Act took account of many more issues. The MMC found that the effects of the practice were that prices (of advertising) were increased; there was less competitive pressure to improve services and standards; consumer choice was reduced; and the freedom of newsagents to take on new business was restricted, thereby adversely affecting the service they could offer to the public. The obligation of exclusivity was therefore held to be against the public interest, although the firm was allowed to discipline newsagents who distributed competing publications selectively to customers of the firm.

A form of service distribution—exclusive franchising—has been examined on three occasions. The Director General has made it clear that franchise systems, whereby an exclusive concession is granted to supply a service, will not be regarded as anticompetitive where there are available substitutes on the market. Even in the absence of competitive pressures the terms of a franchise agreement may offset its anticompetitive effects, such as a provision for periodical competitive tendering, or operating provisions designed to simulate the effects of competition (*British Airports Authority—Gatwick Airport* 1984). In the absence of such factors, an exclusive concession in an uncompetitive market will tend to lead to supracompetitive prices, an effect which was found to have occurred in the *Gatwick Airport* report. In contrast, in *British Railways Board—Godfrey Davis* (1983), the competitive advantage given to the exclusive franchisee gave rise to an insignificant distortion because of the very small proportion of the relevant market which was diverted. In this particular case the market definition was critical to the perceived effect of the conduct; in view of this, it is regrettable that the rather complex definition of the relevant market which was adopted by the OFT was not expressly justified in more detail. The report concerned an exclusive concession granted by British Rail for facilities for car hire at railway stations. The market was defined as 'all business, and a small proportion of leisure, users in the national, and a proportion of the local, [car hire] sectors'.

Pricing and discounting

Pricing policies have been examined on a number of occasions. Predatory pricing was characterised as anticompetitive in the *Scottish and Universal Newspapers* report (1983), where a newspaper publisher provided free advertising for a period of thirteen weeks after the launch of a free newspaper in order to force a competitor out of the market. The practice was regarded as anticompetitive in spite of the short-term reduction in costs to consumers and in spite of the fact that the policy was unsuccessful in diverting custom away from the competitor. In *London Electricity Board* (1982) the firm was found to have been cross-subsidising its retail outlets, which operated at loss-making prices, from its electricity-supply activities, in which it enjoyed a monopoly. The MMC found that other suppliers in the market were also cross-subsidising the sale of the products, but that they had less deep pockets for such support. The practice was not condemned on this occasion because the firm was found to be a price-follower rather than a price-leader, even in submarkets in which it had a dominant share. The distortion of competition was not found to be substantial enough in practice to cause material harm to the market or to consumers.

Discounting practices have been examined by the MMC on a number of occasions. In a general report under section 78 of the Fair Trading Act 1973, the MMC investigated discriminatory discounts granted to retailers, especially in the groceries sector. It found that the pressure placed on suppliers by large retailers to grant discounts had enhanced competition among suppliers. Even though the discounts granted to large retailers did not always reflect cost savings, there was no evidence that the suppliers were subsidising inefficiency on the part of the retailers. The MMC concluded that, on available evidence, the public interest was not adversely affected by discriminatory discounts, and any individual instance where this might not be the case could be dealt with under the 1980 Act (MMC, 1981 II). In reports published under the 1980 Act, loyalty rebates have been branded as anticompetitive, where the discount given does not reflect cost savings made by the discounter. In *Sheffield Newspapers* (1981), the firm offered price reductions to advertisers who placed advertisements with the firm's newspapers for forty-eight weeks out of fifty-two. The intention was to discourage the use of a competing newspaper by advertisers. There was no condition relating to the minimum volume of advertising each week, and the annual discount was low. These factors led the MMC to conclude that the practice did not have the effect of diverting customers away from the competitor, and that it was not an anticompetitive practice within the meaning of the Act. Although a similar system was operated in the television advertising medium by Thames TV, the matter did not proceed beyond the Director General's report (*Thames TV*, 1984). This was because the special circumstances of the market prevented any significant effect flowing from the practice.

The suppression by a dominant magazine publisher of price information in magazine advertisements was found to have the effect of restricting the entry and growth of small mail-order companies in the advertised product market, which would have created a restraint on prices generally (*Holmes McDougall*, 1985). Other practices which have been found anticompetitive include a dominant firm's refusal to deal with a firm which it mistakenly believed to be a competitor (*Essex County Newspapers*, 1983).

Intellectual property rights

The exercise by firms of their intellectual property rights has also been found to give rise to anticompetitive practices. The relationship between antitrust controls and intellectual property rights is problematic. There is a potential conflict between these two, in that the existence and exercise of intellectual property rights may often produce anticompetitive effects, through the monopoly power granted to the holder of the rights. However, there are powerful public policy justifications for maintaining these rights, and indeed some basis for suggesting that the conflict may not be as severe as first appears (Merkin, 1985). In the context of EEC law, the European Court of Justice has developed a workable formula for disposing of the conflict,[10] but there is no settled policy in UK law on the relationship between the two.

The conflict was most apparent in the MMC reports on *Ford* and *BBC/ITP*. In *Ford*, the firm relied on its copyright in vehicle body panels to prevent independent firms from manufacturing and supplying exactly similar panels on the 'after market' for car repairs. Independent firms did indeed engage in such practice, and supplied the panels at greatly reduced prices. Ford consistently refused to grant licences (which it was perfectly entitled to do under copyright legislation) and attempted to stop the practice through litigation. The MMC concluded that Ford's conduct, though lawful, was anticompetitive in that it was an attempt by a dominant firm to prevent competition. The MMC recognised the conflict, and stated that the only possibility for a resolution would be a change in the law to reduce the period during which Ford would enjoy copyright protection. The problem was expressed by the MMC as follows:

> The root of all these difficulties ... [is] that a licence ... is fundamentally an assertion by the licensor and a recognition by the licensee of [an] exclusive right. In this case we have found that the absence of competition resulting from the assertion of that exclusive right would operate against the public interest. There is therefore a conflict between the exclusive right of the owner of the [intellectual property right] and the public interest. A resolution of this conflict which will allow the development of competition requires some modification of the exclusive right not merely its sharing with certain individuals or companies.

The government is presently reviewing the law on intellectual property rights; the *Ford* recommendations will be considered as part of such review. There may have been other options open to resolve the issue (see Frazer, 1985), but the firm agreed to grant licences to all applicants on reasonable terms and at a specified royalty. In this instance, therefore, the requirements of competition policy took precedence over the property rights of the individual firm. This ad hoc resolution of the conflict between the two branches of policy cannot be a long-term stance; suitable statutory reform is eagerly awaited. The issue was raised again in the *BBC/ITP* report, where both firms in the television broadcasting duopoly refused to grant copyright licences to newspapers to publish advance programme information, except on very restrictive terms. The intention of the firms was to protect their own programme publications. The firms' shared monopoly of the broadcasting market was simply being extended to the information market through the use of copyright. The MMC was unable to recommend that this was against the public interest, mainly through a disagreement as to the MMC's function (Frazer, 1986), and there was no resolution of the conflict.

There remain many issues which have not been investigated under the 1980 Act. The Second Green Paper singled out tie-in sales and full-line forcing as being particularly worthy of investigation, and likely always to be against the public interest. As a result of this observation, the MMC examined these practices in a general investigation under section 78 of the Fair Trading Act 1973 (MMC, 1981 I). It found no evidence to suggest that the practices were widespread, or that they were always likely to operate against the public interest. The absence of any investigations into the practices under the complaints-led 1980 Act may well be a confirmation of these findings. The MMC agreed with the literature on the practices that the public interest is most likely to be harmed where the intention of the firm is to extend a dominant position in the tying product to the market for the tied product, or to exercise price discrimination between users of the tying product. On the other hand, ties imposed to maintain standards or to achieve economies are less likely to harm the public interest. Further, the effect of any tie will largely be determined by the degree of dominance enjoyed by the firm in the tying market and the structure of the tied market.

Other investigations

The 1980 Act contains further powers for the control of the conduct and performance of firms. Section 11 provides a mechanism for the investigation of public monopolies,[11] and section 13 gives power to the Secretary of State to require the Director General to investigate any question relating to a price of 'major public concern'. The inclusion of such a power, which has never been exercised, may possibly be explained by the fact that the 1980 Act also abolished the Price Commission, a body which exercised some restraint on prices. The operating methods of the Price Commission were highly complex, and were criticised by industry on this basis as well as on the general principle that prices should be determined by the market. The Second Green Paper recommended that the Price Commission be strengthened as part of competition policy, but the Conservative government, to whom the Green Paper was presented, took the opportunity to abolish the Price Commission as part of its programme to remove market restraints. Section 13 therefore provides for the retention of some power to review individual prices.

In addition to these powers under the 1980 Act, the Secretary of State has residual power to investigate any matter relating to competition or the conduct of firms. Such investigations will be carried out by the OFT and reported on by the Director General. In 1985, as a result of questions raised in the House of Commons, the Secretary of State asked the Director General to instigate a programme of investigations into various aspects of competition in the professions. A report on one aspect of that programme was published in 1986.[12]

Resale price maintenance

Unlike any other anticompetitive practice, resale price maintenance is specifically prohibited under UK law. The Resale Prices Act 1976 consolidates previous law and renders unlawful both collective and individual arrangements for resale price maintenance. Agreements between suppliers to enforce retail prices are regarded as vehicles for the enforcement of price cartels and, as such, as egregious restrictions on competition. It is consequently unlawful under the 1976 Act for suppliers to impose sanctions on dealers as a way of maintaining resale prices. It is also unlawful for a supplier to incorporate minimum resale price provisions in a vertical agreement with a dealer, and any such provisions are void. This prohibition of individual resale price maintenance is more controversial in economic theory. The principal arguments in favour of individual resale price maintenance are that it prevents free-riders and loss-leaders. Free-riding occurs where retailers who sell at low prices through a restriction in pre- and post-sale services benefit at the expense of high-price, high-service retailers. The hypothesis is that consumers will utilise the services of the latter, but purchase from the former. Retailers will therefore be unwilling to commit themselves to the provision of services if there is a danger that their margins or sales will be eroded by undercutting competitors. Loss-leading—the sale of a product at an uneconomic price in order to attract custom into the shop—is also said to undermine the reputation of the supplier of the product, although this argument does not enjoy universal support (Scherer, 1980). The 1976 Act implicitly rejects the free-riding argument by prohibiting individual resale price maintenance. But the loss-leader argument is accepted: firms are permitted to withhold supplies where it can be shown that goods are being sold in this way. The Restrictive Practices Court is also empowered to exempt classes of goods from the legislation. To date, only books and medicaments have been granted such exemption. In common with the restrictive trade practices legislation, unlawful actions under the 1976 Act do not attract criminal liability. The Crown may apply for injunctions to prevent contraventions, and anyone affected by unlawful resale price maintenance may sue in the civil courts for damages. There is no evidence that such private court actions are any more useful in practice than those provided for under the restrictive trade practices legislation.[13]

EEC LAW

The Treaty of Rome does not contain any provision dealing specifically with anticompetitive practices outside the controls on restrictive trading agreements in Article 85 or the monopoly controls of Article 86. However, because of the 'effects' basis of Article 85, and the absence of undue formality in that article, it has proved possible to interpret it in such a way that it is able to confront many of the types of behaviour examined under the Competition Act 1980 in the UK and under the Federal Trade Commission Act in the USA. Arrangements such as selective and exclusive distribution systems, tying and full-line forcing, discriminatory pricing, and the anticompetitive use of intellectual property rights, will all be capable of examination and control under Article 85 and, in the presence of monopoly, under Article 86. These anticompetitive practices will be regulated in the same way as other varieties of restrictive agreement or abuses of a dominant position. There are no special arrangements for their control similar to the Competition Act 1980. Anticompetitive practices of this nature are capable of regulation because it is possible to determine the existence of a mutuality of obligations, and therefore an agreement, under the broad terms of Article 85. Even such conduct as refusal to deal, which appears to be a unilateral practice, will be capable of regulation under Article 85 where it forms part of a wider consensual practice, such as a selective distribution system. The practices considered below are merely examples of the operation of Articles 85 and 86, and are grouped in this chapter so that they may be easily compared to the treatment of similar practices in the other two legal systems.

Distribution systems

The policy of the Commission and the European Court of Justice on selective and exclusive distribution systems has been developed to such an extent that it has proved possible to issue block exemptions[14] relating to many such practices, determining and explaining their legality. An exclusive distribution system will usually comprise an agreement or a series of agreements whereby the supplier agrees to supply only the dealer within a defined area, or whereby the dealer agrees to purchase a class of goods for resale only from the supplier, or whereby the parties enter into mutual obligations in these terms. The potentially anticompetitive nature of these agreements is obvious. An exclusive sales agreement excludes other dealers from selling the product in the area, thereby shielding the exclusive dealer from competition; and an exclusive purchase (solus) agreement will exclude other suppliers from distributing through the tied outlet. Where these anticompetitive effects are realised then they will result in higher prices and a restricted consumer choice. Cross-frontier trade will be obstructed, especially where sales territories are co-extensive with national territories (White, 1984). However, the actual effect of the agreements will depend on the availability of substitutes which compete with the tied product, and on the structure of the relevant markets. Even where exclusive dealing agreements do tend to have anticompetitive effects, they may have countervailing advantages. The block exemptions issued by the Commission on exclusive dealing agreements provide a formula for determining the relationship between the anticompetitive and pro-competitive features of these agreements.

There are two such block exemptions—Regulation 1983/83, which concerns exclusive sales agreements, and Regulation 1984/83, which concerns exclusive purchase agreements. The preamble to Regulation 1983/83 explains the Commission's policy. Exclusive distribution agreements are regarded as having several efficiency advantages: the reduction in the volume of customer contacts enables the supplier to 'concentrate its sales activities' and to deal more easily with cross-frontier trading difficulties. Further, there will usually be marketing and sales advantages and efficiencies. By enabling firms to enter the market only at the manufacturing level, these agreements may also reduce barriers to entry, where the alternative would be a requirement to enter at both levels. This will be especially so where the entering firm is relatively small. The Commission is anxious to promote the interests of small and medium-sized firms, an objective not always justifiable in terms of efficiency. The requirement to enter at all levels will not constitute a barrier where it is possible to raise or divert capital for such an enterprise, on the basis of favourable investment predictions. Small firms will be less able to do this, but this fact does not make the barriers absolute.

The Regulation exempts from the prohibition of Article 85(1) those bilateral agreements whereby the supplier agrees to supply certain goods for resale within the whole or a defined area of the Common Market only to the dealer. However, to benefit from this exemption, the arrangement must be no more restrictive than neccessary, and there must be sufficient competition on the market to offset the potentially anti-competitive nature of the exclusivity. It is permissible for the supplier to be obliged not to sell directly into the dealer's territory in competition with the dealer. It is also possible to require the dealer not to manufacture or distribute competing products, to purchase the relevant products only from the supplier, and to refrain from an active sales policy outside the allotted territory. The dealer may also be obliged to purchase minimum quantities or complete ranges (a practice which the MMC in the UK thought likely to be against the public interest when carried on in the context of obligations of exclusivity—MMC, 1981 II), to sell the goods in presentations dictated by the supplier, and to engage in various sales promotion activities.

Reciprocal exclusive dealing agreements between competing manufacturers will not benefit from the exemption, since such an arrangement will have the effect of a market-dividing agreement. Non-reciprocal agreements between competing manufacturers are also outside the terms of the exemption, unless one of the firms has a turnover of less than 100 million ECU. The exemption will not apply where there is insufficient intra- or inter-brand competition. Thus, where the exclusive supplier is the only source of the particular brand of product in the territory, and there is no alternative source outside the territory, then the exemption will not apply. Nor will it apply where either of the parties places obstacles in the way of trade in the product through other dealers inside or outside the Common Market, by way of the exercise of industrial property rights or otherwise. Inter-brand competition is also protected to a certain degree. The Commission reserves to itself the right to withdraw the exemption in individual cases where certain circumstances apply; one of these circumstances is where the products in question are not subject to effective competition from substitutes. Other such circumstances include the substantial foreclosure of distribution facilities to competing suppliers; and situations where other market participants find it impossible to obtain the particular products from dealers outside the exclusive territory on usual terms. Finally, the marketing conduct of the dealer may lead to the removal of the exemption. Where the exclusive dealer refuses to supply, or differentiates against, categories of purchasers in the territory, then if there is no objective justification for such refusal and the would-be purchasers cannot obtain the goods elsewhere, the exemption may be removed. Similar sanctions will apply where the dealer charges excessively high prices. These last provisions reflect the market power which may be available to an exclusive dealer, especially where the territory is large and the product enjoys a degree of brand loyalty.

There is a separate block exemption in relation to exclusive purchasing agreements, where a reseller of goods agrees to purchase the goods only from the supplier. Agreements of this sort are widespread in the drinks and retail petrol markets, resulting in 'tied' pubs and service stations. Regulation 1984/83 grants a block exemption to such agreements where they comply with the limitations laid down in the Regulation. These are broadly parallel with those in Regulation 1983/83 except that special rules are laid down for beer supply agreements and service station agreements, and maximum terms are fixed for the duration of exclusive supply agreements.

Where agreements cannot benefit from either of the distribution block exemptions, the parties may still apply for individual exemption under Article 85(3). The *Ivoclar* decision (1985) is an example of such tactics.

Selective distribution agreements are not capable of such homogeneous treatment, and the attitude of the enforcing authorities is to be found in both the case law and a block exemption. The latter covers only distribution in the motor industry, a market characterised by the near universality of this method of distribution.[15] In other markets, selective distribution systems will be permitted where a movement from price competition to non-price competition can be justified by the nature of the product. It will be recalled that in the *Bicycles* report, the MMC regarded selective distribution as permissible where the products concerned are of a highly technical nature. The same position is taken by the Commission and the ECJ. Selective distribution systems which aim at the goal of improving non-price competition are therefore not prohibited by Article 85 where the distributed goods are high-quality or highly technical (*AEG-Telefunken* case, 1984). Goods such as watches, hi-fi equipment, cameras, computers, and scientific equipment, as well as cars, may be the proper subject of selective distribution. In these cases it is legitimate to shelter the dealers from price competition so that they will be able to carry out a minimum standard of servicing and related functions. It must be stressed that it is not permissible to ensure high profit margins *per se*; the protection from price competition should be an essential part of the effort to increase non-price competition. Selective distribution systems for goods which do not have the necessary characteristics will contravene Article 85(1), but may be exempted under Article 85(3). In one decision, the Commission held that a selective distribution system for plumbing fittings would infringe Article 85 (*Grohe* decision, 1985).

Where the goods are the suitable subject of such a system, the aim of the system must be the improvement of competition and not its restriction. The ECJ has laid down criteria for assessing the competitive impact of selective distribution systems, and hence their legality under Article 85. Under such policy, dealers must be selected on the basis of objective criteria of a qualitative nature, relating to the technical qualifications of the dealer or the suitability of trading premises (*Metro* case, 1978). These conditions must be laid down uniformly for all potential dealers and must not be used in a discriminatory way. Selection criteria which are not objective or are of a quantitative nature will contravene Article 85(1), but may be exempted under Article 85(3).

Article 85 will apply to selective distribution systems which fall outside the permissible type, even though they appear to be merely unilateral acts on the part of the supplier. The ECJ justifies its claim to control these arrangements by characterising the refusals of the supplier to deal with non-authorised dealers as being part of the contractual arrangements with the authorised dealers, and therefore within the scope of Article 85. The basis for exemption under Article 85(3) generally is described in Chapter 5; in relation to selective distribution systems, no exemption will be given unless there is the possibility for intra-brand competition across national frontiers, so that the system does not have the effect of insulating one part of the Common Market (*Ford (No 2)* decision, 1984). Quantitative criteria are usually frowned upon, but in the *Binon* case (1985), the ECJ suggested that they would be exempted in appropriate circumstances, as are obligations relating to sales effort, servicing standards, display, and stock levels. Most selective distribution systems will be disposed of under the rules laid down in *Metro* (1978). Chard (1982) has undertaken an economic analysis of such systems and, although generally supportive of the economic benefits they entail, calls for a more rigorous individual analysis by the Commission. A similar point is made by Joerges (1984). This is not likely to occur unless the present system can be shown to be working ineffectively.

A related system of distribution is by way of franchising agreements. This method involves a series of vertical agreements between a supplier-franchisor and franchisees, allowing the franchisee to sell the product supplied, under the trade marks or identity of the franchisor. Franchise agreements differ from selective and exclusive distribution systems; they more closely resemble intellectual property licences (Adams and Mendelsohn, 1986). The franchisee accepts the financial risks of the venture, but is able to enter the market more easily by relying on the reputation already accumulated by the franchisor's mark. In addition, the franchisor is able to exploit its reputation more easily. In this way, franchise agreements assist the movement of goods and services across national frontiers (Goebel, 1985). The ECJ has described such a system as 'more than just a method of distribution, this is a manner of exploiting financially a body of knowledge, without investing the franchisor's own capital' (*Pronuptia*, 1986). The ECJ looks favourably on this method of distribution, and it will no doubt increase in popularity as a way of circumventing the restrictions imposed by the ECJ on selective distribution. In the *Pronuptia* case, the ECJ held that franchising systems do not contravene Article 85; any restriction imposed under a franchising agreement which is inherently necessary to maintain the system will be permitted. Restrictions on the franchisee's competitive activities, on the design and location of the sales premises, on the use of know-how, and on the products which may be sold, will all be permitted where they comprise essential elements of the system. However, clauses which divide the market between the participants in the system, or which prevent price competition, must be exempted under Article 85(3) if they are to survive. Territorial protection for the franchisee may well be exempted (*Pronuptia* case, 1986; *Yves Rocher* decision, 1986). It is expected that a block exemption on franchising agreements will be issued by the Commission in due course.

Intellectual property rights

In addition to the regulation of distribution systems, Article 85(1) may also be used in the control of other trading behaviour often classified as anticompetitive conduct. Tying arrangements and discriminatory practices are both cited in the Article as examples of behaviour capable of regulation. The ECJ has also tackled the difficult relationship between antitrust policy and intellectual property rights. The potential conflict between these two facets of policy was mentioned above in the UK context. The nature of the conflict in EEC policy is of an intractable nature for two reasons. First, the fact that intellectual property rights are granted on a national basis means that their exercise is bound to compromise the 'one-market' ideal of the Treaty. Where a firm can use such a right to exclude from the national market goods which have been lawfully produced or circulated in another Member State, the effect will be to repartition the market along national lines. Secondly, there appears to be an internal conflict between articles in the Treaty of Rome. Articles 85 and 86 and Articles 30 to 34 all militate against the restrictive use of intellectual property rights. The first two articles seek to regulate the anti-competitive use of such rights, and Articles 30 to 34 prohibit any activity which hinders the free movement of goods between Member States. However, Article 222 states that the national systems of property ownership will not be prejudiced by the Treaty; and Article 36 provides an exception to the prohibition of Articles 30 to 34 for, *inter alia*, intellectual property rights.

The ECJ saw its task as bringing the exercise of intellectual property rights under control without offending the protective provisions of the Treaty. As a first stage in the development of such regulation, the ECJ confirmed that the anti-competitive aspects of the exercise, or of the licensing, of such rights, might be controlled by Articles 86 or 85 respectively. The ECJ drew a distinction between the *existence* of intellectual property rights and their *exercise*. Within this dichotomy, all aspects of a right which relate to its existence will be undisturbed by the Treaty; but those aspects which relate to its exercise will be capable of regulation if they are anticompetitive. This early policy was limited in scope, in that it relied on the existence of an agreement to which Article 85 may attach, or of the abuse of a dominant position. The mere possession of a patent or other right will not give rise automatically to a dominant position. Where there are effective substitutes for the protected product, the holder of the right will not be able to exercise monopoly power; but where there are no effective substitutes, the possession of intellectual property rights may give rise to considerable market power and the possibility of abuse. In *Ford Body Panels* (1986), for example, the Commission obtained undertakings from a firm that it would grant licences to independent firms that it had excluded from the market by exercising its intellectual property rights. The firm was also required to settle legal proceedings which it had brought against the independent firms for copyright infringement.

Because the requirements of Articles 85 and 86 placed restrictions on the utility of the policy, it was developed to a more sophisticated level by drawing on the principle of the free movement of goods enshrined in the Treaty. Thus, any exercise of intellectual property rights which is either anti-competitive or which hinders the free movement of goods across national frontiers, will be capable of regulation. The distinction between existence and exercise remains critical; the ECJ is unable to prohibit any aspect of the existence of national intellectual property rights. The ECJ has therefore defined those aspects so protected, and refers to them as the 'specific subject matter' of such rights. In relation to patents, for example, the existence of the patent, or its specific subject matter, comprises the 'exclusive right to use an invention with a view to manufacturing industrial products and putting them into circulation for the first time, either directly or by the grant of licences to third parties, as well as the right to oppose infringements' (*Centrafarm* v. *Sterling*, 1974). Any activity or action which falls outside these parameters will be capable of regulation where it offends competition policy or the principle of the free movement of goods.

The most tangible manifestation of this approach to the regulation of intellectual property rights is the doctrine of exhaustion. Under this doctrine, where the holder of rights places goods on the market of one Member State, either directly or through a licensee, then he may not exercise any national rights to prevent those same goods being sold on the market of any other Member State. This concerns the situation where a firm has parallel intellectual property rights in respect of the same product in different Member States. If the firm were allowed to exercise one of those national rights to prevent the import of goods which it had sold in another Member State, the firm would be able to isolate each national market in the protected product. Under the doctrine of exhaustion, all the firm's rights in respect of the goods sold are exhausted at the point they are placed on the market. At this point, the firm is able to reap its 'reward' for the property right, either through direct sales revenues or royalties from licensees, and there would be no justification for permitting any further reward which would have the effect of splitting the Common Market.[16] In *Centrafarm* v *Sterling* (1974), a firm held patents, through subsidiaries, on drugs in the UK and the Netherlands. The drugs were sold at a lower relative price in the UK. The firm attempted to rely on its Dutch patent to prevent a customer which had bought the drugs in the UK from reselling on the Dutch market. The doctrine of exhaustion operated to prohibit such attempt. Of course, the doctrine applies only to those goods which have actually been placed on the market by, or with the consent of, the rights holder. It will not apply to goods of the same description which have not yet been marketed. Nor will it apply to goods which are marketed without the consent of the holder of the rights. Such marketing may be by way of piracy, or even as the result of a compulsory licence being issued against the wishes of the holder of the rights (*Pharmon* v *Hoechst*, 1985). The doctrine will apply to the different types of intellectual property: patents, trade marks, and copyright.

Less satisfactory is a related doctrine, applicable only to trade marks. Under this, the doctrine of common origin, holders of trade-mark rights are not entitled to prevent the import of goods, lawfully produced in another Member State and which bear a trade mark identical to the protected trade mark, where the two identical marks had the same origin. This doctrine was revealed in the *Hag* case (1974), where identical trade marks for decaffeinated coffee were held by one group of companies in Germany, Belgium and Luxembourg. As a result of government sequestration during the Second World War, the ownership of the German trade mark was separated from the other two. When the holder of the German rights exported the product to Luxembourg, the holder of the rights there attempted to prevent the import by reliance on the national right. The ECJ prohibited such a hindrance to inter-State trade. The basis of the ECJ's action was more fully explained in a later case (*Terrapin* v *Terranova*, 1976). It turned on the fact that a basic function of the trade mark—a guarantee that the marked products have precisely the same origin as other products so marked—had already been undermined by the subdivision of the right between different firms. There was therefore no justification in permitting one holder to resist an import of the product by another holder. This rather unsatisfactory doctrine depends on the identical marks having a common origin. Identical marks which were independently developed will not be affected by it.

The doctrine of exhaustion, and to a lesser extent the doctrine of common origin, is a workable solution to the anti-trust/intellectual property conundrum, where the object is to promote cross-frontier trading without removing the benefits of property rights in innovation. It addresses the problem from the viewpoint of the free movement of goods in a unified market, rather than from the viewpoint of competition policy. However, in the field of licensing, competition law is a very active regulator of the use to which intellectual property rights may be put. The early case of *Consten and Grundig* (1966) confirmed that where a licensee was granted absolute protection, within its territory, from parallel imports, then such an arrangement will contravene Article 85. In the important *Maize Seeds* case (1983) the ECJ drew a distinction between 'open exclusive' licences whereby the licensor agrees to grant no further licences in the relevant territory; and those arrangements where absolute territorial protection is con-ferred. Normally, open exclusivity will be permitted. In relation to patent licensing, the development of competition policy has given rise to a block exemption, so that licences which have a net pro-competitive effect will be exempted from the prohibition of Article 85.[17] This block exemption took a very long time to reach the statute book, but contains an innovative procedural method for the clearance of relevant agreements. Under the 'opposition procedure', where firms notify the Commission of a licence which cannot benefit from the block exemption, but which does not contain any specifically prohibited restrictions, the Commission is obliged to raise any objections to the licence within a period of six months. Failure to do so will result in the licence enjoying automatic immunity. This flexible semi-formal approach to decision making has been repeated in later block exemptions.

The advantages of flexibility have been welcomed (Hendry, 1984; Waelbroeck, 1986), but serious doubts have been cast on the legality of the procedure (Venit, 1985; Waelbroeck, 1986; Korah, 1986 I).

Resale price maintenance
The Commission has for some time shown its opposition to resale price maintenance. Article 85 specifically prohibits agreements which 'directly or indirectly fix ... selling prices'; in *Deutsche Philips* (1973) the Commission condemned individual resale price maintenance agreements whereby German retailers were forbidden to sell in other Member States at prices lower than those fixed in Germany. Collective resale price maintenance agreements are also prohibited where they affect trade between Member States. In the *VBBB/VBVB* decision (1982), an agreement between two associations in different Member States, which prevented the sale of books in one Member State at prices below that in the other, had the effect of prohibiting price competition, and thereby limiting the ability of booksellers to increase their share of the relevant markets. As such, it was prohibited under Article 85. In confirming this decision, the ECJ refused to allow the 'loss-leader' argument[18] as a justification for contravening Article 85 (*VBVB and VBBB* v. *Commission*, 1985).

UNITED STATES LAW

US law on anticompetitive practices is contained in two different statutes. Certain specific practices, tying arrangements and price discrimination, are separately prohibited by the Clayton Act. In addition, section 5 of the Federal Trade Commission Act gives comprehensive power to the FTC to regulate all varieties of unfair or anticompetitive trading conduct.

It will be recalled that in the UK it was decided not to prohibit specific forms of anticompetitive behaviour, or even to specify individual examples of behaviour which might be regulated under the Competition Act 1980. Although resale price maintenance was prohibited under previous legislation, the 1980 Act was expressed in very general terms on the basis that the effect of individual practices could only usually be determined by the structure of the relevant market and the economic position of the firm in question. US law has adopted a different approach, by prohibiting three specific varieties of trading behaviour which, it is believed, are inherently likely to be anticompetitive in their effect. Price discrimination and tying arrangements are specifically prohibited under the terms of the Clayton Act, and resale price maintenance is *per se* illegal under long-standing case law.

Price discrimination

Discriminatory prices or discounts are, in certain circumstances, prohibited by section 2 of the Clayton Act, a section usually referred to as the Robinson-Patman Act, which amended the law in 1936. This amendment, passed during a period of intense economic depression, was a response to the growing power of certain retail firms, especially those involved in the groceries market. Large chain stores were exacting high discounts from suppliers, thereby disadvantaging small retailers who, forced to sell at higher prices, were being driven from the market. The lobby power of small business is a constant factor in American politics, and the Robinson-Patman Act was a way of protecting that interest. The objectives of the Act are to promote 'equality of opportunity' (Department of Justice, 1977), in the sense that small firms are able to exact the same prices from suppliers as their larger competitors. But this idea of fairness conflicts with most other provisions of the antitrust statutes, which promote the freedom to determine market behaviour. In this respect the Robinson-Patman Act must be viewed as a distinctive component of antitrust policy.

Liability under the Robinson-Patman Act will occur where sales of like goods to different customers take place at different prices, and where there is a reasonable possibility that this discrimination will lead to competitive injury (*Falls City* v. *Vanco*, 1983). This latter requirement is not restricted to competition between the discriminated firms. The competitive injury may occur at any of three levels. Injury may be to competitors of the seller (primary line injury), to competitors of the purchaser (secondary line injury), or to customers of the purchaser (third line injury). Any differences in price will give rise to a presumption of discrimination, and any substantial discrimination maintained over a period of time will give rise to a presumption of competitive injury. Discrimination may be justified by the seller, or the purchaser, on the basis that it reflects a saving in costs, or that it was made in good faith to meet the lower price of a competitor; both of these defences involve significant difficulties for the defendant.

The effect of the legislation has been the encouragement of price uniformity, and the discouragement of price competition. Particular disadvantages accrue in respect of vertically integrated firms. Where a purchaser operates at more than one stage in the market, it will be unable to enjoy wholesale discounts where this would give it a competitive advantage over its retail competitors. Integrated firms are thus unable to pass on efficiencies to their customers (Gellhorn, 1981). The Act has been roundly criticised for its chilling effect on competition, its anti-efficiency objectives, and its damaging restrictions on the freedom of the market. It is often perceived as a measure to protect competitors rather than one to protect competition. Scherer (1980) goes further, and questions whether the circle of its beneficiaries 'extends much wider than the attorneys who earn sizeable fees interpreting its complex provisions'. For these reasons, the Act is not as vigorously prosecuted by the enforcement authorities as it once was. The Antitrust Division has all but abandoned it to the FTC, and the FTC shows little enthusiasm for it. However, it is still used as a private antitrust weapon by competitors injured by price discrimination.

Tying arrangements

Tying arrangements—agreements to sell one product only if another product is also purchased—are specifically prohibited under section 3 of the Clayton Act. This section proscribes the lease or sale of a commodity on the condition that the lessee or purchaser shall not use or deal in the goods of a competitor, where the effect of such condition is anticompetitive. Ties which involve services rather than commodities are regulated under the general terms of section 1 of the Sherman Act.

Thus, if the lease of photocopiers is tied to the sale of paper for use in the machines, a tie will have occurred. There may be justifications for such a tie, such as maintaining the reputation of the tying product. Alternatively, the tie may have no anti-competitive effect, as where the firm maintaining the tie has no significant market power in the tying market. However, where the firm does have significant power, the tie may be used to extend that power to the market for the tied product. In the *International Salt* case (1947), the court assumed the existence of market power in the tying market from the ownership of patents. Once it was satisfied that the tie affected a volume of business which was not insignificant, the court held that the tie violated section 3. The lack of any real analysis in this case denoted a per se treatment of tying arrangements, wherever it is shown that the firm has sufficient market power in the tying market, and that the tie affects a significant volume of trade in the tied market. More recent treatment of tying arrangements denotes a shift to rule of reason analysis. The *Jefferson Parish* case (1984) was decided in the wake of the shift to rule of reason initiated in the *Sylvania* case (1977).

The major issue in *Jefferson Parish* was the proper characterisation of the agreement as a tying arrangement or an exclusive dealing agreement. General hospital services were tied to anaesthesiological services. This would be a tying arrangement only if the two products were distinct. If the arrangement involved one product only, it could comprise only an exclusive dealing agreement. Both tying and exclusive dealing are dealt with under the same terms of section 3 but, as is explained below, the judicial treatment of these two arrange-ments differs. The majority judgment held that, for separate products to exist, there must be a sufficient demand for the purchase of the tied product separate from the tying product, such that it is efficient to have a separate market for the tied product. The test therefore involves more than a mere definition of the two products; it demands an examination of the efficiencies of separate supply (Pasahow, 1986). The functional integration of the two products will clearly not be dispositive. A different test, outlined in the minority judgment, emphasised the efficiencies of *joint* supply; where significant efficiencies exist in the joint supply of the products, then they will be regarded as a single product under this test, even in the face of separate demand.

The majority regarded the arrangements in *Jefferson Parish* as a tying arrangement, but ruled that such arrangements will be per se unlawful only where the seller has sufficient market power in the tying market to 'force' the tie on the purchaser, and where the tie forecloses a substantial volume of commerce in the tied market. Where no such dominant power exists in the tying market then the rule of reason will be applied to determine the competitive impact of the tie. The minority would have removed the per se element altogether, and Pasahow (1986) suggests that this view may well prevail in the future. The Department of Justice's Vertical Restraints Guidelines, discussed below, treat tying arrangements separately from exclusive dealing agreements and other vertical restraints. However, the Guidelines do appear to adopt the minority test of distinctness laid down in *Jefferson Parish*, so more arrangements are likely to be regarded by the Antitrust Division as exclusive dealing agreements rather than as tying arrangements. Where arrangements are classified as tying agreements, the Guidelines state that no challenge will be made if the firm imposing the tie has a market share of 30 per cent or less (unless there is clear evidence that competition in the tied market is being unreasonably restrained). Even where the firm does have such a market share, unless it also has dominant power, approaching monopoly proportions, then the tie will be analysed under the rule of reason to determine its competitive impact.

Resale price maintenance

Antipathy towards resale price maintenance has been one of the clearest lines of policy in US antitrust. Horizontal price-fixing agreements have always been regarded as per se illegal under the Sherman Act, and a per se rule against vertical resale price maintenance was developed in the first such case to come before the Supreme Court, *Dr Miles* (1911). In that case, the attempts of the manufacturer to control the pricing conduct of its independent retailers was regarded as wholly anti-competitive. Judicial antipathy towards resale price maintenance has remained constant, although the statutory prohibition was interrupted for some time by the passage of 'fair trade' laws exempting most resale price maintenance arrangements from the prohibition of the Sherman Act.

However, the ability of firms to choose their own customers is a highly valued freedom, and the decision in the *Colgate* case (1919) confirmed the legitimacy of unilateral refusals to deal. Where refusals to deal really are unilateral, and not part of some boycott or other restrictive agreement, then no antitrust liability will ensue. Unlike UK law, therefore, it is permissible for manufacturers to rely on their *Colgate* right, and refuse to deal with a dealer which has failed to observe its suggested resale price. The *Colgate* doctrine has suffered some setbacks over the years, and at one point it was thought that it would not be possible to terminate a dealership to support resale price maintenance unless the facts of the case displayed 'Doric simplicity' in their similarity to the facts in *Colgate*. However, since the *Monsanto* case (1984), it would appear that the *Colgate* doctrine is still perfectly viable in relation to vertical resale price maintenance, so long as the refusal to deal is truly a unilateral act of the manufacturer, and so long as there is no hint of an agreement with other, observant, dealers. In spite of this, *Dr Miles* remains as strong as ever, although Marks and Jacobson (1985) suggest that the language used in the *Monsanto* case may well invite a further attack on that rule. It is the ambition of the Antitrust Division to remove the per se prohibition of resale price maintenance in favour of a rule of reason analysis. However, the continuing hostility of Congress to any such development will most likely ensure the continued vitality of the rule in *Dr Miles* for some time yet.

Distribution systems

Restrictions in vertical agreements, such as distribution systems, must be separated for antitrust purposes into price restrictions and non-price restrictions. The attitude of the Supreme Court to vertical restrictions has been somewhat inconsistent over the years, but since the *Sylvania* case (1977) all non-price restrictions in vertical agreements are reviewed under the rule of reason. Price restrictions continue to be per se illegal under the rule in *Dr Miles* (1911). The position taken in the *Sylvania* case was opposite to that taken in the previous landmark case, *Schwinn* (1967). In the earlier case, the Supreme Court held that all restrictions imposed by a supplier after it has parted with the goods, in respect of their resale 'are so obviously destructive of competition that their mere existence is enough [to give rise to liability]'.

However, in *Sylvania* the Court took a more sophisticated line, in distinguishing between inter-brand and intra-brand competition, in the same way that such a distinction is made by the European Commission in its policy on distribution restrictions. In this case, the supplier restricted resale of the goods to specific premises of its dealers in an attempt to increase the efficiency of distribution. No obligations of exclusivity were imposed on the dealers, and no guarantee was given that their franchised area would be protected. The Court was unwilling to condemn these restrictions on a per se basis because of the complex relationship between the potential reduction of intra-brand competition and the simultaneous increase in inter-brand competition. The reduction in intra-brand competition caused through a decrease in the number of dealers will not give rise to the possibility of exploitation where consumers are able to turn to competing products.

It is only the absence of effective competition from substitutable products that would permit dealers to exploit the reduction in intra-brand competition. The check on that power from competing products forces the supplier and dealer to pass on the efficiencies gained from vertical restrictions. Distribution will be improved through the greater willingness of protected dealers to invest resources into the network and to provide (costly) advice and other customer services. For all these reasons, the Court concluded that per se analysis was inappropriate for non-price vertical restrictions. The *Sylvania* judgment expressly maintained the distinction between price and non-price restrictions. Many economists dispute that such distinction should be maintained (e.g. Phillips and Mahoney, 1985), and in the *Monsanto* v. *Spray Rite* case (1984), the Department of Justice intervened to attempt to persuade the Supreme Court to drop the distinction, and to analyse all vertical restraints under the rule of reason. The case concerned the termination of a dealership, allegedly because the dealer had engaged in price-cutting. The Department asked the Court to consider the question of resale price maintenance under the rule of reason, since the economic effects of such practice may not differ from those produced by the restrictions examined in *Sylvania*. The Court refused to consider this point in the context of the particular appeal, and the distinction remains. Restrictions in any distribution system relating to the territory in which, or the customers to which, goods may be resold will be assessed according to their impact on intra- and inter-brand competition.

Exclusive distribution systems will usually be permitted where they comprise no more than an obligation on the supplier to supply no other dealer in the territory, where sufficient inter-brand competition exists and where the dealer is free to sell outside the territory. However, exclusive dealing agreements where the dealer agrees not to deal in competing products will fall to be considered under section 3 of the Clayton Act. This section applies to exclusive dealing agreements as well as tying arrangements, where their effect is anticompetitive. A long-standing case on exclusive dealing agreements, *Standard Oil and Standard Stations* (1949), held that such agreements will be unlawful only where it can be demonstrated that competitive activity has diminished or probably will diminish. It will be recalled that, in applying section 3 to tying contracts it is sufficient to show that the volume of business affected is not insignificant and that competitors are foreclosed from a substantial market. However, in relation to exclusive dealing agreements, the correct test was held to be whether the agreements covered a substantial portion of the relevant market.

This departure from the approach adopted in tying cases was justified by a belief in the potential efficiencies of exclusive dealing agreements, as opposed to tying arrangements which 'serve hardly any purpose beyond the suppression of competition'. The competitive injury test for exclusive dealing agreements was refined by the concurring opinion in the *Jefferson Parish* case (1984), which stated that exclusive dealing agreements will be unreasonable only where a 'significant fraction' of buyers or sellers are frozen out of the market. The Supreme Court in *Standard Oil and Standard Stations* was unwilling to examine the competitive impact of the exclusive dealing agreements. It felt that serious difficulties would be involved in assessing the impact of such agreements as opposed to other possible market structures, such as vertical integration. The Court's rejection of a full rule of reason analysis was based on the specific nature of the prohibition in section 3: '[w]e are faced, not with a broadly phrased expression of general policy, but merely a broadly phrased qualification of an otherwise narrowly directed statutory provision'. Nevertheless, courts must still examine the relevant market to determine the economic justification for the individual agreement, a requirement clearly pointed to in the *Tampa Electric* case (1961). Steuer (1986) has found that lower courts in more recent cases have been willing to undertake a closer analysis of the competitive impact of exclusive dealing agreements, and have shown a greater understanding of their pro-competitive effects.

Distribution by way of franchise agreements was developed in the US and is now widely used in restaurant outlets and other markets. The essence of the franchise relationship—'a complex marketing alliance' (Keyes, 1986)—does not offend antitrust principles. However, the clustering of the elements in a franchise agreement may be regarded as a tying arrangement. Items such as ancillary products or the purchase of land may be tied to the sale of the franchised product or the licence of the relevant trade mark. In order to determine their legality, franchise ties will be assessed in the same way as any other tying agreement. However, Keyes (1986) points to the difficulty in determining the correct market in which to measure the market power of the franchisor. Without proof of sufficient market power, the test for illegality laid down in *Jefferson Parish* (1984) cannot be satisfied. It is therefore likely that franchise agreements will escape successful challenge on this ground.

A significant development in the policy on distribution systems was the publication in 1985 of the Department of Justice's *Vertical Restraints Guidelines*.[19] These were published with the intention of clarifying the Department's policy towards vertical restraints, so that firms would be encouraged to adopt restraints which have pro-competitive effects. The Guidelines apply only to non-price restraints and tying arrangements; their major impact is on customer and territorial restraints, exclusive dealing, and tying arrangements. The Guidelines dispose of certain practices as being always legal. Selective distribution systems are considered to be uncontroversial, as are agreements which contain restrictions on the location of the dealer, or which assign 'primary responsibility areas', or which require dealers to pass over profits to dealers in other territories.[20]

As to other types of restriction, the Department will consider their potential competitive impact by balancing their pro-competitive aspects against their anticompetitive effects. The Department is clearly convinced that vertical restraints are in the main pro-competitive, and the tenor of the Guidelines is that anticompetitive effects (in the form of the facilitation of collusion, or the exclusion of rivals) will not usually be found (cf. Steiner, 1985). Among the potential benefits of vertical restraints, the Guidelines list: lower distribution costs, the facilitation of entry, the promotion of customer service through the elimination of free-riders, the protection of the supplier's investment in the dealers, flexibility in the allocation of risk between firms, the improvement of product quality and safety, and the reduction of transaction costs.

The evaluation of the competitive impact of vertical restraints is carried out by the Department at two stages. Stage one comprises a 'market structure screen'. A rough definition of the market is undertaken, and where the agreement is insignificant within the context of that market, no further action will be taken. Agreements which are not screened out at this stage will be more closely examined. The insignificance of agreements is calculated according to a fairly precise, and rather complex, formula. Under this, territorial and customer restraints, and exclusive dealing agreements, will not be challenged where the market share of the firm imposing the restraint is no greater than 10 per cent. Neither will a challenge be made where the 'Vertical Restraints Index' (VRI) is under 1,200 and the 'coverage ratio' is below 60 per cent in the same market; or where the VRI is under 1,200 in both markets (supplier and distributor); or where the coverage ratio is below 60 per cent in both markets. The VRI is a measure of the impact of the restraint on the market, and is calculated by summing the squares of the respective market shares of each firm engaged in the restraint at the same level in the market. Thus, if there are four suppliers who impose the restraint and each has a market share of 10 per cent, the VRI would be (10 × 10) × 4 = 400. The coverage ratio is the percentage of each market which is involved in the restraint. In the above example, the coverage ratio in the suppliers' market will be 40 per cent.

Stage two of the Department's evaluation involves a more careful market definition and a further examination of competitive effect. The Department is mainly concerned with ease of entry into both markets as a limitation on the adverse impact which may flow from vertical restraints. Where data on entry conditions do not dispose of the matter, the Department will consider a range of other factors.

The Guidelines have been savagely criticised by Congress, by antitrust practitioners and by the National Association of Assistant Attorneys General. The main thrust of the criticism is that the Guidelines are not an accurate reflection of the case law, and are a disguised attempt by the Department to erode the distinction between price and non-price restraints. Although the Department's intervention in the *Monsanto* case did clearly indicate its desire that vertical price restraints be evaluated according to the rule of reason, the Guidelines expressly state that they do not extend to price restrictions. Congress also criticised the Guidelines' belief that there is little anticompetitive threat from diminishing intra-brand competition. This criticism ignores the limiting effect of inter-brand competition on the power of protected dealers. One other criticism was that the Guidelines are too simplistic when they state that certain vertical restrictions (such as selective distribution) are 'always legal'. Rodino's speech summed up the mood of Congress: 'The Department's attempts to repose in suppliers almost exclusive authority to control the actions of independent distributors and retailers ... is ... contrary to existing law, congressional intent, and contrary to the most fundamental notions of free enterprise, which the antitrust laws serve to protect'. There is evidence to suggest that practitioners and courts are not yet relying on the Guidelines in their analysis of vertical restraints.

Intellectual property rights
The argument that a potential conflict exists between
intellectual property rights and antitrust has never been fully
accepted in the US. The opinion of courts and commentators
has been divided between those who view the monopoly
aspects of intellectual property as inherently anticompetitive,
and those who regard the two policies as directed towards the
same objective (see Kaplow, 1984). The latter view is currently
ascendant in government circles. The Deputy Assistant
Attorney General at the Antitrust Division recently denied any
friction at the interface between intellectual property rights
and antitrust. The antagonism of the Supreme Court to patent
licensing was, he claimed, based only on the semantic labelling
of patents as monopolies. This antagonism ignored 'the underlying nature and importance of ... any intellectual property
rights system to a viable, dynamic free market' (Rule, 1986).
The Antitrust Division has now abandoned its antagonistic
policy towards patent licensing, a policy of per se illegality
which was based on a collection of principles known as the
'nine no-nos'.[21] Current policy is based on welfare
considerations only and is dictated by the rule of reason
approach demanded by *Sylvania*. The pro-competitive aspects
of intellectual property rights are now emphasised, especially
the prevention of free-riding and the reduction in transaction
cost in moving information to its most valued uses. The
Vertical Restraints Guidelines, although not applicable to
intellectual property licences, indicate a favourable view of
them. Rule (1986) confirms the Antitrust Division view that
intellectual property licences increase consumer welfare by
allowing owners to deploy their technologies in the most
effective way. Any restriction of competition among licensees
will not give rise to antitrust liability under this view since,
even with restrictions, the licences give rise to a greater
dissemination of the technology. This laissez-faire attitude to
intellectual property is disturbed only where the licensor
enjoys substantial market power such that competing technologies may be excluded from the market.
   The permissive attitude of the Antitrust Division is not
always reflected in the courts, but the *Windsurfing* case (1986)
in the Court of Appeals for the Federal Circuit indicated a

238 Monopoly, Competition and the Law

movement towards rule of reason in the examination of intellectual property licences. The Court held that there must be a determination in each case that the licence restricted competition unlawfully. Rosen (1986) suggests that courts will in future examine the pro- and anti-competitive aspects of restrictions more closely, and will have especial regard to the promotion of inter-brand competition.

The role of the Federal Trade Commission

Section 5 of the Federal Trade Commission Act overlays the entire area of antitrust policy. The Act was passed in 1914 partly as a response to the decision of the Supreme Court in *Standard Oil* (1911). The intention of Congress was to maintain flexibility in the coverage of antitrust policy, and to provide an alternative method of adjudication and enforcement to the courts. Section 5 is drafted in astonishingly wide terms: in its amended form it prohibits 'unfair methods of competition in or affecting commerce, and unfair or deceptive acts or practices in or affecting commerce'. Enforcement of the section is within the exclusive jurisdiction of the FTC. The enforcement process, described in Chapter 5,[22] is administrative rather than judicial, although there is a right of appeal to the courts. The two legs of the prohibition—'unfair methods of competition' and 'unfair or deceptive acts'—cover both competition and consumer protection and provide a dual role for the FTC. In this respect, as in many others, it resembles the Office of Fair Trading in the UK.

The very wide terms of section 5 have caused problems in interpreting the scope of the FTC's jurisdiction. The historical development of this interpretation has been fully described in an American Bar Association monograph on the FTC (ABA, 1981). Even today, there is still uncertainty over the exact nature of the FTC's role. It is clear that section 5 duplicates everything in the Sherman and Clayton Acts, so that a violation of those Acts will automatically give rise to a violation of section 5. It is also clear that the mandate of the section goes further than the scope of the Sherman and Clayton Acts. The section will cover any practice which violates the spirit or the policy of those statutes, even though it does not violate the letter. Particularly, any practice which may be regarded as an antitrust violation in its incipiency, will be covered by the section. Thus, any act which would *lead* to an antitrust violation may be regulated under section 5 (*FTC* v. *Motion Picture Advertising*, 1953).

It may well be that the section goes further still. In the *Sperry and Hutchinson* case (1972), the Supreme Court stated in clear terms that the FTC had authority under section 5 to define and proscribe an unfair competitive practice even though it does not infringe the letter or the spirit of the antitrust laws, since it is open to the FTC to consider wider public values. However, the clear wording of this judgment has not resolved the meaning of the section because the statement was largely irrelevant to the outcome of the case, and therefore not binding (ABA, 1981). The scope of the section remains ambiguous, but at its very least it is wider than the terms of the antitrust Acts. The presence of section 5 ensures a flexibility of response to potentially damaging anticompetitive activities. But the partner of flexibility is uncertainty, and critics of the section point to the inability of firms and their advisors to determine the boundaries of lawful behaviour. Practices which clearly do not violate the Sherman and Clayton Acts may well be held to violate section 5. The policy adopted by Congress was for a flexible antitrust weapon that would enable intervention to take place wherever it is likely that competition will be injured, even though the practice may not be covered by the Sherman or Clayton Acts. A degree of uncertainty must be accepted as being inherent in any such system.

NOTES

1. The close connection between the wording of Article 85 and section 2 of the 1980 Act was recognised by the MMC in the *Sheffield Newspapers* report. Cmnd 8664 (1982).
2. See Chapter 4.
3. The Anti-Competitive Practices (Exclusions) Order 1980. SI 1980/979. A later Order removed immunity from charter flight services—The Anti-Competitive Practices (Exclusions) (Amendment) Order 1984. SI 1984/1919.
4. SI 1980/979.
5. *Ibid.*

6. *Ibid.*
7. *Ibid.*
8. The undertakings given were wide-ranging, obliging the firm to grant licences to independent firms to manufacture certain products at a royalty, and on terms, specified at length in the undertakings. Similar undertakings were given to the European Commission.
9. See above p. 40.
10. See below p. 222.
11. Public bodies are defined very widely in the Act.
12. Director General of Fair Trading, *Advertising and Charging Rules of the Professions Servicing the Construction Industry* (OFT, 1986).
13. See above p. 130.
14. Regulation 1983/83, OJ 1983 L 173/1; and Regulation 1984/83, OJ 1983 L 173/5. For a full description of the Regulations, see Korah (1984).
15. Regulation 123/85. OJ 1984 L15/16.
16. The doctrine does not depend on the concept of sufficient reward. Where a firm takes the decision to market goods on a national market which does not provide patent protection, the rights will still be exhausted on that marketing. The decision to sell in such circumstances will be presumed to have been made on a sound commercial basis: *Merck* v. *Stephar* (1981).
17. Regulation 2349/84 OJ 1984 L 219/15.
18. See above p. 214.
19. Department of Justice, *Vertical Restraints Guidelines*, 50 FR 6263 (1985).
20. See Oppenheim, Weston and McCarthy (1981) for a description of these practices.
21. Oppenheim, Weston and McCarthy (1981) at p. 885.
22. The procedures of the FTC in its administration of section 5 are very fully described in ABA (1981).

7 Extraterritoriality

The constant improvement during this century in the conditions for international trade means that even small firms are able, and encouraged, to trade outside the country in which they are established. International trade vitalises the competitive process and provides a limit to the power of firms which possess local monopolies. The ability of firms to trade across frontiers may of course be limited by the imposition of protective tariffs and other barriers, but in the absence of such obstacles, the merging of national markets can only be beneficial in terms of its effect on competition. However, this internationalisation does pose certain problems for the control of anticompetitive behaviour. Firstly, foreign competition must be taken into account in the process of market definition. Secondly, policy makers must decide whether the activities of firms outside the national territory should be subject to control where the effect of such behaviour can be felt on the national market.

A claim to exercise the powers of State outside the national territory will involve the infrastructure of international law. There are several recognised bases in international law for the exercise of jurisdiction. Of these, the ones relevant to antitrust enforcement are the 'territorial' and 'nationality' principles. Under the territorial principle, a State may claim jurisdiction in respect of any acts committed on its territory. Conspiracies and other forms of anticompetitive behaviour which actually take place in a national territory will clearly give rise to jurisdiction, whatever the nationality of the firms involved. The nationality principle permits a claim to jurisdiction by a State in respect of the activities of its nationals, wherever that activity may be committed. These principles are invoked so commonly that they are firmly established in international law (Akehurst, 1984). However, the effects doctrine, under which jurisdiction is claimed in respect of the activities of foreigners abroad where the economic effect of such activities is felt within the State concerned, has not been accepted by all States, and its position in international law is subject to doubt (cf. Leenen, 1984). The doctrine is keenly supported and prosecuted in the US, and resisted with equal vigour in the UK. Rosenthal and Knighton (1982) have found that these deeply held opposing views have led to an increase in tension between certain States and a deflection of investment away from the US. Although the claims of the US are more moderate than they were, there seems to be no ready solution to the conflict (cf. Lowe, 1985), which has already caused the UK to take radical defensive measures.

The attitude of the UK has been one of consistent hostility to the idea of an effects doctrine, both for its own legal system and for those of other States. A clear statement of this policy is to be found in an *aide memoire* submitted by the UK government to the European Commission in connection with the *Dyestuffs* decision (1969).[1] This decision was addressed to a number of firms, including ICI in the UK; at this date, the UK had not yet joined the EEC. The UK government expressly objected to the Commission assuming jurisdiction over a UK firm, supposedly on the basis of the effects doctrine. The objection was based on the view that the effects doctrine was unsupportable in international law, more especially so where firms may be subject to penal sanctions. The UK government held the view that antitrust jurisdiction could only be assumed on the basis of the nationality or territorial principles.

This hostility to the effects doctrine is also revealed in the UK antitrust statutes. They demonstrate a clear reluctance to exercise any control over the activities of firms outside the UK, or over the domestic activities of UK firms the effect of which is felt only overseas. A prime example of this is section 90 of the Fair Trading Act 1973, which contains the only mandatory feature of the control of monopolies, mergers, and anti-competitive practices. The section provides the Secretary of

State with a power to issue orders to remedy any injury to the public interest brought about through monopoly practices, merger activity, or anticompetitive practices. However this power is limited in relation to any activity which takes place outside the UK. In such cases the order will only have effect where its addressee is a citizen of the UK, or a company incorporated in the UK, or a person carrying on business there. This last criterion is not defined, but where defined in other areas of law, requires a physical presence in the UK. Another indication of the Fair Trading Act's domestic parameters is provided by section 7(3), which defines a monopoly firm in the services sector by reference to the market share which it enjoys. Under this definition, a firm is taken to supply services in the UK only if it has a place of business in the UK, or controls the relevant activities from the UK, or is a company incorporated there.

The control of restrictive trade practices is similarly limited to domestic affairs. The only agreements covered by the Restrictive Trade Practices Act 1976 are those in which at least two UK firms are party (with or without foreign firms). The jurisdiction of the Restrictive Practices Court to restrain the operation of restrictive agreements is confined to firms carrying on business in the UK or their trade associations.[2] Indeed, the RPC has no jurisdiction to assess restrictions in agreements which relate to the manufacture or supply of goods, or the supply of services, outside the UK. Where agreements have an exclusively overseas application, then neither the 1976 Act nor the Competition Act 1980 will apply at all.

The UK has responded with hostility to claims by other States to jurisdiction based on the effects doctrine. In antitrust enforcement, it is the claims of the US authorities that have provoked the most defensive response by the UK. The continued claims of the US to assume jurisdiction over UK firms were characterised as an attempt by the US to export its economic policy to unwilling recipients in foreign countries. The two countries were unable to settle the matter through diplomatic negotiations lasting several decades, and as a result the UK government enacted the Protection of Trading Interests Act 1980. The Act does not specify the US as its intended target, but in the parliamentary debates leading to its enactment it was made abundantly clear that the Act was intended to be a defence against the 'wide extent and fundamental uncertainty of the claimed reach of United States law through this pernicious extraterritorial effects doctrine'.

The 1980 Act enables the Secretary of State to prohibit a UK firm from complying with any requirement or regulation of a foreign country where it is being applied extraterritorially in a way which might damage the trading interests of the UK. There are similar powers to prohibit compliance, in similar circumstances, with a request by a foreign court for the production of documents. The liability of UK firms to treble damages claims under US antitrust law is a feature which successive UK governments have found particularly irksome, and the Act provides that no multiple damages judgments of foreign courts may be enforced in the UK. Further, where a UK firm has been obliged to pay treble damages, the Act gives it a right to recover the 'multiple' portion of the damages in UK courts. The Act has been used only once in the context of antitrust,[3] in relation to the action brought in the US courts by Laker Airways against several other airlines, on the basis that the defendants had engaged in a predatory pricing conspiracy to drive Laker into liquidation. The defendants attempted to persuade the UK courts to prohibit Laker from pursuing the US action, an attempt which was ultimately defeated in the House of Lords (*Laker* case, 1984). However, the Secretary of State intervened under the 1980 Act and prevented the UK defendants from complying with the US antitrust laws in the context of the case, or from producing any documents to the Department of Justice, the grand jury, or the court.[4] The additional element in this case was that the uncertainty created by the US actions was delaying the privatisation of British Airways.

In the EEC, there is a difference of opinion between the Commission and the European Court of Justice as to extra-territoriality. The Commission has always supported the notion of an effects doctrine for the extraterritorial application of Articles 85 and 86. It stated this decisively in the *Dyestuffs* decision (1969), a stance which prompted the UK government to deliver its sharply-worded *aide memoire*, referred to above.

The Commission has continued to claim such effect. In its Eleventh Report on Competition Policy (1981), it stated that the Articles 'apply to restrictive or abusive practices by undertakings situated in non-member countries where their conduct has an appreciable impact within the common market'. This was a slight retreat from a previous statement that jurisdiction could be claimed where the effects of an agreement 'spread' to the EEC (Commission, 1972). In the *Aluminium Imports* decision (1985), the Commission held that the interests of the EEC in maintaining an undistorted competitive structure were so fundamental that they should override all but the most important interests of a non-Member State.

The ECJ has never adopted such a bold stance; its policy was stated in the *Dyestuffs* case (1972). The Advocate General[5] urged the adoption of an effects doctrine wherever a trading practice caused a direct and immediate restriction of competition on the Community market, so long as the effect of the conduct was both foreseeable and substantial. The Court confirmed that the mere fact that one party to a restrictive agreement is situated outside the EEC will not prevent the application of Article 85. However, the ECJ was unwilling to accept even the moderate version of the effects doctrine proposed by the Advocate General. It did, however, assume jurisdiction on a different basis. Although ICI was established outside the EEC, it did have subsidiary companies within the EEC. ICI relied on the legal distinction between a parent company and its subsidiary in order to distinguish their respective legal liabilities. This position was forcefully reiterated by the UK government in its *aide memoire*. The ECJ did not accept that the separate legal personality of a subsidiary would dispose of the possibility that the actions of the subsidiary might be imputed to the parent company. In the application of Article 85, agreements between a parent and a subsidiary are not usually regarded as 'agreements between undertakings'. This is because a subsidiary, especially where it is wholly owned, will not usually have any real autonomy to determine its activities; it will usually act, ultimately at least, at the behest of the parent company, its major or only shareholder. For antitrust purposes therefore, the two companies are regarded as one economic unit. In view of this unity, the activities of a subsidiary are taken to be indistinguishable from the activities of the parent. Jurisdiction against the parent may therefore be claimed where it has a presence in the EEC through a subsidiary or other agent. Only where it can be shown that the subsidiary has real autonomy of action on the market, can such a claim to jurisdiction be resisted. Even the limited jurisdictional claim of the ECJ involves a number of procedural problems relating to the process of investigation and the enforcement of judgments outside the EEC (see Whish, 1985).

US antitrust policy, in common with other aspects of US commercial policy, is firm in its support for the effects doctrine. The *Alcoa* case (1945) found sweeping jurisdiction for US courts to apply the Sherman Act over foreign firms. The court held that 'any state may impose liabilities, even upon persons not within its allegiance, for conduct outside its borders which the state reprehends'. Any conduct prohibited by the Sherman Act which has 'some effect' on US imports or exports could be regulated under the effects doctrine so interpreted. This broad claim for jurisdiction was significantly toned down in the *Timberlane* case (1976), where the court developed a 'jurisdictional rule of reason'. The court took account of the resentment which such claims provoked in foreign countries, and regarded a test based only on the presence of effects on the US market to be too narrow a basis for extraterritorial jurisdiction. The court considered that a finding of a significant effect was a minimum requirement on which to base jurisdiction, but that courts should take account of comity and the needs of other nations, in deciding whether to exercise that jurisdiction. Factors such as the nationality of the parties, the relative significance of the effects on the US as compared with those felt elsewhere, and the foreseeability of those effects, must be considered by the court in order to assess the potential for conflict if jurisdiction were to be asserted.

The approach adopted in this case was adopted by the Department of Justice, but not by all other courts. In the *Uranium* cases (1980), the court rejected this balanced approach and asserted jurisdiction on the basis of the effects felt on the US market (see Kestenbaum, 1982, for an account of the litigation). This case was the last straw for the UK government, and it led directly to the enactment of the Protection of Trading Interests Act 1980. The Sherman Act has now been amended to provide for a balancing test. The minimum criterion for the assertion of jurisdiction is a direct, substantial and foreseeable effect on domestic US trade, or import or export trade. This imposition of a 'soft' approach to extraterritoriality has not silenced the critics. Of particular concern is the fact that the balancing of important national interests takes place in a US court, a forum not universally considered to be appropriate.

NOTES

1. The text of the *aide memoire* is set out in Lowe, *Extraterritorial Jurisdiction* (Grotius Publications, 1983).
2. Restrictive Trade Practices Act 1976, sections 2(3) and 35(4).
3. The only other occasion concerned US action in relation to foreign suppliers on the Soviet oil pipeline project.
4. Protection of Trading Interests (US Antitrust Measures) Order. SI 1983/90.
5. The Advocate General fulfils an official role in the European Court of Justice, through the delivery of an opinion on the law relating to the case. The Court is not obliged to follow this opinion, but it usually does.

Bibliography

American Bar Assoc. (ABA) (1981) *The FTC as an Antitrust Enforcement Agency*, Monograph 5, 2 vols (ABA).

Adams (1985) I) 'European and American Antitrust Regulation of Pricing by Monopolists', 18 *Vanderbilt Journal of Transnational Law* 1.

Adams (1985 II) 'Antitrust Constraints on Single Firm Refusals to Deal by Monopolists in the EEC and the United States', 20 *Texas International Law Journal*, 1 (1985).

Adams and Mendelsohn (1986) 'Recent Developments in Franchising', *Journal of Business Law* 206.

Akehurst (1984) *A Modern Introduction to International Law*, 5th edn. (George Allen and Unwin, London).

Areeda (1980) 'Predatory Pricing', 49 *Antitrust Law Journal*, 897.

Areeda (1983) 'Justice's Merger Guidelines: The General Theory', 71 *California Law Review*, 303.

Areeda (1985) 'Changing Contours of the Per Se Rule', 54 *Antitrust Law Journal*, 27.

Areeda and Turner (1975) 'Predatory Pricing and Related Problems Under Section 2 of the Sherman Act', 88 *Harvard Law Review*, 697.

Ashley (1983) 'Predatory Pricing Under Article 86 of the Treaty of Rome', 32 *International and Comparative Law Quarterly*, 1004.

Atiyah (1979) *The Rise and Fall of Freedom of Contract* (Clarendon Press, Oxford).

Attorney General (1955) *Report of the Attorney General's National Committee to Study the Antitrust Laws*, 31 March.

Baden Fuller, 'Article 86 EEC: Economic Analysis of the Existence of a Dominant Position', 4 *European Law Review* 423 (1979).

Baker (1984) 'The 1984 Justice Department Guidelines', 53 *Antitrust Law Journal*, 327.

Baker and Blumenthal (1983) 'The 1982 Guidelines and Preexisting Law', 71 *California Law Review* 311.

Baxter (1983) 'Responding to the Reaction: The Draftsman's View', 71 *California Law Review*, 618.

Bellamy and Child (1978) *Common Market Law of Competition*, 2nd edn. (Sweet and Maxwell, London).

Blake (1960) 'Employee Agreements Not To Compete', 73 *Harvard Law Review*, 625.

Bishop (1981) 'Price Discrimination Under Article 86: Political Economy in the European Court', 44 *Modern Law Review*, 282.

Blecher (1985) 'The "New Antitrust" As Seen by a Plaintiff's Lawyer', 54 *Antitrust Law Journal* 43.

Bork (1966) 'Legislative Intent and the Policy of the Sherman Act', 9 *Journal of Law and Economics*, 7.

Bork (1985) 'The Role of the Courts in Applying Economics', 54 *Antitrust Law Journal* 21.

Bork and Bowman (1965) 'The Crisis in Antitrust', 65 *Columbia Law Review*, 363.

Borrie (1986) 'Restrictive Practices Control in the UK', *Journal of Business Law*, 358.

Boyer (1983) 'Form as Substance: A Comparison of Antitrust Regulation', 32 *International and Comparative Law Quarterly*, 904.

Brozen (1974) 'Entry Barriers: Advertising and Product Differentiation', in *Industrial Concentration: The New Learning*, ed. Goldschmid, Mann and Weston (Little, Brown, Boston).

Brummer (1981) 'Reagan Sets a Takeover Explosion', *Guardian*, 15 July.

Calvani (1985) 'Non-Price Predation: A New Antitrust Horizon', 54 *Antitrust Law Journal*, 409.

Campbell (1982) 'The Competition Mission: Guiding Principles and Future Directions', 51 *Antitrust Law Journal*, 541.

Cann (1985) 'Section 7 of the Clayton Act and the Pursuit of Economic "Objectivity"', 60 *Notre Dame Law Review*, 273.

Chapman (1981) 'The Monopolist's Refusal to Deal: An Argument for the Rule of Reason', 59 *Texas Law Review*, 1107.

Chard (1982) 'The Economics of the Application of Article 85 to Selective Distribution Systems', 7 *European Law Review* 83.

Clanton (1983) 'Focusing the Enquiry: Specificity in the Merger Guidelines and Elsewhere', 71 *California Law Review*, 430.

Clanton (1984) 'Recent Merger Developments: Coming of Age Under the Guidelines', 53 *Antitrust Law Journal*, 345.

Clark (1940) 'Toward a Concept of Workable Competition', 30 *American Economic Review*, 241.

Clarkson and Muris (1981) 'Commission Performance, Incentives and Behaviour', in *The Federal Trade Commission Since 1970*, ed. Clarkson and Muris (Cambridge University Press, Cambridge).

Claydon (1986) 'Joint Ventures—An Analysis of Commission Decisions', 7 *European Competition Law Review*, 151.

Commission of the European Communities (1966) 'Memorandum on the Problem of Concentration in the Common Market', *Studies Series: Competition*, No. 3.

Commission of the European Communities (1972) 'Notice on the Importation of Japanese Products', OJ 1972 C 111.

Coombes (1970) *Politics and Bureaucracy in the European Community* (George Allen and Unwin, London).

Corbin (1982) *Corbin on Contracts* (West Publishing, US, 1962) and Kaufman Supplement (West Publishing, Minnesota).

Cunningham (1974) *The Fair Trading Act 1973, Consumer Protection and Competition Law* (Sweet and Maxwell, London).

Davis (1986) 'Horizontal Merger Policy', 54 *Antitrust Law Journal*, 1261.

Demsetz (1974) 'Two Systems of Belief About Monopoly', in *Industrial Concentration: The New Learning*, ed. Goldschmid, Mann and Weston (Little, Brown, Boston).

Demsetz (1982) *Economic, Legal and Political Dimensions of Competition* (North-Holland, New York).

Department of Justice (1977) *Report on the Robinson Patman Act* (Department of Justice, USA).

Director General of Fair Trading (1986) *Annual Report 1985* (HMSO, London).

Elzinga (1977) 'The Goals of Antitrust: Other than Competition and Efficiency, What Else Counts?', 125 *University of Pennsylvania Law Review*, 1191.

Fairburn (1985) 'British Merger Policy', 6 *Fiscal Studies*, 70.

First Green Paper (1978) *A Review of Monopolies and Mergers Policy*, Cmnd. 7198.

Flynn (1977) 'Antitrust Jurisprudence: A Symposium on the Economic, Political and Social Goals of Antitrust Policy', 125 *University of Pennsylvania Law Review*, 1182.

Flynn (1983) '"Reaganomics" and Antitrust Enforcement: A Jurisprudential Critique', *Utah Law Review*, 269.

Fox (1983) 'The 1982 Merger Guidelines: When Economists are Kings?', 71 *California Law Review*, 281.

Frazer (1985) 'Beating Panels: The Monopolies and Mergers Commission Report on Ford Motor Co. Ltd.', 8 *European Intellectual Property Review*, 235.

Frazer (1986) 'Unchanging Times: The Monopolies and Mergers Commission Report on the BBC and ITP', 7 *European Competition Law Review*, 96.

Galbraith (1952) *American Capitalism: The Concept of Countervailing Power* (Houghton-Mifflin), Boston.

Gellhorn (1981) *Antitrust Law and Economics in a Nutshell*, 2nd edn. (West Publishing, Minnesota.)

Gellhorn (1982) 'Regulatory Reform and the Federal Trade Commission's Antitrust Jurisdiction', 49 *Tennessee Law Review*, 471.

George (1985) 'Monopoly and Merger Policy', 6 *Fiscal Studies*, 34.

George and Joll (1975) 'The Legal Framework', in *Competition Policy in the UK and EEC*, ed. George and Joll (Cambridge University Press, Cambridge).

Glassman (1980) 'Market Definition as a Practical Matter', 49 *Antitrust Law Journal*, 1155.

Goebel (1985) 'The Uneasy Fate of Franchising under EEC Antitrust Laws', 10 *European Law Review* 87.

Goldschmid (1973) 'Antitrust's Neglected Stepchild', 73 *Columbia Law Review* 1193.

Gyselen and Kyriazis (1986) 'Article 86 EEC: The Monopoly Power Measurement Issue Revisited', 11 *European Law Review*, 134.

Halverson (1980) 'Emerging Antitrust Issues Affecting the Conduct of Dominant Firms', 49 *Antitrust Law Journal*, 893.

Handler and Lazaroff (1982) 'Restraint of Trade and the Restatement (Second) of Contracts', 57 *New York University Law Review* 669.

Harris and Jorde (1983) 'Market Definition in the Merger Guidelines: Implications for Antitrust Enforcement', 71 *California Law Review*, 464.

Harris and Jorde (1984) 'Antitrust Market Definition: An Integrated Approach', 72 *California Law Reivew*, 1.

Hay (1985) 'Antitrust and Economic Theory: Some Observations from the US Experience', 6 *Fiscal Studies*, 59.

Henderson (1924) *The Federal Trade Commission: A Study in Administrative Law and Procedure* (Yale University Press, New Haven.)

Hendry (1984) 'Block Exemption for Certain Categories of Patent

Licensing Agreements', 9 *European Law Review*, 441.

Heydon (1971) *The Restraint of Trade Doctrine* (Butterworths, London).

Hilton (1919) 'A Study of Trade Organisation and Combinations in the UK', in *Report of Committee on Trusts*, Cd. 9236 (HMSO, London).

Hurwitz and Kovacic (1982) 'Judicial Analysis of Predation: The Emerging Trends', 35 *Vanderbilt Law Review*, 63.

Jentes (1980) 'Assessing Recent Efforts to Challenge Aggressive Competition as an "Attempt to Monopolize"', 49 *Antitrust Law Journal*, 937.

Joerges (1984) 'The Administration of Art. 85(3) EEC Treaty: The Need for Consultation and Information in the Legal Assessment of Selective Distribution Systems', 7 *Journal of Consumer Policy*, 271.

de Jong (1975) 'EEC Competition Policy Towards Restrictive Practices', in *Competition Policy in the UK and EEC*, ed. George and Joll (Cambridge University Press, Cambridge).

Joshua (1983) 'The Element of Surprise: Competition Investigations Under Article 14(3) of Regulation 17', 8 *European Law Review*, 3.

Kaplow (1984) 'The Patent-Antitrust Intersection: A Reappraisal', 97 *Harvard Law Review*, 1815.

Katzmann (1980) *Regulatory Bureaucracy: The Federal Trade Commission and Antitrust Policy* (MIT Press, Mass.).

Kauper (1983) 'The 1982 Horizontal Merger Guidelines: Of Collusion, Efficiency and Failure', 71 *California Law Review*, 497.

Kay (1983) 'The Meaning and Measurement of Market Power', 4 *European Competition Law Review*, 163.

Kestenbaum (1982) 'Antitrust's "Extraterritorial" Jurisdiction: A Progress Report on the Balancing of Interests Test', 18 *Stanford Journal of International Law*, 311.

Keyes (1986) 'The Market Power Requirement in Franchise Tie-Ins', 54 *Antitrust Law Journal*, 1239.

Korah (1975) *Competition Law of Britain and the Common Market* (Paul Eleck, London).

Korah (1980) 'Concept of a Dominant Position Within the Meaning of Article 86', 17 *Common Market Law Review*, 395.

Korah (1984) *Exclusive Dealing Agreements in the EEC* (European Law Centre, London).

Korah (1986 I) *EEC Competition Law and Practice*, 3rd edn. (ESC Publishing, Oxford).

Korah (1986 II) 'EEC Competition Policy—Legal Form or Economic Efficiency', *Current Legal Problems*, 85.

Leenen (1984) 'Extraterritorial Application of the EEC Competition Law', *Netherlands Yearbook of International Law, 139.*

Leigh and Guy (1976) 'Exclusive Agency Agreements in the EEC', 1 *European Law Review*, 282.

Letwin (1967) *Law and Economic Policy in America* (Edinburgh University Press, Edinburgh).

Lipner (1986) 'Horizontal Mergers, *General Dynamics* and its Progeny: Requiem for a Presumption', 27 *South Texas Law Review*, 381.

Lowe (1985) 'The problem of Extraterritorial Jurisdiction: Economic Sovereignty and the Search for a Solution', 34 *International and Comparative Law Quarterly*, 724.

MacDonell (1919) 'Notes as to the Law Relating to Combinations', in *Report of Committee on Trusts*, Cd. 9236 (HMSO, London).

Malin and Lawniczak (1982) 'A Comparison of the American Sherman Antitrust Act and the British Restrictive Trade Practices Act: The Trade A. ociation Experience', 59 *University of Detroit Journal of Urban Law*, 147.

Mann (1974) 'Advertising, Concentration and Profitability: The State of Knowledge and Directions for Public Policy', in *Industrial Concentration: The New Learning*, ed. Goldschmid, Mann and Weston (Little, Brown, Boston).

Marks and Jacobson (1985) 'Price-Fixing: An Overview', 30 *Antitrust Bulletin*, 199.

Markus and Levi (1985) 'The Urge to Merge', *The Observer*, 8 December.

McCarty (1985) 'Merger Policy and Enforcement at the Federal Trade Commission: the Lawyer's View', 54 *Antitrust Law Journal*, 103.

McGee (1974) 'Efficiency and Economies of Size', in *Industrial Concentration: The New Learning*, ed. Goldschmid, Mann and Weston (Little, Brown, Boston).

McNulty (1968) 'Economic Theory and the Meaning of Competition', 82 *Quarterly Journal of Economics*, 639.

Meeks (1977) *Disappointing Marriage: A Study of the Gains from Merger* (Cambridge University Press, Cambridge).

Merkin (1985) 'The Interface between Anti-trust and Intellectual Property', 6 *European Competition Law Review*, 377.

Merkin and Williams (1984) *Competition Law* (Sweet & Maxwell, London).

Monopolies and Mergers Commission (1981 I) *Full-Line Forcing and Tie In Sales*, HC 212 (HMSO, London).
Monopolies and Mergers Commission (1981 II) *Discounts to Retailers*, HC 311 (HMSO, London).
Monopolies and Restrictive Practices Commission (1955) *Collective Discrimination*, Cmd. 9504.

Neah (1968) *Report of the White House Task Force on Antitrust Policy*.
Needham (1969) *Economic Analysis and Industrial Structure* (Holt, Rinehart and Winston, New York).
Noble (1982) '"No Fault" Monopolization: Requiem or Rebirth for *Alcoa*?', 17 *New England Law Review*, 777.
(Note) (1982) 'Antitrust Implications of Employee Non-Compete Agreements', 66 *Minnesota Law Review* 519.
(Note) (1985) '60 Minutes with J. Paul McGrath', 54 *Antitrust Law Journal* 131.

O'Brien and Swann (1968) *Information Agreements, Competition and Efficiency* (Macmillan, Basingstoke).
OECD (1966) *Report by the Committee of Experts on Restrictive Business Practices on Information Agreements*, (OECD, Paris).
Office of Fair Trading (1976) *A Guide to Registration* (HMSO, London).
Office of Fair Trading (1985) *Mergers* (HMSO, London).
Office of Fair Trading (1986) *Anti-Competitive Practices* (HMSO, London).
Oppenheim, Weston and McCarthy (1981) *Federal Antitrust Laws*, 4th edn. (West Publishing, Minnesota).

Pasahow (1986) 'Tying and the Single-Product Issue', 54 *Antitrust Law Journal*, 1219.
Pass and Sparkes (1980) 'Dominant Firms and the Public Interest: A Survey of the Reports of the MMC', 25 *Antitrust Bulletin*, 437.
Pertschuk (1977) *Hearings–Subcommittee on Antitrust and Monopoly*, Washington.
Phillips and Mahoney (1985) 'Unreasonable Rules and Rules of Reason: Economic Aspects of Vertical Price-Fixing', 30 *Antitrust Bulletin*, 99.
Pollock (1985) 'The "New Antitrust"—Its Implications for the Practitioner', 54 *Antitrust Law Journal*, 51.
Posner (1971) 'A Program for the Antitrust Division', 38 *University of Chicago Law Review*, 500.

Posner (1976) *Antitrust Law: An Economic Perspective* (University of Chicago Press, Chicago).

Posner (1977) *Economic Analysis of Law*, 2nd edn. (Little, Brown, Boston).

Potter (1985) 'Centralized European Merger Regulation: A Viable Alternative', 26 *Virginia Journal of International Law*, 219.

Prentice (1983) 'Illegality and Public Policy', in *Chitty on Contracts*, ed. Guest (Sweet and Maxwell, London).

Pryce (1973) *The Politics of the European Community* (Butterworths, London).

Ramsay (1987) 'The Office of Fair Trading', in *Regulators and Public Law*, ed. Baldwin and McCrudden (Weidenfeld and Nicolson, London).

Reich (1980) 'Emerging Per Se and Rule of Reason Principles in the Supreme Court', *Antitrust Law Symposium 1980*).

(Report) (1919) Committee on Trusts, *Report*, Cd. 9236 (HMSO, London).

Reynolds (1983) 'Merger Control in the EEC', 17 *Journal of World Trade Law*, 407.

Rhoades (1983) *Power, Empire Building and Mergers* (Lexington Books, New York).

Richardson (1969) *The Policy-Making Process* (Routledge and Kegan Paul, London).

Robinson (1980 I) 'Tougher Line on Mergers Forecast', *The Times*, 2 July.

Robinson (1980 II) 'Recent Antitrust Developments—1979', 80 *Columbia Law Review*, 1.

Rogers (1963) *Comparative Aspects of Anti-Trust Law in the United States, the United Kingdom and the EEC* (British Institute of International and Comparative Law, London).

Rosen (1986) 'Licensing Restrictions in the US and the European Economic Community', 55 *Antitrust Law Journal*, 383.

Rosenthal and Knighton (1982) *National Laws and International Commerce* (Routledge and Kegan Paul, London).

Rostow (1960) 'British and American Experience with Legislation Against Restraints of Competition', 23 *Modern Law Review*, 477.

Rowe (1985) 'Antitrust in Transition: A Policy in Search of Itself', 54 *Antitrust Law Journal*, 5.

Rule (1986) 'The Administration's View: Antitrust Analysis After the Nine No-No's', 55 *Antitrust Law Journal*, 365.

Scheffman (1985) 'Merger Policy and Enforcement at the Federal

Trade Commission: The Economist's View', 54 *Antitrust Law Journal*, 117.

Scherer (1977) 'The Posnerian Harvest: Separating the Wheat from the Chaff', 86 *Yale law Journal*, 974.

Scherer (1980) *Industrial Market Structure and Economic Performance*, 2nd edn. (Houghton Mifflin, New York).

Schumpeter (1942) *Capitalism, Socialism and Democracy* (Harper, New York).

Schwartz (1983) 'The New Merger. Guidelines', 71 *California Law Review* 575.

Second Green Paper (1979) *A Review of Restrictive Trade Practices Policy*, Cmnd. 7512 (HMSO, London).

Sharpe (1983) 'Merger Control in the United Kingdom', 4 *European Competition Law Review*, 171.

Sharpe (1985) 'British Competition Policy in Perspective', 1 *Oxford Review of Economic Policy*, 80.

Shaw and Simpson (1985) 'The Monopolies Commission and the Process of Competition', 6 *Fiscal Studies*, 82.

Siegfried and Sweeney (1982) 'The Social and Political Consequences of Conglomerate Mergers', in *Mergers and Acquisitions*, ed. Keenan and White (Lexington Books, New York).

Siragusa (1979) 'The Application of Article 86 to the Pricing Policy of Dominant Companies: Discriminatory and Unfair Prices', 16 *Common Market Law Review*, 179.

Steiner (1985) 'The Nature of Vertical Restraints', 30 *Antitrust Bulletin*, 143.

Steuer (1986) 'Exclusive Dealing After *Jefferson Parish*', 54 *Antitrust Law Journal*, 1229.

Stevens and Yamey (1965) *The Restrictive Practices Court* (Weidenfeld and Nicolson, London).

Stocking (1961) *Workable Competition and Antitrust Policy* (Vanderbilt University Press, Nashville).

Sullivan (1977 I) 'Revisiting the "Neglected Stepchild": Antitrust Treatment of Postemployment Restraints of Trade', *University of Illinois Law Forum*, 621.

Sullivan (1977 II) *Antitrust* (West Publishing, New York).

Sullivan (1980) 'Emerging Per Se and Rule of Reason Principles in the Supreme Court', *Antitrust Law Symposium 1980*.

Swann (1973) *Competition in British Industry: Case Studies* (Loughborough University Press, Loughborough, Leics.).

Swann (1974) *Competition in British Industry* (George Allen and Unwin, London).

Swann (1979) *Competition and Consumer Protection* (Penguin Books, Harmondsworth).

Tebbit (1984 I) *Hansard, Written Answers* [213] 5 July.

Tebbit (1984 II) 'Ministerial Statement', in *Looking Ahead,* ed. Office of Fair Trading (OFT, London.)

Temple Lang (1979) 'Monopolization and the Definition of "Abuse" of a Dominant Position under Article 86 EEC Treaty', 16 *Common Market Law Review,* 345.

Temple Lang (1981) 'Community Antitrust Law—Compliance and Enforcement', 18 *Common Market Law Review,* 335.

Thorelli (1954) *The Federal Antitrust Policy: Origination of an American Tradition.*

Toepke (1982) *EEC Competition Law* (John Wiley and Sons, Chichester, Sussex).

Tollison (1980) *The Political Economy of Antitrust* (Lexington Books, New York).

Turner (1980) 'The Role of the "Market Concept" in Antitrust Law', 49 *Antitrust Law Journal,* 1145.

Van Bael (1985) 'The Antitrust Settlement Practice of the EC Commission', 23 *Common Market Law Review* 61.

Van Rijn (1983) 'Intra-Enterprise Conspiracy and Article 85 of the EEC Treaty', in *Essays in European Law and Integration,* ed. O'Keefe and Schermers (Kluwer, Deventer).

Venit (1985) 'The Commission's Opposition Procedure', 22 *Common Market Law Review,* 167.

Vogelenzang (1976) 'Abuse of a Dominant Position in Article 86: The Problem of Causality and Some Applications', 13 *Common Market Law Review,* 61.

Waelbroeck (1976) 'New Forms of Settlement of Antitrust Cases and Procedural Safeguards: Is Regulation 17 Falling into Abeyance?', 11 *European Law Review,* 268.

Walker (1981) 'Product Market Definition in Competition Law', 11 *Federal Law Review,* 386.

Warren-Boulton (1985) 'Merger Policy and Enforcement at the Antitrust Division: The Economist's View', 54 *Antitrust Law Journal,* 109.

Weaver (1977) *Decision to Prosecute: Organisation and Public Policy in the Antitrust Division* (MIT Press, Mass.).

Werden (1985) 'A Closer Analysis of Antitrust Markets', 62 *Washington University Law Quarterly,* 647.

Whish (1985) *Competition Law* (Butterworths, London).

White (1984) 'The New Block Exemption on Exclusive Dealing', 9 *European Law Review,* 356.

Wilberforce, Campbell and Elles (1966) *The Law of Restrictive Trade Practices and Monopolies*, 2nd edn. (Sweet and Maxwell, London).

Zimmerman (1982) 'The Antitrust Division's Decree Review and Private Litigation Programs', 51 *Antitrust Law Journal*, 105.

Index

259

Undertaking, 161–2

Vertical Restraints (*see also*
  under individual restraints)
  beneficial effect, 235
  competitive impact, 235–6
  guidelines, *see* Vertical
    Restraints Guidelines
  non-price restrictions, 231–2
  price restrictions, 231–2

rule of reason, 231–3
Vertical Restraints Guidelines
  adoption, 234
  approach, 230
  competitive impact,
    measurement, 235–6
  criticism, 236
  market definition, 235, 236
  selective distribution, 234–5
  Vertical Restraints Index,
    235–6